CW01221597

Tales and Recipes
from a
Travelling Cook

Tales and Recipes *from a* Travelling Cook

Iain Hewitson

Food photography by Greg Elms
Additional photography by George Krawat

ALLEN & UNWIN

A SUE HINES BOOK

Thanks to my girlfriend Ruth Krawat for all her help, hard work and patience while I, as usual, changed my mind and ideas continually.

First published in 2000

Copyright text © Iain Hewitson 2000
Copyright food photography © Greg Elms & Allen & Unwin 2000
Copyright additional photography © George Krawat 2000
Copyright author photograph © James Penlidis 2000

All rights reserved. No part of this book may be reproduced or transmitted in any form or by any means, electronic or mechanical, including photocopying, recording or by any information storage and retrieval system, without prior permission in writing from the publisher. The *Australian Copyright Act* 1968 (the Act) allows a maximum of one chapter or 10% of this book, whichever is the greater, to be photocopied by any educational institution for its educational purposes provided that the educational institution (or body that adminsters it) has given a remuneration notice to Copyright Agency Limited (CAL) under the Act.

A Sue Hines Book
Allen & Unwin Pty Ltd
83 Alexander Street
Crows Nest NSW 2065 Australia
Phone: (61 2) 8425 0100
Fax: (61 2) 9906 2218
E-mail: info@allenandunwin.com
Web: www.allenandunwin.com

National Library of Australia
Cataloguing-in-Publication entry:

Hewitson, Iain.
Tales and recipes from a travelling cook.

Includes index.
ISBN 1 86508 301 1.

Hewitson, Iain – Journeys – Australia. 2. Cooks – Australia – Travel – Anecdotes. 3. Cookery. I. Title.

641.5

Food photography by Greg Elms
Additional photography by George Krawat
Cover author photo by James Penlidis
Styling by Fiona Hammond
Designed and typeset by text-art
Printed by South China Printing Company, Hong Kong

10 9 8 7 6 5 4

The author and publishers would like to thank the following for the generous loan of props: Supply & Demand, Minimax, Roost, Chapel Street Bazaar and Song.

Contents

Who called the cook a bastard?   *vi*
Kitchen essentials   *vii*
Tiptoeing with the leprechauns   *1*
Bring on Morocco   *17*
Strange brew   *41*
Bung it on the barbie   *57*
An Australian revolution   *109*
Should east meet west?   *143*
Salads of all shapes and sizes   *177*
An Indian sojourn   *211*
Spanish fusion   *231*
Good old Aussie tucker   *249*
I hate desserts   *305*
Index   *335*

Who called the cook a bastard? 'I don't know, but what I would like to know is who called the bastard a cook?'

an old Australian shearer's joke

A joke which was, I'm sure, in my early days in kitchens, often repeated behind my back. Because way back then, instead of concentrating on food that I was capable of producing (or for which the components were freely available), to the detriment of my poor friends and, to a lesser extent, my customers, I was obsessed with the notion of reproducing the great dishes of Europe, most of which I had only read about.

In my defence, I would like to lay a certain amount of blame at the door of the kindly soul who gave me my first-ever serious cookbook—*Great Recipes From the World's Great Restaurants*. A book which, unfortunately, opened the eyes of a young Huey to delights such as truffles and foie gras, and simple little numbers such as 'Pheasant Under Glass' and 'Escalopes of Wild Salmon in Sorrel Sauce'. All at a time in the Antipodes when a half-way decent chicken, or even a piece of really fresh fish, was a pretty rare commodity.

But thankfully, after a few failures (the most notable being a rare breast of duck which was so tough that it flew from the table when I attempted to cut it) it was decided that it was time I began travelling and actually began tasting those recipes that I was so intent on recreating. And, needless to say, I quickly discovered that these were not the dishes the locals sat down to daily. Instead, they mostly ate simply, concentrating more on the quality and freshness of the raw ingredients, rather than on any complicated or over-the-top cooking process. A philosophy which, to the joy of both patrons and mates alike, I quickly embraced.

And to this day, except on that very odd occasion when I get a little carried away, I basically cook pretty simple food. Sure, it must have lots of flavour and care must have been taken with the marketing, where all good cooking begins. But fairly uncomplicated it is. And that is what this book is all about. Buying what is at the height of its season and then combining it with ingredients that complement rather than obscure. And at all times keeping in mind that recipes are not set in concrete, so adaptation to suit your likes and dislikes, your purchases or even your budget is quite acceptable.

And on the subject of more recent travels, one of the best things about being on television and travelling the world in search of new and fascinating food experiences was the fact that I actually did come across some new and fascinating food experiences. These are, of course, included in this book (along with some of the funnier moments to boot).

Kitchen essentials

Pots and pans
Pots should have heavy bottoms, tight-fitting lids and good solid handles. Three or four different sizes would be nice and always, always have one extra-large pot for blanching, braising and the like. Pans should also have nice solid handles. One large heavy-bottomed version plus a couple of different sizes in non-stick would be good. Plus, of course, one omelette or crêpe pan.

Knives
Don't scrimp when it comes to buying knives. Buy the best because, if you look after them, they are a lifetime investment. Buy a steel at the same time and ask the shopkeeper to show you how to use it if you don't already know. Always wash them in the sink (not the dishwasher) after use, keep them in a knife bag or block and buy only those that are needed—at home, all you should really need is a cook's knife, a paring knife and a carving knife.

Bits and pieces
Good salt and pepper grinders are essential. As is, to me, a garlic press, parmesan shaver, bulb baster, salad dryer, lemon zester, olive pitter, meat and deep-frying thermometers and one of those things that slices beans into long slivers (I've forgotten its name). Also, a bench slicer or mandolin makes life very easy, as does a manual coffee grinder, which I use for grinding spices.

Fancy bits and pieces
In my kitchen, the wok and ridged grill are also essential items. And, I don't know how I ever survived without my food processor and blender. I also use, on a regular basis, my electric mixer, rice cooker and the microwave, which may not perform exactly as the manufacturers claim but is a good kitchen tool none the less.

And let us not forget
Solid whisks, a good set of pastry cutters, ladles, stainless-steel spoons, storage jars, wooden spoons, measuring jugs, juicers, cake tins, bowls and baking sheets of various sizes, spatulas, rubber gloves and lots of tea towels to put in our back pockets.

Tiptoeing with the leprechauns

IRELAND WAS A surprise. I must admit I went there expecting stodgy, old-fashioned food. And although I am sure that nouvelle cuisine never was and never will be a huge hit with the Irish, I was thrilled to discover that even the most traditional of dishes were now lighter and fresher. In fact, what we ate was modern-day peasant cooking, which was still robust and full of flavour but had far more delicate sauces and lots of fresh, crunchy vegetables to lighten the load.

And let us not forget Ireland's produce—simply wonderful!

- Irish stew with a touch of Paris
- Beef in Guinness
- Cashel blue cheese and vegetable soup
- Black pudding with Irish creamy mash (champ)
- Myrtle Allen's Irish brown bread
- Brussel sprout colcannon

- **Boxty with smoked salmon and horseradish and chive sour cream**
- **Dublin coddle**
- **Aherne's pot of seafood**
- **Irish whiskey syllabub**
- **Irish coffee**

Irish stew with a touch of Paris (for 4)

'The Cook's Journey' researchers had discovered that the best Irish stew in Ireland was supposedly served at The Common's Restaurant in Dublin. So we arranged for the chef to cook it for us, only to be slightly embarrassed when we arrived and discovered that he was actually a Frenchman. Still, he was a terrific cook and the Irish stew was, thankfully, absolutely delicious.

	Preheat oven to 200°C.
3–4 lamb necks	Remove meat from bone, trim off all sinew and most of the fat, and cut meat into even cubes (or ask your butcher to do this for you). Then put in a large pot and cover with water.
1 carrot, peeled and diced **2 celery stalks, diced** **1 large onion, peeled and diced** **2 leeks, well washed and diced** **6 spring onions (green onions), diced** **freshly ground salt and pepper**	Throw all the vegies in the pot with plenty of seasoning.
8 black peppercorns **6 juniper berries** **2 star anise**	Tie spices in muslin and add to the pot. Bring to the boil, cover tightly with both foil and a lid, and place in the oven. Cook for 50–60 mins, or until the lamb is tender.
4–6 large floury potatoes, scrubbed but not peeled	Meanwhile, put spuds on the lower rack of the oven and cook until they are tender. Remove and leave until cool enough to handle, then peel and roughly mash. Add mash to pot and mix in well.
chopped parsley	Serve stew sprinkled with parsley and with plenty of crusty bread.

The creation of the black gold

In Ireland, I think what entertained me most was the fact that everywhere I went within a 500-kilometre radius of Dublin just happened to be the birthplace of the black elixir—Guinness. First up, Seamus, the barman at the historic Cashel Palace Hotel in the shadow of Castle Rock, the ancient crowning site of Munster, looked me dead in the eyes and asked me to trust him as he relayed the most compelling story of its creation right there in the hotel's backyard. And, I have to tell you, I was convinced. That is until Patrick at the Dublin Arms told me Seamus was talking rubbish and that the black gold was actually created in No. 43, right next door, and was first sold at the very spot we were standing on. A tale which also seemed pretty damned plausible. But then again, Michael, Sean, Brendan and seemingly every second Irish publican were pretty believable too, especially after a few pints of the blessed stuff.

Beef in Guinness (for 4–6)

Preheat oven to 190°C.

vegetable oil
1 kilo well trimmed stewing steak,
    cut into 1.5 cm cubes
freshly ground salt and pepper

Heat a little oil in a large, heavy-bottomed pot. Brown the beef on all sides, in two or three lots, adding more oil as necessary. Remove, set aside and season.

3 medium onions, sliced
2 rashers of bacon, sliced

Add a little more oil to the pot and heat. Add onions and bacon and cook gently until golden, scraping up all the brown bits from the bottom.

1 tbsp brown sugar
2 tbsp tomato paste
1 cup beef stock (packet is fine)
1 bottle Guinness (333 ml)

Put these ingredients in the pot along with the beef and vegies. Mix, cover tightly with foil and a lid, and put in oven for 1¼–1½ hours until the beef is tender.

freshly ground salt and pepper
champ (see page 7)

Check seasoning and adjust if necessary, ladle stew into bowls and serve with creamy mash (champ) and plenty of crusty bread.

> **Try this with different styles of beer—each will impart a very different flavour. And, remember, stews and braises are even better when reheated the following day.**

Cashel blue cheese and vegetable soup

(for 6–8)

½ **bunch of celery, diced**
2 medium-sized carrots, peeled and diced
2 medium-sized onions, peeled and diced
3 medium-sized potatoes, peeled and diced
chicken stock (packet is fine)

Put vegies in large pot and just cover with the stock. Bring to boil and simmer until vegies are tender.

freshly ground salt and pepper
200 g blue cheese, rind removed and cubed
freshly chopped parsley

Check, adjust seasoning, and ladle soup into bowls. Throw in the cubes of cheese, sprinkle with parsley and serve immediately.

> **As the cheese melts, it adds wonderful highlights to this simple soup.**

Black pudding with Irish creamy mash (champ)

(for 4)

The Irish certainly love their potatoes. At almost every meal (including breakfast), there are three or four different spud dishes. And, when I asked one of their leading chefs what would happen if he instead just served one, he replied that not only would the customers storm the kitchen, he would rather quickly be right there on the unemployment line.

1 kilo potatoes, peeled and cubed
¼ cup milk
¼ cup cream
unsalted butter
½ cup of the sliced green part of spring onions (green onions)
freshly ground salt and pepper

vegetable oil
300–400 g black pudding, cut in thick slices
tomato chutney
chopped parsley

Cook spuds in lightly salted water until tender, and drain well. Bring milk and cream to the boil with a good dollop of butter. Turn off, add spring onion greens, cover and let sit while the potatoes cook. Then drain and mash the potatoes, adding cream mixture little by little. Season to taste.

When the potatoes are almost ready, heat a little oil in a large pan and fry the black pudding in two or three lots, until crisp on the outside and hot within. Then place a mound of mash on each plate, put the pudding slices around and add a dollop of chutney and chopped parsley.

> **Forget the diet. Traditionally, champ had an indent in the top into which you added another generous dollop of butter. The potato was then eaten from the outside in, dipping each forkful into the butter.**

Acting the part

Famed Irish actor (and drinker) Peter O'Toole was asked what his favourite three dishes from his homeland would be. Without a pause, he answered that his Number 1 choice would have to be Guinness. His Number 2 choice would be the same. And, also without hesitation, Number 3 would have to be Guinness as well.

Myrtle Allen's Irish brown bread (makes 1 loaf)

For years I had been whipping up loaves of a terrific, very easy bread from *Beard on Bread*, a great little book written many, many years ago by renowned American foodie, James Beard. But it was not until I got to Ireland that I discovered who the mythical Myrtle Allen is, to whom the recipe was credited. She is, in fact, regarded as the mother of modern Irish cooking, with her restaurant, Ballymaloe House in County Cork, famous both for its cuisine and the amazing gardens which supply a great deal of the kitchen's ingredients. The property is also home to the Ballymaloe Cooking School run by author and TV presenter, Darina Allen, Myrtle's daughter-in-law.

3¾ cups stone-ground wholemeal flour	Place flour in bowl and put in a warm oven (gas with pilot on only, or electric on very low).
1½ tbsp dry yeast 1 cup warm water 2 tbsp molasses 1 tbsp salt	Dissolve the yeast in the water and then whisk in the molasses and salt. Add this mix to the flour, then mix in up to 1 cup water (mixture should be firm, but not too dry).
1 cup warm water	Put dough in lightly oiled bread tin, let rise once by one-third of its original size and then cook in a preheated 200°C oven for 50 mins. (Check that it is ready by turning out and rapping the bottom of the loaf with your knuckles—it should sound hollow.) Then leave, out of the tin, in the turned-off oven for 10 mins.

> **With only one rising, this is one of the simplest breads around—it also makes the best toast, and is worth making for that alone. (Get out the Vegemite.)**

Brussel sprout colcannon (for 4 patties)

Traditionally colcannon was served on the eve of All Saints Day, when a wedding ring was pushed into one of the patties. Legend has it that the recipient would supposedly marry within 12 months. (Maybe that's the reason I've married a fair few times—I've eaten far too much colcannon.)

4 floury potatoes	Peel and cube the potatoes. Boil in lightly salted water until tender, drain and roughly mash.
vegetable oil **1 medium-sized onion, sliced** **2 rashers of bacon, sliced** **6 brussels sprouts, cored and finely sliced**	Heat a little oil in a pan and sauté the onion, bacon and sprouts for 5–10 mins.
1 egg **freshly ground salt and pepper** **chopped parsley**	Mix egg into the potato and onion mix. Then add seasoning and parsley, and form into patties. Cook in an oiled pan until crusty on both sides and hot within.

> **Wonderful with any grill or fry-up and particularly good with lamb's fry or calf liver.**

Boxty with smoked salmon and horseradish and chive sour cream (for 4–6)

1 cup cold mashed potato
1¼ cups grated raw potato, squeezed dry in a towel
¾ cup plain flour
1 tsp baking powder
½ tsp salt

Mix all these together.

½ cup buttermilk
vegetable oil

Add buttermilk little by little to potato mixture until firmish. Make into patties and fry in an oiled pan. Drain well on kitchen paper towels.

½ cup sour cream
1 tbsp chopped chives
horseradish cream
6–8 slices smoked salmon

Mix the sour cream with the chives and horseradish cream to taste. Top patties with salmon and horseradish cream.

Boxty on the griddle
Boxty in the pan
If you don't eat your Boxty
You'll never get a man

An old Irish ditty

Dublin coddle

(for 4)

8 thick pork sausages
vegetable oil

Bring large pot of water to the boil. Add sausages, turn down heat and simmer just until firm to the touch. Drain well. Heat a little oil in a large pan and brown the sausages in two lots. Remove and set aside.

2 rashers of bacon, sliced
2 medium-sized onions, sliced
2 cups sliced cabbage

Add a little more oil to pan if necessary, and sauté the bacon and onion until soft. Add cabbage, and toss.

4 medium-sized potatoes, peeled and thickly sliced
freshly ground salt and pepper
Dijon mustard
chopped parsley

Lay potatoes in bottom of lightly oiled Dutch oven or casserole. Top with onion mix, season well and almost cover with water. Place sausages on top, cover and simmer gently until potatoes are tender. (You can also cook this in a 190°C oven.) Remove the sausages and reduce the liquid over a high heat, if necessary. Check seasoning, mound vegie mix on plates and top with sausages. Sprinkle with parsley and serve with mustard on the side.

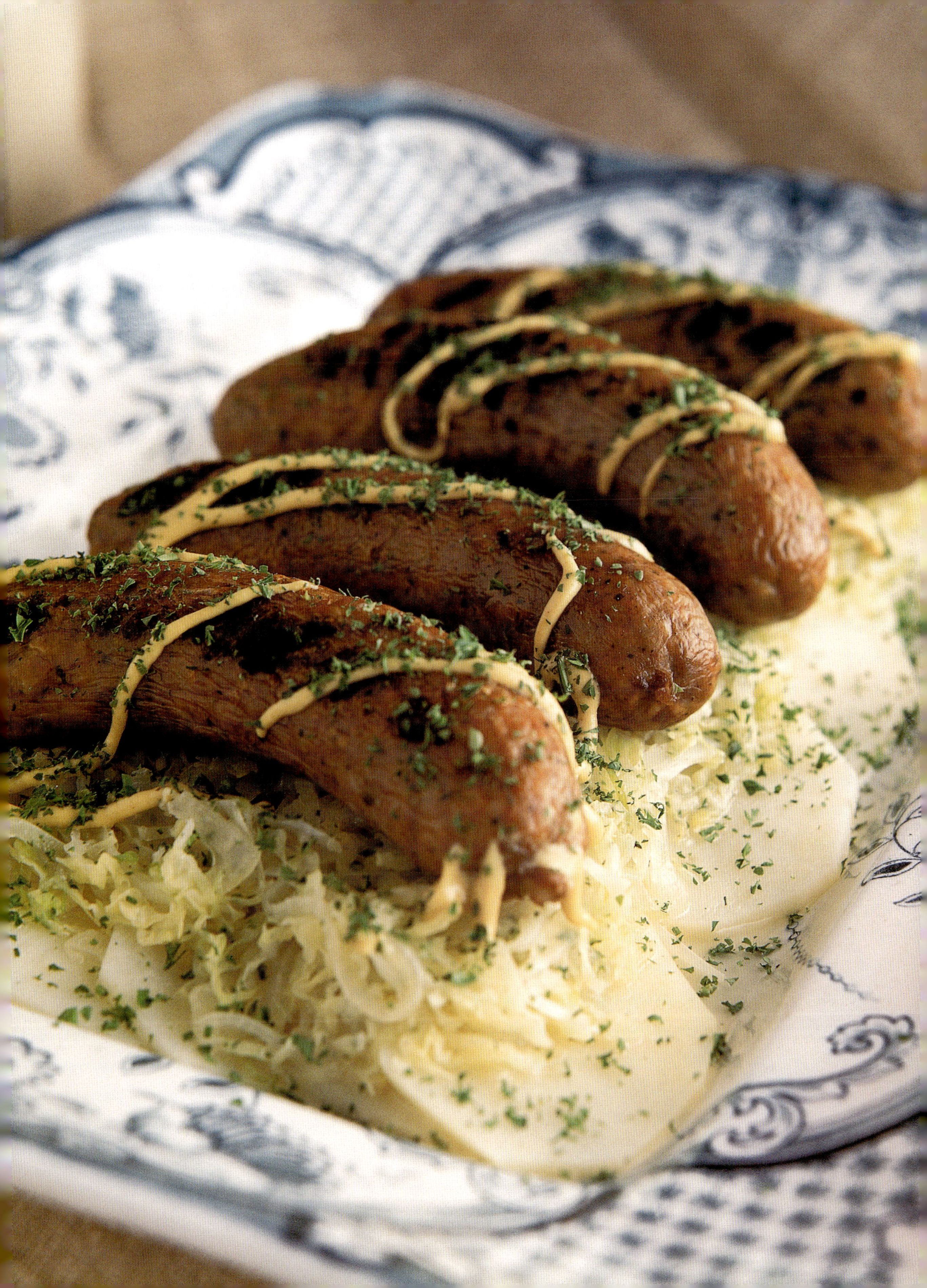

Aherne's pot of seafood (for as many as you like, depending on the size of the pot)

Ireland's flavoursome vegetables and salad leaves (many of them organically grown) are truly wonderful—as is the meat, cream, butter and cheese from the famous lush pastures.

But it is the fish and shellfish which are truly the stars of the show. Rarely have I tasted seafood that is quite so fresh as was demonstrated by this terrific seafood pot cooked for me at Youghal in Waterford County by Aherne's terrific chef, David Fitzgibbon. (And, because I can hear you all asking: yes, Youghal is where the original Moby Dick movie was filmed and, to this day, they still talk of the great 'wrap' party to which the whole town was invited.)

---

1 cup white wine
⅔ cup olive oil
⅔ cup fish stock
    (bought or home-made)
2 whole garlic cloves

Put these ingredients in a large, heavy-bottomed pot, with a tight-fitting lid, and bring to the boil.

mussels in the shell
oysters in the shell
clams in the shell

Add raw seafood, cover and cook for a few minutes.

cooked crayfish, cut in thick slices
cooked prawns
cooked bugs, cut in half
cooked yabbies
raw scallops, on the half shell
chopped chives
leaves of fresh dill

Add remaining ingredients and cook, covered, for another 2–3 mins until hot and then place seafood in bowls, along with all juices (you may need to give the shellfish a bit of a hand with a knife to completely open the shells). Serve with finger bowls, plenty of napkins, and mayonnaise and crusty bread on the side.

❝ This is bloody difficult to eat, but well worth the effort. And, do remember, the seafood must be spotlessly fresh so you can substitute different types depending on availability. ❞

And the perfect finish to any meal—a couple of Irish favourites

Irish whiskey syllabub (for 4–6)

zest and juice of 1 lemon
6 tbsp honey
8 tbsp Irish whiskey

In a bowl, mix together and leave for one hour to develop flavours.

2 cups thickened cream
Dutch cocoa

Whisk half the cream into the lemon mixture and continue whisking until mixture begins to thicken. Then whip the rest of the cream and carefully fold in. Place in bowl and sprinkle with cocoa.

Irish coffee

Heat the glasses by pouring boiling water into them. Leave for a few seconds then tip out. Put 1 tsp sugar in the bottom of each glass and add strong black coffee to about two-thirds of the way up. Mix with a spoon, and add 1 nip of Irish whiskey. Then whip thickened cream lightly and, using two large spoons, float this on the top. Sprinkle with a little raw sugar.

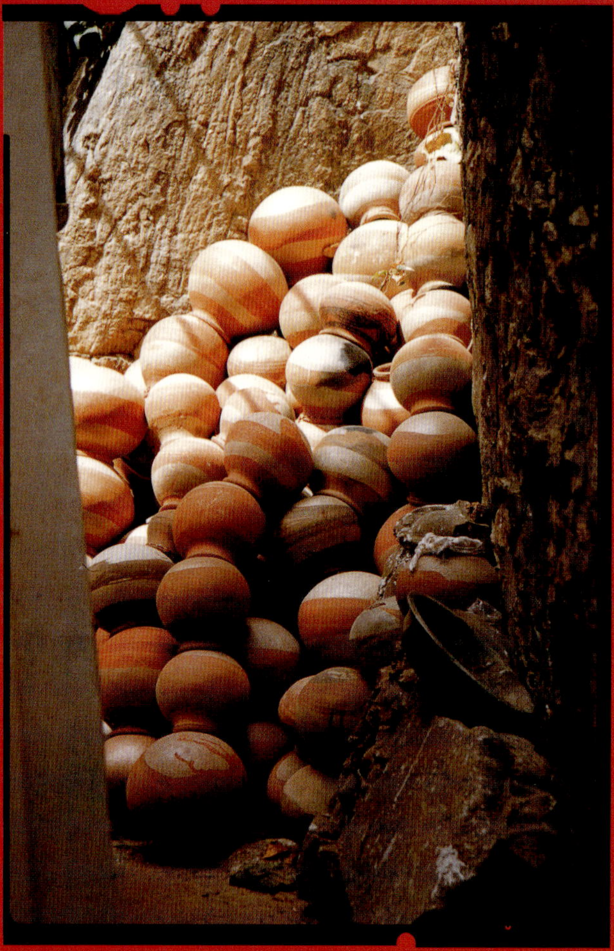

Bring on Morocco

I AM OFTEN ASKED about my favourite food and, I must admit, this is a question I answer with ease. Because all I demand of my food is that it has real flavour. Not for me the insipid or those nouvelle-cuisine-inspired little numbers. No, what I want is a dish that contains different highlights intent on making almost every mouthful a new taste experience. A view which certainly explains my liking for the food of Morocco, because this is food which is almost guaranteed to do exactly that.

- Chermoula-marinated chicken in the style of Huey
- Mustapha's hot and spicy steamed fish
- Couscous salad
- Moroccan swordfish steaks with preserved lemon salsa
- Pot roasted quails with lemons and raisins

- A salad of barbecued vegies, orange couscous and harissa yoghurt
- A Moroccan orange, fennel and olive salad
- Tagine of pork chops with spiced apples
- Preserved lemon and garlic mayonnaise
- Moroccan keftas (meatballs) in tomato sauce
- Harira with kefta and ham hock
- Spiced lamb with pita bread and mint yoghurt
- Homemade pita bread (well worth the effort)
- Lamb tagine with sweet potatoes

Chermoula-marinated chicken in the style of Huey (for 4)

Chermoula is a much used, much loved marinade from Morocco. And, while this version would not achieve the highest approval rating from most Moroccan chefs, I feel that the mango chutney, soy and sambal not only add a bit of extra tang, but some extra body as well.

½ cup coriander leaves ½ cup flat-leaf parsley ¾ cup olive oil ½ tbsp ground turmeric ½ tbsp sambel oelek 1 tsp ground cumin 2 tbsp Indian mango chutney 2 tbsp lemon juice 1 tbsp soy sauce freshly ground black pepper	Whiz all this up together.
8–12 boneless chicken thighs	Put in the marinade and mix in well. Leave for an hour or so. Preheat oven to its highest degree. Put chicken in baking dish and cook for 10–12 mins until the juices run clear when meat is pricked with a fork. Serve with a simple salad and some harissa yoghurt (see page 28) if you like.

> **You could also make this into a great salad by reserving some of the marinade for a dressing. Slice the chicken and toss it with some sliced capsicum, tomato wedges, boiled baby potatoes and the reserved marinade.**

The developing palate (part 1)

My first introduction to Moroccan food was when many, many years ago, I worked in a kitchen with a very talented Moroccan chef, Mustapha. But sadly his talents were not appreciated because he had this habit of, in a classical French restaurant, adding chillies, exotic spices and his beloved harissa (which he kept in a jar in his pocket) to such dishes as Soupe à L'oignon Gratinée, Coq au Vin and Boeuf Bourguignonne. To be fair, I actually felt that he improved the dishes out of sight, but in this I was almost alone: the head chef, François, a rather staid Frenchman, did not agree and Mustapha's stay was as brief as it was exciting.

Mustapha's hot and spicy steamed fish

(for 1 or 2)

1 plate-sized baby fish (about 250–300 g), cleaned and scaled	Fill a wok or large pot one-third with water. Put a bamboo steamer on top and bring to the boil. Place fish on a plate which will fit in steamer, and cut 3 slashes crossways on each side.
leaves from ¼ bunch coriander, well washed 3 garlic cloves, peeled 3 small chillies 2 tsp ground cumin 2 tsp castor sugar ½ tbsp rock salt	Whiz up everything into a paste, smear all over fish and place in steamer. Cover and cook for 10–12 mins (check to see if it's ready by making a small cut behind head).
juice of 2 limes	Serve fish with all the juices poured over and a couscous salad (see page 22) on the side.

> **Coriander, as you will soon realise, is about my favourite herb. But, for those of you who are not as keen as I am, just substitute a mixture of soft herbs such as basil, parsley and mint.**

Couscous salad (for 4)

1 cup chicken stock (packet is fine) 1 tsp ground cinnamon 1 tsp turmeric pinch of ground chilli pinch of ground cloves	Bring stock and spices to the boil.
1 cup couscous	Add couscous and cook over a low heat for a minute or two, fluffing with a fork. Set aside to cool.
2 tbsp toasted, flaked almonds 2 tbsp each diced red and green capsicums 2 tbsp diced cucumber 2 tbsp diced red onion 2 tbsp preserved lemon, diced (optional—see page 24)	Put couscous in bowl, add remaining ingredients and toss well.

Moroccan swordfish steaks with preserved lemon salsa

(for 4)

½ cup olive oil
3 garlic cloves
1 tsp ground paprika
1 small chilli, chopped
2 tbsp chopped mint
2 tbsp chopped parsley
a splash of soy sauce
juice of 1–2 lemons
freshly ground pepper

Whiz up as a marinade.

4 swordfish steaks (each 160–180 g)

Pour most of the marinade over the fish and leave, turning two or three times, for 30–40 mins.

4 pieces preserved lemon, bought or home-made (see page 24)
1 red onion, finely sliced
2–3 tbsp virgin olive oil
1 tbsp red-wine vinegar
harissa (see page 26) to taste
1 tbsp chopped parsley

For the salsa, discard lemon flesh and cut skin into fine slivers. Mix with onion, oil and vinegar and harissa to taste. Then mix in the parsley.

Grill, barbecue or pan-fry the fish, keeping it a little under-done, and serve with salsa on the side and a dribble of the reserved marinade over the top.

Preserved lemons

Not a bad staple for any pantry. Scrub 10 lemons well and cut into quarters. Place in a bowl and mix well with 250 g kitchen salt. Put a layer of the salt in a clean preserving jar and pack the lemons in, skin side out, pressing on them firmly to release juices as you do so. Top up the jar with extra lemon juice to cover the lemons, seal and leave for a month or so before using. They will last in the fridge for 2 or 3 months.

Pot-roasted quails with lemons and raisins

(for 4)

This mildly spiced dish is proof that not all Moroccan food will blow your head off. Actually, in many cases the dishes are extremely subtle but on the side is served that fiery staple, harissa, a chilli paste which you add at your own discretion.

Preheat oven to 180°C.

8 quails
vegetable oil

Tuck the quail wings under their bodies and push toothpicks through the legs and the points of the breasts. Heat a little oil in large heavy-bottomed pot and brown the quails all over. Remove.

2 cups chicken stock (packet is fine)
2 tbsp raisins
2 lemons, pips removed and finely sliced
2 tsp finely chopped garlic
1 tsp ground turmeric
freshly ground salt and pepper

Pour off oil, add these ingredients and whisk well. Return quails in one layer, with breasts upwards. Cover and cook on the middle rack of the oven very, very gently for 20 mins (turning down heat if necessary—the liquid should be just trembling).

2 tbsp chopped coriander
lemon juice (optional)

Take out quails and keep warm. Add coriander to the pot and reduce the liquid to a syrup. Check seasoning, adding a little lemon juice if necessary.

Remove toothpicks, place quails on plates and pour cooking juices over the top. Serve with couscous (see page 22) and harissa (see page 26) on the side.

❝ **You could also use chicken thighs, and to make it into a one-pot dish add some green vegies such as sugar peas, beans or broccoli towards the end.** ❞

A touch of spice

Harissa can be bought in many good delis or supermarkets. But if you want to make your own, just roast 2 tbsp coriander seeds and 1 tbsp cumin seeds in a hot, dry pan for a few minutes over moderate heat. Then process or blend to a paste along with 3 tbsp olive oil, 4 small fresh chillies, 2 garlic cloves and a pinch of salt. This mix will keep for months in the fridge.

A proverbial pain in the arse

I know some restaurant customers can be a bit difficult, but this particular one at Fleurie took the cake. Ringing at 4 pm on the day of his booking, he informed us that he was a vegetarian and expected something special. So, as usual, we went to a lot of trouble and not only made a cappuccino of various mushrooms and arranged for some vegie-stuffed naan bread to be brought hot from the tandoor oven at our other restaurant (Champagne Charlies), but also prepared a selection of stuffed vegies such as onions, zucchini flowers, squash and baby pumpkins—each with a different stuffing. Well, to say the least, we were a little annoyed when the customer decided that this wasn't to his liking and ordered a steak instead.

A salad of barbecued vegies, orange couscous and harissa yoghurt

(for 4 as a main, 6–8 as a starter)

I have nothing against vegetarians. To me they are not second-class citizens, and my restaurants have always attempted to cater to their needs. But I do sometimes get upset by their dietary habits. Because to me there is nothing terribly appealing about brown rice and beans, nut cutlets or even endless bowls of pasta. Especially when I know there are some wonderful vegetable alternatives out there, including this classy dish which, in true Moroccan style, involves a whole spectrum of contrasting flavours.

---

4 zucchini, washed
1 red and 1 green capsicum, seeded and cored
1 sweet potato, peeled
½ large eggplant, washed
olive oil
freshly ground salt and pepper

Cut vegies into neat shapes (remembering to slice the sweet potato fairly thinly). Toss with a little oil and seasoning, and set aside.

harissa (see page 26)
½ cup plain yoghurt

Mix harissa into yoghurt, to taste.

1 cup orange juice
1 tsp ground cinnamon
2 tbsp olive oil
1 cup couscous
2 tbsp raisins
a good dollop of soft butter

Bring orange juice, cinnamon and olive oil to the boil. Pour over the couscous and raisins, and mix well. Leave for 3 mins until swollen, then stir in the butter and fluff with a fork. (This can be done in advance and reheated in the microwave.)

1 handful frisée lettuce or rocket leaves

Barbecue or grill the prepared vegies until crisp-tender. Put the couscous on plates, top with the leaves and then the vegies, and sprinkle with the spiced yoghurt.

A Moroccan orange, fennel and olive salad

(for 6–8)

4 oranges

1 red onion
1 small fennel bulb

1 handful rocket leaves, washed and dried
24 small black olives
freshly ground salt and pepper
virgin olive oil
sherry vinegar
chopped parsley

Peel oranges, cut off pith and cut flesh into thin slices. Place in fridge for 1 hour.

Slice onion finely. Remove hard core from fennel and slice very finely.

Scatter rocket on a platter. Top with sliced orange, onion and fennel, and the olives. Then season and sprinkle generously with oil and a little sherry vinegar. Sprinkle with parsley and, if you like, serve with preserved lemon and garlic mayo on the side (see page 32).

Tagine of pork chops with spiced apples

(for 4)

I must admit that I have never been a great fan of the meat and fruit mix. A dislike which I credit to a short period of residency in Queensland in that era when nothing appealed more to a Queensland chef than a pile of fruit salad on top of anything that had once mooed, bleated or even squawked. (This habit has now, thankfully, long gone.) But there are exceptions to this rule: duck is one that quickly springs to mind and it is true that this bird has a natural affinity with fruits such as oranges, apricots and peaches. It is also hard to beat venison with cherries as long as the cherries are fresh. And let us not forget pork with apples, which is definitely a marriage made in heaven.

Preheat oven to 180°C.

4 large well-trimmed pork loin chops

Place in one layer in a large casserole or baking dish.

1–2 onions, finely sliced
vegetable oil

Sauté onions in oil until soft and then scatter on top of the chops.

3 Granny Smith apples, peeled, cored and cut in thick wedges
1–2 tbsp honey
juice of ½ lemon

Place apple on top and drizzle with honey and then lemon juice.

½ tsp ground allspice
½ tsp ground cinnamon
½ tsp ground cayenne
½ tsp salt

Now sprinkle with the salt and spices. Pour ¼ cup water around the edges, cover tightly and cook for 40–50 mins, until chops are tender.

1 handful rocket leaves
olive oil
balsamic vinegar
freshly ground salt and pepper
preserved lemon and garlic mayo
    (optional—see page 32)

Place chops and all juices on a platter, then dress the rocket with the oil, vinegar and seasonings, mound in the centre of the chops and serve with the mayo on the side.

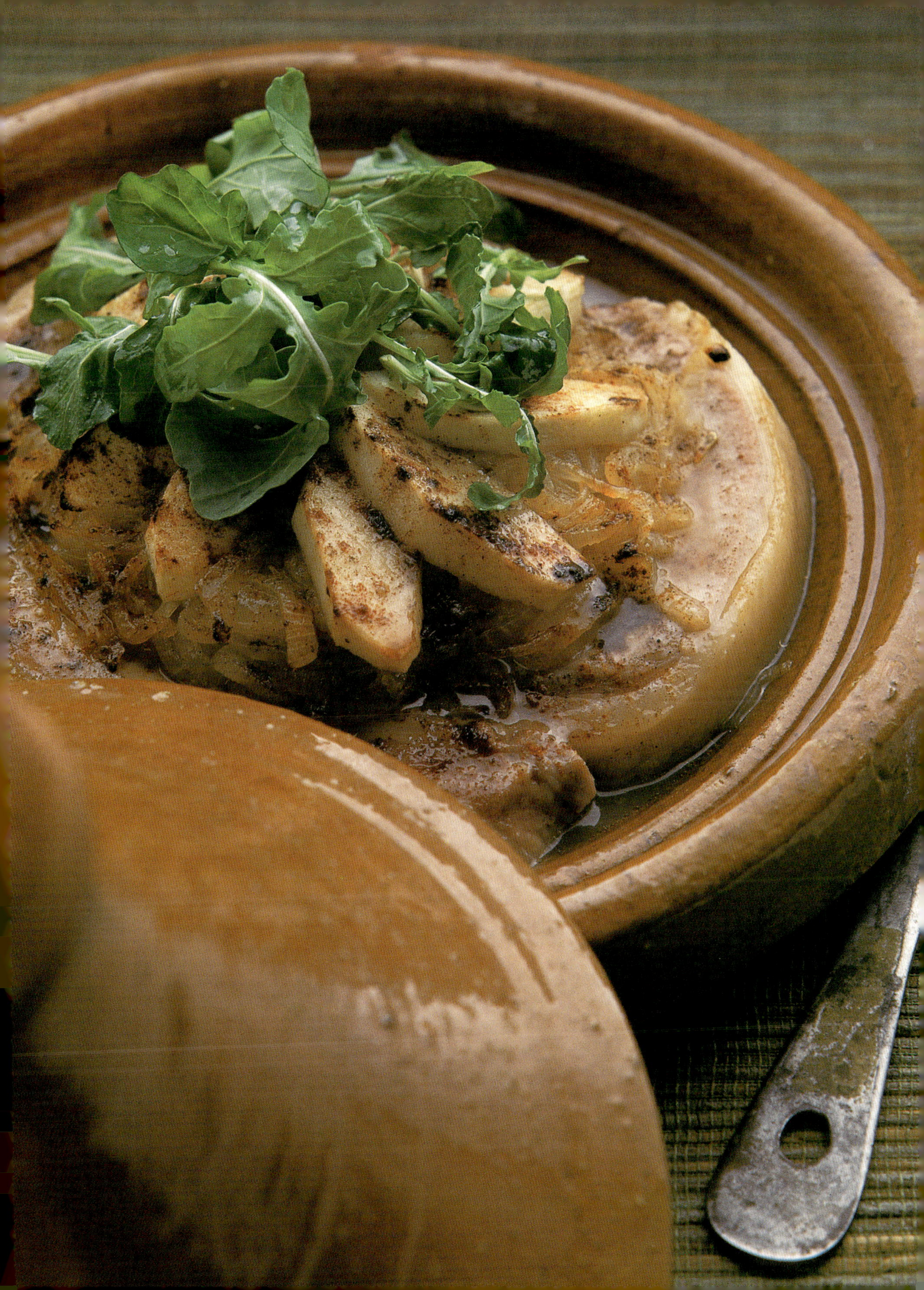

Preserved lemon and garlic mayonnaise

3 garlic cloves, unpeeled

Put in microwave at 100 per cent for 1 min. Squeeze out the pulp and chop.

1 cup mayonnaise (see page 182)
2 pieces preserved lemon, diced finely (see page 24)
1 tbsp chopped parsley

Mix with the mayo, lemon and parsley.

Moroccan keftas (meatballs) in tomato sauce

(for 4–6)

	Preheat oven to 210°C.
olive oil 2 medium-sized onions, finely chopped 4 garlic cloves, finely chopped	Heat a little oil in heavy-bottomed pot and sauté onions and garlic until soft. Remove half and set aside.
2 cups drained canned tomatoes, chopped 1 tsp ground cumin 1 tsp sweet paprika 2 tsp sugar freshly ground salt and pepper 1 tbsp sambal oelek	Add all this to the pot and simmer gently until sauce thickens. Set aside.
500 g lean minced lamb ⅓ cup yoghurt ½ tbsp sambal oelek ½ tbsp sweet paprika ½ tbsp ground cumin 3 tbsp chopped coriander freshly ground salt and pepper	Mix these together in a bowl, along with the reserved garlic and onion. Then roll into meatballs approx. 3 cm in diameter. Place on an oiled oven tray and bake until lightly browned and firm to the touch (approx. 7–8 mins).
2 tbsp chopped parsley 2 tbsp chopped basil	Pour off any fat from the keftas and mix them into the tomato sauce along with the herbs. Put into ovenproof dish and bake for 15 mins, stirring once or twice.
mint yoghurt (see page 228)	Either sprinkle the yoghurt over the top of the keftas or serve on the side.

❝ **When making meatballs, check the seasoning by frying a little ball first. And forget the old-fashioned floured hands—instead, place a bowl of cold water nearby and dip your fingers into this as you proceed to roll the meat mixture into balls of the desired size.** ❞

Harira with kefta and ham hock (for 8)

More of a stew than a soup, harira is traditionally served to end the fast during Ramadan.

¾ cup haricot beans
½ cup dried broad beans
¾ cup lentils

Cover with cold water, soak overnight and drain.

2 garlic cloves, chopped
1 medium-sized onion, chopped
1 medium-sized carrot, diced
1 large potato, diced
2 celery stalks, diced
olive oil

Heat a little oil in a large heavy-bottomed pot and sauté the vegies until the onion is soft.

2 smoked ham hocks
1 tsp sweet paprika
1 tsp ground turmeric
1 tsp ground cumin
½ tsp ground cayenne
freshly ground pepper
1 cup canned tomatoes, drained and chopped
1.5 litres chicken stock (packet is fine)

Add along with pulses and stock to well cover. Bring to boil and simmer for at least one hour, until hocks are very tender. Remove hocks and, when cool enough to handle, cut into chunks and return to soup.

1 cup cooked or canned chickpeas (see page 39)
Moroccan keftas (see page 33)
2 pieces preserved lemon skin, bought or homemade, sliced (see page 24)
2 tbsp chopped flat-leaf parsley
2 tbsp chopped coriander
freshly ground salt
2 cups water

At same time, roll and bake the meatballs until browned (this can be done in advance) and add to soup along with the rest of the ingredients. Simmer gently for 5–10 mins. Serve in deep bowls.

The tagine

A tagine is a conical-topped glazed earthenware cooking vessel (the cone keeps all the steam in, ensuring a very tender, flavoursome result). But these days a tagine can refer to almost any Moroccan stew, whether it is cooked in the traditional dish or not. So keep in mind that if you don't happen to have a tagine lurking in your cupboard, a heavy-bottomed casserole or baking dish will do almost as well.

Spiced lamb with pita bread and mint yoghurt (for 8–10)

Loosely based on Morocco's most famous lamb dish, the Berber m'choui, the idea here is that you wrap the meat up in the pita along with a dollop of yoghurt and a squeeze of lemon. (You could also, as they do in Morocco, serve bowls of mint and coriander sprigs, ground cumin, cayenne and sea salt alongside, which the guests can add at their own discretion.) And do keep in mind that this is a dish designed to be eaten with the fingers. So, please, plenty of napkins.

2 garlic cloves, crushed 1 tbsp ground coriander 2 tsp ground cumin 1 tsp ground cinnamon 1 tbsp minced fresh ginger ¼ cup olive oil juice of 1½ lemons freshly ground salt and pepper	Mix all together to make a marinade.
1 leg of lamb, about 2 kilos	Rub marinade all over the lamb and refrigerate overnight, turning two or three times. Preheat oven to 160°C. Place lamb on a rack and cook to the desired degree (about 2¼ hours for medium-rare). Then rest, loosely covered, for 15 mins.
pita bread, bought or home-made (see page 37) mint yoghurt (see page 228) lemon wedges	Warm plenty of pita, slice the lamb and serve in the centre of the table with a bowl of the yoghurt and lemon wedges.

Homemade pita bread (well worth the extra effort)

310 ml warm water
1½ tbsp dried yeast
1½ tbsp sugar

Mix these together and leave until mixture bubbles (approx. 5 mins).

430 g plain flour
½ tsp salt
185 ml olive oil

Combine these in a large bowl with the yeast mixture and mix to form a rough dough. Then tip out onto a floured surface and knead vigorously, for 10 mins or until it becomes a smooth, elastic ball. Return dough to an oiled bowl, cover and leave to rest until doubled in size. Turn it out, punch it down and knead for 5 mins.

Divide dough into 12 lumps and roll these into balls. Then press down with a rolling pin and roll into ovals 5 mm thick. Place on greaseproof paper, cover and leave for 20 mins. When puffed, cook on an un-oiled flat grill or in a non-stick pan, until lightly coloured.

" **For the bread-making process see page 9.** "

Lamb tagine with sweet potatoes (for 4–6)

2 garlic cloves, crushed 1 tsp ground cumin ½ tsp ground coriander 1 tsp ground paprika 2 pinches cayenne freshly ground salt 2 tbsp chopped parsley juice of 1 lemon 4 tbsp olive oil 1 tbsp honey	Mix everything together.
1 kilo cubed lean lamb	Mix lamb with above spicy mixture and leave for an hour or two.
	Preheat oven to 190°C.
olive oil	Heat a little oil in a large, heavy-bottomed pot and, in three or four lots, brown the lamb. Add more oil as necessary. Set meat aside.
1 large onion, chopped 2 garlic cloves, chopped 1 tbsp curry powder ½ tbsp ground cumin 1 cinnamon stick	Wipe out the pot, add a little more oil and the onion, and sauté until soft. Then add the spices and stir for a minute or two.
3 cups chicken stock (packet is fine) 1 cup canned tomatoes, drained and chopped	Add stock and tomatoes, along with the lamb, mix well, bring to the boil, cover and put in oven.
2 sweet potatoes, peeled and cut in fairly large chunks	After 45 mins add sweet potatoes and cook for about another ¾ hour, until lamb is tender.
1 cup cooked chickpeas 2 tbsp raisins chopped parsley	When ready, add chickpeas and raisins, cook for a few minutes more and serve tagine sprinkled with parsley.

❝ To cook chickpeas, soak them overnight in cold water, then drain, cover with fresh water and simmer for about an hour, until tender. Don't ever add salt during the cooking process, as this toughens them. You can also (but don't tell anyone I told you) use canned chickpeas. ❞

An addiction to garlic

❝ Tomatoes and oregano make it Italian, wine and tarragon make it French, sour cream makes it Russian, lemon and cinnamon makes it Greek, soy sauce makes it Chinese, garlic makes it good. ❞

from *The Alice's Restaurant Cookbook* by Alice May Brooks

I'm sure that anyone who has ever watched me on TV will realise that I'm seemingly hopelessly addicted to this humble bulb. In fact, I think my favourite meals of all time are those which are served by the admirable Alice Waters for her annual garlic festival at her Californian restaurant, Chez Panisse, where every course, including dessert, features copious quantities. Truly wonderful stuff, although I must admit that as yet I have not reached such culinary heights. But I have at least been able to follow her school of thought, which states that even the smallest amount of garlic will improve most dishes. Unlike Alice though, I do understand that there are those among us who do not quite share the obsession. In garlic's defence, I would like to point out that we are talking about one of the truly ancient vegies, which even rates a favourable mention in the Old Testament (Numbers XI:5). Over the years garlic has also been thought of as a sure-fire cure for everything from leprosy and TB to baldness and the common cold, not to mention its supposed properties as an aphrodisiac. Although I must admit I have often wondered about the turn-off factor associated with its strong and rather pungent odour.

Strange brew

The cooking of New Orleans is truly distinctive. It is a fascinating, heady spicy mix of French, African and Spanish cuisines with, to boot, the odd touch from the Caribbean.

But, I must admit, on my very first visit to this lively city I found myself faced with a little bit of a dilemma. Confronted by a menu with names almost as distinctive as the cuisine itself, what could I order without making a right fool of myself and finding that I had, in fact, just chosen the restaurant proprietor as my main course. I mean, what the hell was Gumbo Ya Ya, Big Mamou, Cajun Popcorn, Dirty Rice, Macque Choux or a Po-Boy? Even Blackened Redfish, the house specialty, sounded decidedly unappetising. While I was damned if I was going to order the one thing I did recognise, Hush Puppies, because whether or not this was a Louisiana delicacy, I found nothing appealing about a pair of shoes on my plate.

Still, intrepid gourmet that I am, I woosed out and said to the waiter 'Bring me whatever you like'. I then discovered that Hush Puppies are tasty, fried morsels, Gumbo is a terrific spicy soup chockful of lots of goodies and Cajun Popcorn is actually crispy, crunchy fried shrimp generously sprinkled with Tabasco.

- Prawn and sausage gumbo ya ya
- Chicken and beans in a spicy gumbo sauce
- Cajun groper fillets with fried watermelon and raita
- Oyster and corn macque choux
- The po-boy
- The peacemaker
- Prawn and cheese hush puppies
- Blackened fillet steak on a bed of corn and peas with a garlic and chilli butter
- K-Paul's cheese and chilli bread

Prawn and sausage gumbo ya ya (for 4–6)

While a Gumbo is technically a soup, it is in anybody's language a pretty hearty one and is best served as a main course with plenty of hot, crusty bread.

½ cup ghee or vegie oil
½ cup plain flour

Heat oil in a large heavy-bottomed pot, add the flour and cook, stirring constantly over medium heat until a rich brown. (This is a Cajun roux.)

2 garlic cloves, chopped
2 large onions, chopped
1 red and 1 green capsicum, cored, seeded and diced
2 celery stalks, diced

Add vegies to the roux, turn down heat and cook gently for 5 mins.

2 bay leaves
2 tsp salt
½ tsp ground black pepper
½ tsp ground cayenne
½ tsp dried thyme
½ tsp dried oregano

Add herbs and spices to the pot, mix in well and cook for 2 mins.

4 cups chicken stock (packet is fine)
1½ cups canned tomatoes, drained and chopped
3 thick sausages, cut into chunky pieces

Add all this, whisk well, bring to a simmer and cook for 15–20 mins (adding more stock if necessary).

8 large green prawns in the shell
Tabasco sauce

Then add the prawns and a generous amount of Tabasco, and simmer until prawns are firm to the touch and have changed colour.

1½ cups cooked long-grain rice
chopped parsley

Heat rice in microwave (or in a pan) and place in 4–6 large deep bowls. Ladle gumbo over the top, sprinkle with parsley and serve with more Tabasco on the side.

The cajun roux

Unlike the French roux, a Cajun roux is cooked over a high heat and because of that develops a distinctive nutty flavour which adds real Cajun character to many Louisiana dishes. But be careful, it is very easy to burn (which will make it bitter), so use a nice heavy pot, stir constantly and, if any problems arise, just turn down the heat and cook it slowly for a longer period of time.

Chicken and beans in a spicy gumbo sauce

(for 4)

1 tsp ground cumin 1 tsp sweet paprika 1 tsp ground cayenne 1 tsp salt 1 tsp garlic powder 1 tsp onion powder	Mix these together.
8 chicken thighs vegetable oil	Dust thighs with most of the spice mix. Heat a little oil in a large, heavy-bottomed pot and brown chicken on both sides. Remove.
1 medium-sized onion, chopped 1 garlic clove, crushed 2 celery stalks, diced 2 red capsicums, cored, seeded and diced	Add a little more oil to the pot and sauté the onion and garlic until soft. Then add the other vegies and toss for a minute or two.
1 small can peeled tomatoes, drained and chopped ½ cup white wine	Add these to the pot and boil for 10 mins.
2 cups dried haricot beans, soaked overnight in cold water 2 cups chicken stock (packet is fine) Tabasco sauce	Drain beans and add to the pot along with the stock, Tabasco to taste and a little of the remaining spice mix. Simmer for 15 mins then return the chicken, cover and simmer for approx. 20 mins until chicken is cooked (adding a little more stock, if necessary).
chopped parsley	Place in 4 bowls, sprinkle with parsley and serve with Tabasco on the side.

> **I cooked this lighter variation in New Orleans and, if I have to say so myself, the locals were pretty impressed. (They scoffed the lot.)**

Cajun groper fillets with fried watermelon and raita

(for 4)

Almost every café, restaurant and bar in New Orleans serves their version of Blackened Fish. Yet it is not, surprisingly, a traditional dish, but in fact a fairly recent creation by local hero, Chef Paul Prudhomme, which can be easily whipped up at home. But be warned, the first time I did so I almost burnt the kitchen down. So, make sure that your kitchen exhaust is working efficiently and your stove-top is situated well away from the nearest smoke alarm. Otherwise, the grill plate on the barbie outside may be a better, and safer, option.

2 tsp dried oregano **2 tsp dried thyme** **1 tbsp garlic powder** **1 tbsp onion powder** **1 tsp ground cayenne** **1½ tsp ground sweet paprika** **1 tsp salt**	Mix herbs and spices together.
8 groper fillets (each 80–100 g) **vegetable oil**	Place spice mix on a large plate and press fish into it on both sides. Then heat oil in a large pan until almost smoking, add fish and turn heat down. Cook until fish is opaque in centre (check by making a cut with a small knife), turning over once or twice. Cook the fish in two or three lots, if necessary.
12 wedges of watermelon, about 5 mm thick **plain flour** **mint and cucumber raita (see page 220)**	At the same time, dust watermelon with flour and cook in another oiled pan until lightly coloured on both sides. Place on plates, top with fish and garnish with raita.

> **You can buy a commercial Blackened Fish mix if you like—there are many on the market, including Paul Prudhomme's own (and mine).**

A breakfast treat—oyster and corn macque choux (for 6–8)

This is essentially a spicy Cajun mix of scrambled eggs, vegies and a splash of hot sauce. And the locals regard it not only as a hangover cure but, when oysters are included, as an aphrodisiac as well. The best of both worlds, you might say!

3 corn cobs, husk and silk removed **2 tomatoes, cored and diced** **4 basil leaves, sliced** **1 tbsp chopped parsley** **freshly ground salt and pepper**	Over a bowl, cut the kernels from the cobs and then use a sharp knife to scrape the cobs to get all the juices. Mix with the other ingredients.
unsalted butter **½ red capsicum, cored, seeded and diced** **½ spring onion (green onion), sliced**	Melt a little butter in a large, heavy-bottomed pan and sauté capsicum and spring onion until lightly brown. Add corn mix and toss for a minute or two.
8–10 large eggs **⅓ cup cream**	Whisk these together, season and add to the pan, stirring constantly with a fork until soft curds form.
Tabasco sauce **12–16 large oysters**	Add Tabasco to taste and then toss the oysters through, just to warm them.
12–16 thin slices prosciutto **chopped parsley**	Place prosciutto in circles on plates and mound the macque choux in the centre. Sprinkle with parsley.

> **Be warned—this can be pretty addictive stuff and may become habit-forming, particularly if accompanied by the odd Bloody Mary or two.**

A town after my own heart

Actually, it is not surprising that the food in New Orleans is so good. Because this is a town simply dedicated to the better things in life. Just walk around the French quarter at almost any time of the day or night and you will be entertained by great jazz seemingly being played in every bar and on every corner. At the same time your taste buds will be tantalised by wonderful odours emanating from huge black cauldrons bubbling right there on the sidewalks full to overflowing with crawfish (similar to yabbies), or by the many oyster bars with their open windows piled high with the succulent bivalves just waiting to be shucked. Or even by the aroma of gumbo, which appears to waft along every city street at certain times of the day.

Airlines—please take note

Tabasco sauce is certainly one of the stars of Louisiana. First created in 1865, after the Civil War, by Edmund McIhenny (and still, to this day, produced by the McIhenny family) it is seemingly sprinkled on everything from oysters and eggs to roasts and grills. A miniature bottle of this red-hot stuff has even become an integral part of the field rations of the American armed forces. Which is a pretty terrific idea, because I'm sure a generous slurp of Tabasco could enliven the most boring and bland food. (Maybe the airlines could take a leaf out of their book and include those miniatures with all airline meals—now there's an idea.)

The po-boy (for 4)

Made either as individual sandwiches or in a whole French stick split in half, the Po-Boy is classy junk food which is stuffed with anything from roast beef and gravy to crumbed fish seasoned liberally with Tabasco. And the name—this comes from the 1914 New Orleans streetcar strike, when several thousand young streetcar workers could hardly afford to eat and two 'poor boys', Benny and Clovis Martin, came up with the idea of filling stale bread with reheated leftovers along with a gravy or sauce to moisten the bread.

Thai sweet chilli sauce
sambal oelek
1 cup mayonnaise (bought or home-made, see page 182)

Add chilli sauce and sambal to the mayo to taste, and set aside.

sliced leftover roast meat or poultry with gravy

Reheat the meat gently in the gravy (adding a little water if necessary).

8 thick slices country-style bread
unsalted butter
3 iceberg or cos lettuce leaves, sliced
3 tomatoes, sliced
½ **red onion, finely sliced**

Toast the bread, butter it lightly and top 4 of the slices with mayo, lettuce, tomatoes and onion, and then with the meat and a little of its gravy. Sprinkle with more mayo and top with the other slice of bread.

> **The Thai chilli sauce I use for this is the speckled one which is, for some strange reason, dubbed Sweet Chilli Sauce for Chicken. I say 'for some strange reason' because directly underneath this description it is deemed to be perfect for a large variety of seafood with hardly a mention of the chicken—obviously something has been lost in the translation.**

The peacemaker

(for 4–6)

According to legend, this sandwich is so called because, after a night spent in the bars of the French quarter, the husband brought this special treat home in an attempt to appease his wife—I wonder whether it worked?

---

1 cup breadcrumbs
plain flour
freshly ground salt and pepper
2 eggs
Tabasco sauce
milk
2–3 dozen large Pacific oysters

In 3 bowls, put the crumbs, the plain flour mixed with seasonings, and the eggs whisked with Tabasco and a little milk. Then crumb the oysters by dipping each one in flour, then egg mix and finally, firmly, in crumbs. Set aside.

Preheat oven to 180°C.

1 French stick
melted butter

Cut loaf in half lengthways and hollow out some of the soft centre. Paint inside with the butter and bake in oven until crisp.

4 cups vegetable oil

Heat oil to 180°–190°C and fry the oysters until golden. Drain well.

Tabasco sauce
tartare sauce (see page 290)
crisp lettuce leaves, shredded
sliced tomato

Add Tabasco to the tartare, to taste, and spread generously in hollow bread bases. Top with lettuce, tomato and oysters, and press top of the bread back on firmly. Cut into 4 or 6 pieces crossways.

> **EAT LOUISIANA OYSTERS FOR LONGER LOVING**

bumper sticker from New Orleans' famous Acme Oyster House

Prawn and cheese hush puppies (for 8)

Absolutely nothing to do with the shoes of the same name (although, in one New Orleans restaurant, the fritters were rather leathery), Hush Puppies are supposedly called that because of the hunters' habit of feeding them to their dogs to stop them barking. And, I must admit, if I was hand-fed these delicious morsels I would most probably stop barking too.

240 g unsalted butter
1 tsp salt
1 garlic clove, crushed
500 ml water

Put these in a saucepan and boil until butter is completely melted.

240 g flour

Add flour to the pan all at once over heat and stir continually with a wooden spoon until mixture comes away from the sides and forms a loose ball, and there is a light coating on the bottom of the pot. Then allow to cool slightly.

5 large eggs
2 tsp Dijon mustard
150 g commercial grated parmesan
4 cooked prawns, chopped finely
150 g grated tasty cheese
2 chopped spring onions (green onions)

Add eggs to the batter one at a time, mixing well between each addition. Then mix remaining ingredients in well.

6 cups vegetable oil
extra parmesan grated
chopped parsley
chilli mayonnaise (see page 50)

Put oil in a wok or large heavy-bottomed pot and heat to about 180°–190°C. With a teaspoon, drop spoonfuls of the batter into the hot oil and cook until golden (don't overcrowd the oil). Then drain well on paper towels, sprinkle with a little parmesan and parsley, and serve with chilli mayonnaise.

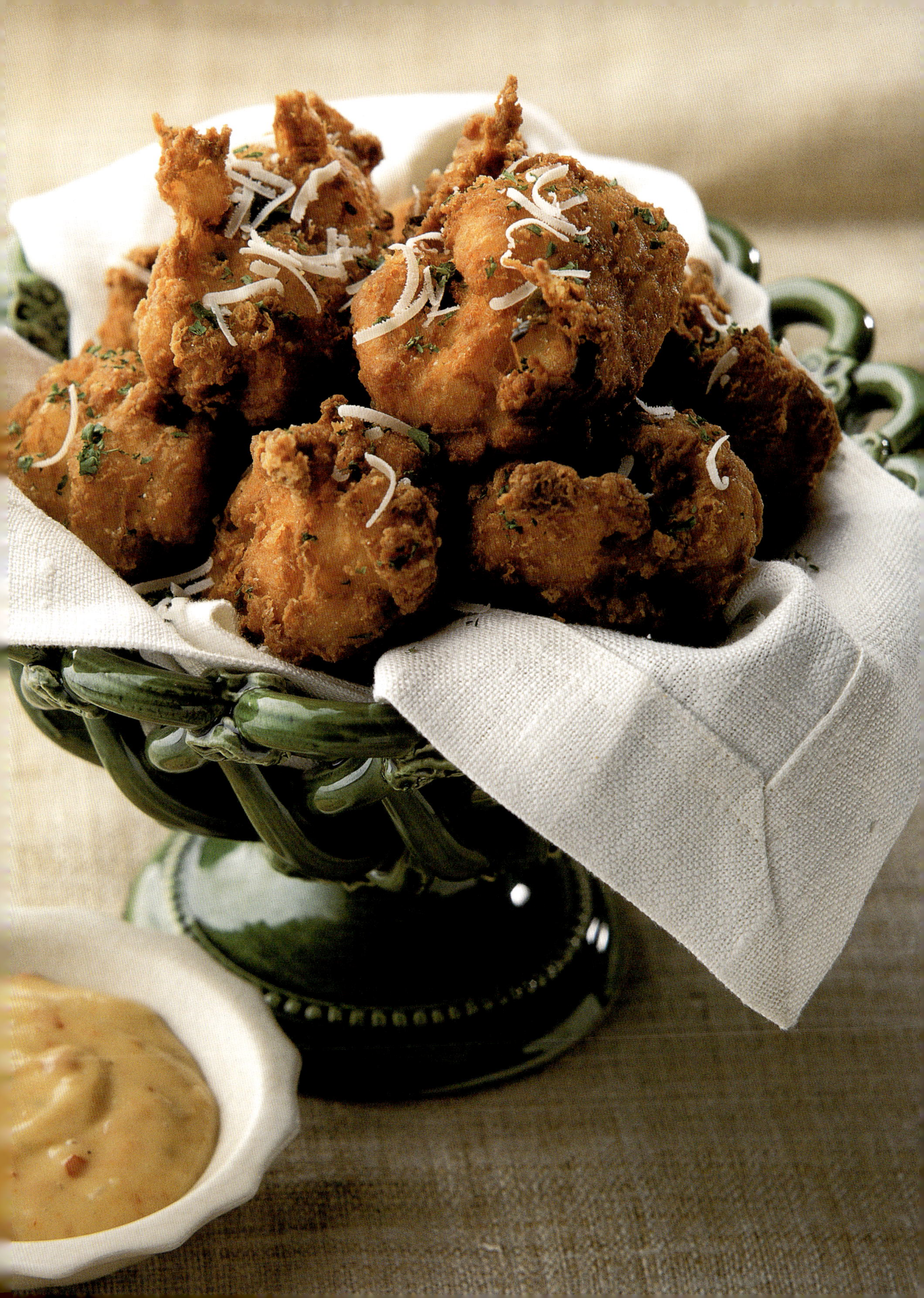

Blackened fillet steak on a bed of corn and peas with a garlic and chilli butter (for 4)

100 g soft, unsalted butter
2 garlic cloves, crushed
a squeeze of lemon juice
1–2 chillies, seeded and very
 finely chopped

Mix together and set aside.

Blackened spice mix (see page 46)
4 x 180 g fillet steaks, trimmed of
 all fat and sinew
vegetable oil

Put spice mix on a plate and press steak into it, on both sides. Heat oil in a pan, until almost smoking. Add beef and seal on both sides, then turn down heat and cook steaks to the desired degree. When beef is ready, set aside in a warm spot to rest.

3 corn cobs, kernels removed
1 cup tiny fresh peas
 (or frozen ones)

Cook the corn and peas briefly in a large pot of lightly salted boiling water. Drain well and place in a circle on 4 plates. Top with steaks and put a generous dollop of the flavoured butter on top.

The inevitable Chinese fix

As is my wont, even in New Orleans there came a day when I just had to have an Asian fix. So the crew, in their wisdom, left it up to me to find a halfway-decent Chinese establishment. Which may be an easy task in almost any Aussie city, but in New Orleans it turned out to be quite a difficult chore. And, I must admit, my chosen restaurant was less than inspiring: not only was the food dreadful (Australia circa 1950, with tonnes of MSG and nary a fresh vegie in sight) but, as the crowning glory, the Chinese tea came not in a pot but in a McDonald's milkshake container with tea bags of a definite commercial bent hanging over the sides.

K-Paul's cheese and chilli bread

My version of the delicious bread that is served at K-Paul's Louisiana Kitchen. This is the perfect accompaniment to almost any Cajun or Creole food. And taking a leaf from K-Paul's (where it is baked right there in the middle of the dining room) I always cook it at the very last moment, so that those wonderful fresh bread aromas still linger throughout the house as my guests arrive.

Preheat oven to 190°C.

15 g dried yeast
400 ml tepid water

Mix yeast with water. Allow to prove for 10 mins.

4 small chillies
4 spring onions (green onions)
500 g plain flour
240 g tasty cheese, grated
1 tbsp sambal oelek
2 tsps salt
1 tbsp olive oil
½ tsp sugar

Finely slice chillies and spring onions, and combine with remaining ingredients in a large bowl. Stir in yeast mixture. Prove, covered, until doubled in size.

Knock back dough and place in oiled bread tin. Leave until dough fills the tin.

eggwash (see below)

Brush top of loaf with eggwash and bake for 30–40 mins.

> **An eggwash is made by combining a beaten egg with a little milk or water and is brushed over the dough before baking.**

Bung it on the barbie

I LOVE TO BARBECUE. Even after taking into account the fact that, traditionally, our backyards tended to be perfumed by burning fat and, dare I say it, fly spray, there was still always something about the smoky aroma of food cooking over hot coals which instantly whetted my appetite. And while it can be said that familiarity breeds contempt, although I have seemingly spent half my life slaving over a hot barbie, this form of cooking is still one of my favourites.

But I must admit that in recent years, my barbie feasts have evolved from that old-fashioned 'let's burn some meat' form into rather lean and mean little numbers. Like most Australasian food, the humble barbie has reinvented itself, soaking up the foodie ideas of the world like a sponge. So, no more burnt snags and fatty chops, and definitely no more blackened steaks (unless in the Cajun style). Instead, the new age version tends to lean towards the Mediterranean, Asia or the Caribbean, with herb-packed marinades, well trimmed cuts of meat and starring roles for everything from baby fish and sardines to spatchcocked chickens and boned legs of lamb.

I have also stopped thinking of the BBQ as something that is, purely and simply, fired up on the weekends or for those special backyard parties. Instead, I now think of it as just another piece of kitchen equipment which can be easily used to whip up sauces, cook vegetables with a difference, or even create the complete family meal (as long as it is not snowing outside). And just to show that I really am the new age barbie cook, the fly spray has even been replaced—by a good old-fashioned fly swatter.

- Lamb cutlets 'scottadito'
- Butterflied leg of lamb in a mustardy marinade
- John Wilson's hot-smoked lamb topside
- Herby Moroccan marinated lamb cutlets
- Garlic and rosemary studded leg of lamb
- Tuscan fillet of beef with mushrooms and olive butter
- A lo-cal lamb salad with minted yoghurt
- Huey's terrific steak sanga
- Huey's favourite BBQ butter
- T-bone steaks with Maggie Beer's slow-roasted onions
- Barbecue roasted rib-eye of beef with mustard crust and horseradish sour cream
- Mixed grill—Italian-style
- Beef on a stick
- Indian pork and veal koftas in flat bread
- Texas-style BBQ baby back ribs

- Tuscan barbecued rolled pork
- Wolfgang Puck's marinated kangaroo with mint vinaigrette
- Spatchcocked chicken with garlic butter and fresh basil
- Calypso chook
- Real simple chicken breasts with a lemon-spiked herb marinade
- A piquant BBQ mayo
- Kick-arse chicken tortilla with avocado salsa
- Salmon on a bed of charred radicchio with a tapenade butter
- Whiting with an Italian herb relish
- Bahamian baby fish
- Stuffed squid (calamari) with Sicilian parsley, garlic and olive oil dressing
- Barbecued sweetcorn salsa
- Grilled marlin with roasted salsa
- Sardines on toast with a twist
- Barbecued oysters with sausages
- Tolarno's bloody mary oyster shooters
- Barbecued corn on the cob with gremolata butter
- Witloof in an Italian manner
- Barbecued potatoes with crispy bacon and sour cream
- Some vegie quick picks
- Pumpkin with soy-honey caramel
- Big juicy mushrooms with basil oil
- What about a few of the classic BBQ salads revisited?

Lamb cutlets 'scottadito' (for 4)

A traditional Italian favourite, where the idea is that you trim the cutlets well, cook them briefly over high heat and then eat them with your fingers. (And, just in case you are wondering, *scottadito* means 'burning fingers', which is exactly what happens.)

Preheat BBQ.

1 cup olive oil
juice of 1 lemon
freshly ground salt and pepper
1 tbsp chopped parsley

Whisk these ingredients together for a marinade.

4 racks of lamb, trimmed of all fat and sinew (make sure your butcher has removed the chine bone)

Cut racks into cutlets and clean them by scraping the bones with a sharp knife to remove any meat or fat. Then give each cutlet a whack with a meat mallet and pour marinade over, leaving them for 20–30 mins (but no more, as this amount of lemon will begin to cook them). Cook to the desired degree (about 2 mins each side for medium-rare) and serve immediately.

❝ **If you have trouble doing it yourself, ask your butcher to trim the racks for you—but resist the temptation to buy pre-cut cutlets, as it is then almost impossible to trim them to the degree required.** ❞

The spit on your gravy BBQ

My friends in the supermarket business may not be too keen on this idea, but my mate Filthy Phil (one of the original members of 'I Spit on your Gravy', a band whose behaviour was, to say the least, appalling) told me of the Gravy's famous barbies which, according to him, were always a huge hit. It seems that, in typical Gravy fashion, they hadn't actually got around to buying a BBQ. So they instead used a supermarket shopping trolley, which they turned on its side and propped up with bricks, then lit a fire in the middle. The cooking was then performed on the bars of the trolley and, according to an informed source, the food was either burnt or raw, but the participants were too p....d to notice.

Butterflied leg of lamb in a mustardy marinade

(for 6–8)

1 cup olive oil
2 tbsp Dijon mustard
½ tbsp sambal oelek (Asian chilli paste)
generous splash of soy sauce
juice of 1 lemon
freshly ground pepper

Whisk everything together.

1 small leg of lamb (ask your butcher to butterfly it for you)

Place lamb on bench, give it a few whacks with a meat mallet and trim off any excess fat. Put into the above marinade and leave for 1–2 hours.

Preheat BBQ.

Place lamb on hottest part of the BBQ and cook for 10 mins, turning over once or twice. Move to a more moderate part of the barbie and cook to the desired degree (about 30–35 mins in total for medium-rare). Remove from heat, rest for 5 mins and carve.

❝ Of course, you can serve this with a green salad or some jacket potatoes, but I love, in an American vein, candied sweet potatoes alongside. Just scrub some sweet potatoes and cook in boiling salted water, until tender when pierced with a skewer. Drain, cool and cut into thick slices. Then, when lamb is almost ready, barbecue until golden, regularly brushing with liquid honey. ❞

John Wilson's hot-smoked lamb topside

(for 4–6)

My mate John Wilson is an expert on smoking (and that is not of the B&H variety). He was, until recently, the driving force behind Sydney firm Mohr Foods who, in my opinion, produce about Australia's best smoked salmon.

1 garlic clove, peeled
2 lamb topsides, trimmed well
freshly ground salt and pepper

6 heaped cups hardwood sawdust
½ cup tarragon leaves
1 garlic head, separated but left whole
1 tbsp coriander seeds
1 tbsp whole black peppercorns

Set a kettle BBQ with indirect fire, and light it.

Rub garlic all over meat, season and leave for 30 mins.

Mix sawdust with the other ingredients and add enough water to form a ball. When BBQ fire has died down, spread out and cover with 2 cm of sawdust mix and ensure there is enough draft to let the coals smoulder. (If coals aren't smouldering or are flaring, adjust the ventilation vents.)

Place lamb on rack, and put lid on. After 20 mins increase the draft, giving the lamb a smoked flavour. Cook to the desired degree (approx. 20 mins for medium-rare), rest for 5 mins, slice, and serve with lettuces dressed with olive oil.

Herby Moroccan marinated lamb cutlets (for 4)

½ cup vegetable oil
1 cup soft herbs, such as coriander, parsley, basil, etc.
a splash of soy sauce
½ tsp each ground cumin and turmeric
2 fresh chillies
2 tsp honey
juice of ½ lemon
freshly ground pepper

Whiz up to make a marinade.

4 racks of lamb, all fat and sinew removed, and chine bones removed

Cut racks into cutlets and flatten slightly with a meat mallet. Pour above marinade over and leave for an hour or two, turning a few times. Barbecue to the desired degree, brushing with the marinade as you do so. Serve with couscous (see page 22) or a simple green salad.

> **This marinade is one of my absolute favourites, which also works well with a leg of lamb. Just pour over a well-trimmed leg, massage it in, then refrigerate overnight, turning it once or twice, before roasting in a hot oven.**

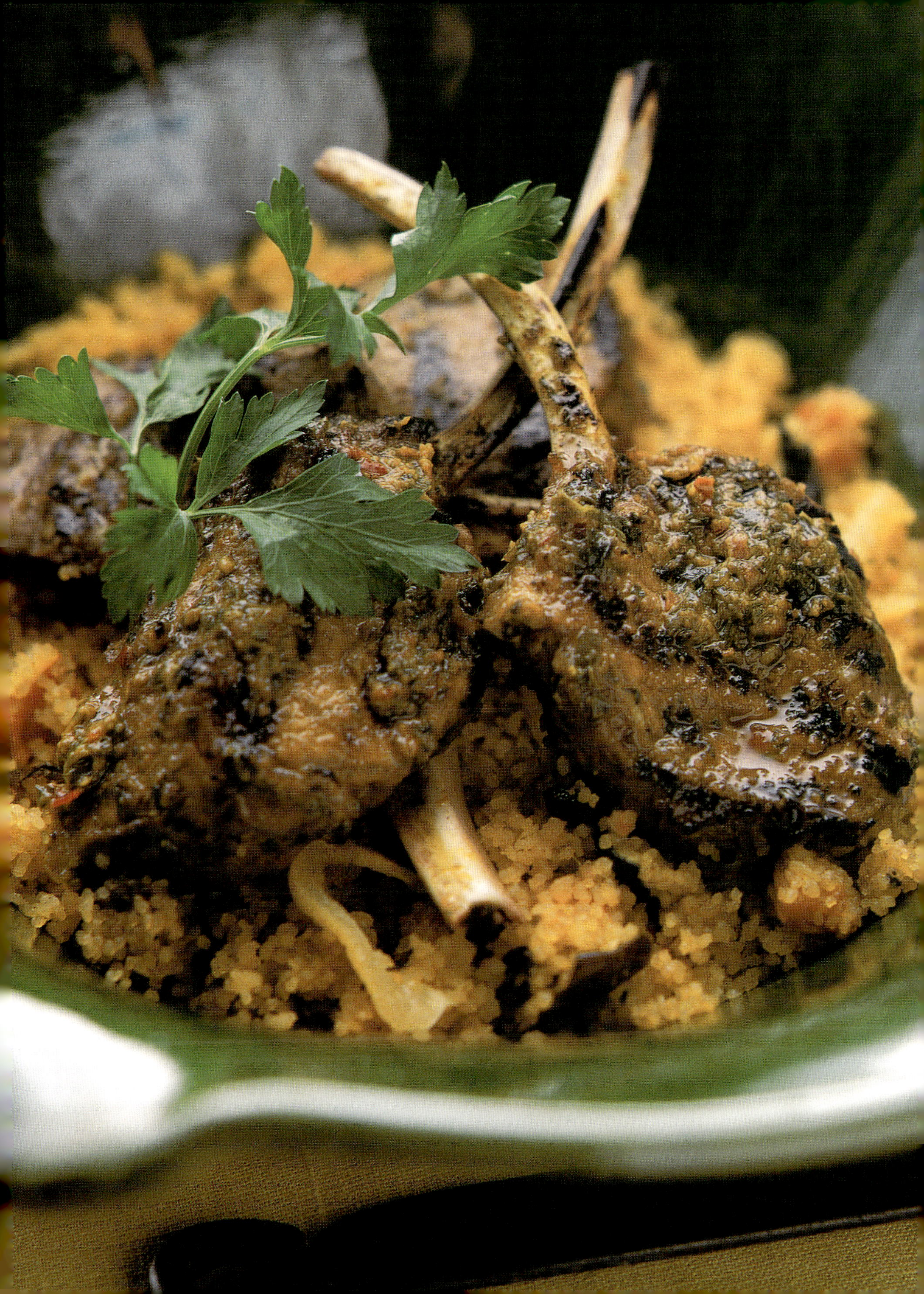

Garlic and rosemary studded leg of lamb

(for 6–8)

1 butterflied leg of lamb
12 small slivers of garlic
12 rosemary sprigs

Place lamb on bench, give a few whacks with a mallet and trim any excess fat or sinew. Lay skin side down on bench and make 12 small cuts about 5 mm deep in the meat. Push a sliver of garlic and a rosemary sprig into each.

½ cup olive oil
2 tbsp honey
2 tbsp rosemary needles
4 garlic cloves, crushed
splash of soy

Mix these together, pour over lamb and leave overnight, turning once or twice.

Preheat BBQ.

Put lamb on hottest part of BBQ for 10 mins, turning once or twice. Move to a more moderate part and cook to the desired degree (about 30–35 mins in total for medium-rare), brushing regularly with the marinade. When meat is ready, remove from heat, rest for 5 mins and carve into thin slices.

> **In 1492, when Columbus discovered the New World, he also discovered something far more important. The Arawak Indians were cooking meat over pits of fire—a process that they called Barbacoa. Obviously, this is the origin of barbecuing as we know it today.**

Tuscan fillet of beef with mushrooms and olive butter (for 4)

1 garlic clove, crushed
squeeze of lemon
2 anchovies
8 pitted black olives
100 g soft unsalted butter

600–700 g centre cut beef fillet, left in one piece and trimmed well
8 large flat mushrooms, peeled and stalks removed
olive oil

freshly ground salt and pepper
chopped parsley

Preheat BBQ.

Process everything except the butter. Then mix in the butter, roll in foil or greaseproof paper and place in freezer for 15 mins or so.

Brush beef and mushrooms all over with oil. Cook beef to the desired degree (approx. 15–18 mins for medium-rare), adding mushrooms when the meat is almost ready.

Place beef and mushrooms in a tray, top with some slices of the flavoured butter and leave in a warm spot for 5 mins.

Slice beef, place on plates, season and pour all the juices from the tray over the top, along with some chopped parsley.

Rest that meat

Resting meat (or poultry or seafood) after cooking will always produce a far better result. This is because the cooking heat forces the juices into the centre and, when the meat is allowed to relax, these same juices settle throughout, resulting in a far more tender product.

A lo-cal lamb salad with minted yoghurt

(for 4)

	Preheat BBQ.
2 loins of lamb, trimmed of all fat and sinew olive oil freshly ground salt and pepper	Brush the lamb lightly with oil and season. Barbecue to the desired degree (approx. 8–10 mins for medium-rare) and set aside to rest in a warm place for 5 mins.
6 ripe red tomatoes, cored and cut into thick slices ¼ telegraph (continental) cucumber, peeled and cut into thick slices ¼ red onion, finely sliced extra-virgin olive oil	Place tomato slices in a circle on a large plate (or on 4 individual ones). Top with cucumber and then the onion. Sprinkle very lightly with oil, and season.
½ cup low-fat yoghurt juice of ½ lemon 2 tbsp finely chopped fresh mint a pinch of cayenne 1 garlic clove, crushed	Mix together.
4 sprigs of mint	Slice lamb and place neatly on the salad, along with any juices. Sprinkle with yoghurt mix and garnish with mint sprigs.

❝ Isn't it great when a dish is not only good for you, but it tastes bloody good to boot? ❞

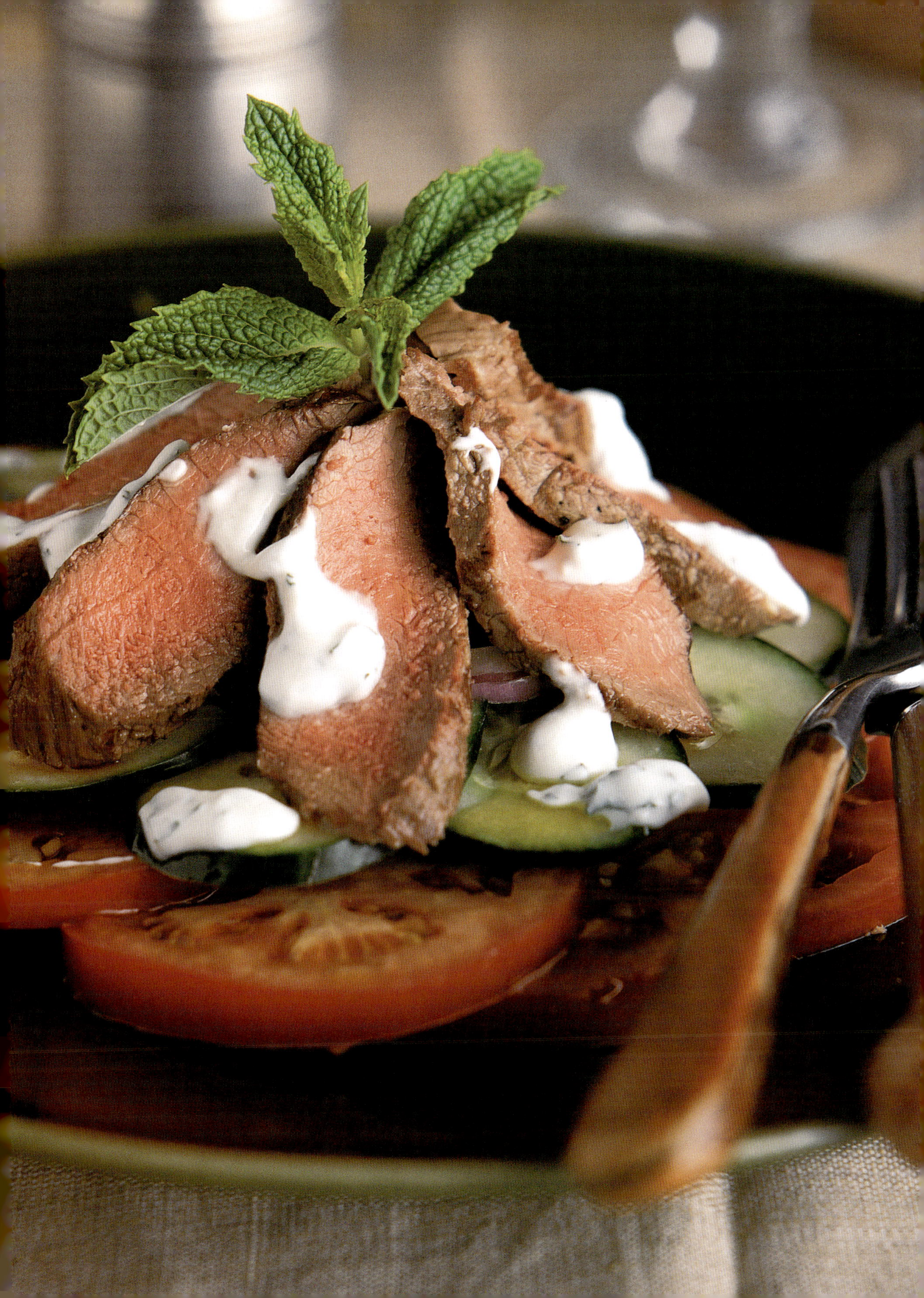

Huey's terrific steak sanga (for 4)

Preheat BBQ.

2 medium-sized onions, peeled and thickly sliced
freshly ground salt and pepper
vegetable oil

Season onions, brush with oil and cook over moderate heat until golden-brown and slightly charred on the edges.

4 x 100 g slices of beef rump or rib eye, trimmed very well
4 rashers of rindless bacon
3 ripe tomatoes, cored and cut into thick slices
8 thick slices country-style or sourdough bread

Cook steak to desired degree.
Cook the bacon at the same time and, when both are ready, quickly cook the tomato slices and 4 pieces of the bread on both sides.

Dijon mustard
4 large crisp lettuce leaves
Huey's favourite BBQ butter (see page 71)

Place bread on individual plates and smear generously with mustard. Top each with a lettuce leaf, some of the onion, a few tomato slices, steak, a bacon rasher and some butter. Then grill the other 4 slices of bread and place on top.

Huey's favourite BBQ butter

1 tsp chopped parsley
2 pinches ground paprika
2 pinches dried tarragon
1 tsp Dijon mustard
3 tbsp fresh tomato purée
2 garlic cloves, crushed
4 anchovies
2 tsp capers
6 pitted black olives

Whiz up in a processor and remove to a bowl.

500 g unsalted butter
lemon juice
Tabasco sauce
freshly ground salt and pepper

Add butter to the above mixture gradually, until smooth and well mixed. Then add lemon juice, Tabasco and seasonings to taste and roll in greaseproof paper. Keep in freezer until needed.

T-bone steaks with Maggie Beer's slow-roasted onions (for 4)

I first tasted these delicious onions when Maggie cooked them for me on the front lawn of her, now sadly departed, Pheasant Farm restaurant in the Barossa Valley. She served them with barbecued kangaroo, but I have found they work just as well with any red meat. (I also ate them one night on toast for supper when I had got carried away and cooked a few too many—delicious!)

4 medium-sized brown onions, skin on
olive oil
freshly ground salt and pepper

Cut onions in half crossways, brush generously with oil and season well. Cook in 160°C oven for 2 hours or until they caramelise.

Preheat BBQ.

⅓ cup olive oil
1–2 garlic cloves, crushed
6 sprigs rosemary
4 x 200 g T-bone steaks, well trimmed
freshly ground salt and pepper

Combine oil, garlic and rosemary. Marinate steaks in this for 30–45 mins, turning once. Then barbecue to the desired degree. Remove to 4 plates and season.

2–4 tbsp good red-wine vinegar (such as Hill-Smith)
2–4 tbsp olive oil
chopped parsley

Peel caramelised onions, cut in two and sprinkle with vinegar, oil and parsley to taste. Serve alongside the steaks.

The cooking of the steak

When cooking steaks, always make sure that the grill or BBQ is preheated—otherwise the meat will stew and toughen. And, for god's sake, don't play with them! At the very most, turn them over once or twice and never, ever flip them over the first time until they are well crusted on the bottom.

Barbecue roasted rib-eye of beef with mustard crust and horseradish sour cream

(for 8+)

Preheat kettle BBQ with indirect fire.

1 whole beef rib-eye fillet
freshly ground salt and pepper
Dijon mustard

Trim fillet of any excess fat, season well and smear top and sides generously with mustard. Place on rack with drip tray underneath, and roast, covered, to the desired degree. When cooked, remove from BBQ, cover loosely with foil and rest for 10 mins.

sour cream
prepared horseradish cream
1 tbsp snipped chives

Mix together to taste. Then slice meat, against the grain, into thick slices and serve with any juices and the horseradish sour cream.

> " A meat thermometer takes all the worries out of this recipe. Just insert into the centre of the roast and cook to 60°C for rare and 70°C for medium. "

Mixed grill—Italian style (for 4)

I have always been a great fan of the mixed grill. Even from an early age, a plate piled high with different goodies appeared the perfect dish and one which I, as the budding gastronome, ordered on almost every visit to our local greasy spoon.

But, I have to admit, the rest of the family didn't quite see my passionate interest in this culinary Everest in quite the same way as I. Brother Don, to this day, insists that my menu choice had more to do with pure greed than with any supposed development of a fine palate. (And he can talk—in those days, this former president of the Champagne Academy couldn't even look at a steak unless it was well done and generously sprinkled with sauce of a definite commercial bent.)

Still, fortunately for both of us, our tastes did eventually mature. And whilst I still enjoy the mixed grill, these days it is far more likely to be the Italian version, which is simplicity in itself, combining three or four different varieties of well trimmed meat cooked briefly over charcoal and served with little more than a wedge of lemon. And, surprisingly, I don't even miss that tomato sauce!

	Preheat BBQ.
4 thick Italian sausages	Put sausages in simmering water and simmer gently until firm. Drain, then barbeque sausages over moderate heat, turning regularly until well browned.
4 thick pieces centre-cut fillet steak (approx. 80 g each), trimmed of all fat and sinew **4 well trimmed double lamb cutlets** **4 large flat field mushrooms, peeled** **olive oil** **freshly ground salt and pepper**	Brush meat and mushrooms with oil and barbecue over high heat to the desired degree, seasoning once sealed and removing to the side when almost ready. (Turn while cooking to create attractive grid marks.)
4 slices calf or lamb liver, trimmed of all fat and sinew	Oil liver, season and cook briefly over high heat. (The liver must, at the most, be pink inside—otherwise it will be dry and tasteless.)
chopped parsley **lemon wedges**	Arrange meat and mushrooms on plates, sprinkle with parsley and serve with lemon wedges on the side.

Oh dear

When I operated Memories of the Mediterranean Restaurant at Rockman's Regency Hotel in Melbourne, we received a review from one of our more waspish restaurant reviewers. After much difficulty, she finally found something to complain about—the Mediterranean mixed-meat grill, according to her, had too much meat in it. Most of my comments were, of course, unprintable, but I do remember mentioning to my staff that it was a little like complaining that bouillabaisse, the famous seafood soup from the South of France, had too much fish in it!

Beef on a stick (for 6–8)

When I first began working in restaurants, the shish kebab was one of the most popular menu items. Maybe, in the customers' case, this was due to the fact that its rather exotic name invoked romantic images of the kasbahs of North Africa, the Greek Islands or even the court of the Russian tsars, where the meat traditionally arrived flaming on the swords of the palace guards.

But for whatever reason (even for me) the shish kebab was a popular menu choice. That was until all images of romanticism were dispelled by me being given the task of preparing the blessed things. It was then I realised why these skewers were so popular with the restaurateurs, because every meat scrap, no matter how old, sinewy or smelly became a part of this exotic treat with the supposition that, once it had been marinated for a day or two, who would know.

Of course I now knew and for many years after, I wouldn't touch anything that had even been near a stick or a skewer. That is, until I travelled overseas and discovered that, fortunately, it was only in New Zealand and Australia that the shish kebab was treated so shabbily—and that when they were made from lean, lightly marinated cubes of meat, seafood or poultry and cooked over glowing coals they were absolutely delicious.

¼ **cup olive oil**
splash of soy sauce
2 garlic cloves, crushed
½ **handful fresh herbs, such as parsley, mint and basil**
freshly ground pepper
squeeze of lemon

Whiz up to make a marinade.

1 kilo chuck steak, well trimmed and cut into 2 cm cubes

Toss meat in marinade and leave for 1 hour.

Preheat BBQ.

button mushrooms
cubes of onion, capsicum and eggplant, cut to approx. the same size as the beef

lemon wedges

Thread beef and vegies on the skewers and cook, turning and brushing with the marinade at regular intervals, until meat is crusty on the outside and cooked to the desired degree inside.

Serve with lemon wedges.

> **This works just as well with lamb or chicken, and I have even made a super version using large, fresh scallops. But, in that case, I only left them in the marinade for 15 minutes.**

> **If using wooden skewers, soak them in cold water before they go on the BBQ. This will stop them bursting into flames as the meat cooks (which is not a bad idea).**

Indian pork and veal koftas in flat bread (for 4)

vegetable oil
¼ onion, finely chopped
1 garlic clove, crushed

250 g pork and veal mince
2 tbsp Indian lime pickle
a little beaten egg
salt and freshly ground pepper
2 tbsp chopped parsley

½ cup plain yoghurt
1 tbsp chopped coriander
Indian lime pickle

4 pieces pita bread
2–3 Cos lettuce leaves, sliced
8–12 slices tomato
8–12 slices telegraph
 (continental) cucumber

Heat a little oil and gently sauté onion and garlic until soft.

Mix these ingredients with the sautéed onion and garlic and then, using your hands, divide into 4–8 portions. Take each portion and roll along a skewer to make a sausage shape. Cover and refrigerate for at least 2 hours to firm.

Mix yoghurt and coriander with lime pickle to taste. Set aside.

Preheat BBQ.

Cook the koftas on an oiled grill plate over medium-high heat. When they are almost ready, heat the pita bread on the BBQ. Cut off one edge of each piece of bread and stuff this 'pocket' with lettuce, tomato, cucumber and kofta. Sprinkle with the yoghurt mixture.

Not every American needs a barbie

I must admit that when it comes to the cooking of steaks (or, in fact, almost any red meat), I am closer to the raw to bloody brigade than I am to those who prefer them well cooked.

But even I was amazed when a well dressed Texan wandered into one of my restaurants and gave a whole new meaning to a rare steak. His demands were actually very simple. All he wanted was a plate that had been placed in a hot oven for exactly 10 minutes, a 200 g well trimmed piece of our best steak, a generous dollop of butter (unsalted of course) and some freshly ground pepper.

My first reaction was pretty understandable but, more out of curiosity than anything else, I decided to bow to his demands. I then watched in amazement as he smeared the steak with butter and pepper before 'cooking' it on the well heated plate.

Obviously, here was a man who thought Beef Tartare and Carpaccio were for wimps, because as the whole room came to a stop he proceeded to demolish this piece of decidedly raw beef in large chunks with little more than the occasional addition of extra seasoning.

He then paid the bill, tipped $20, asked for his compliments to be passed on to the chef (for what?) and strolled from the dining-room with nary a backward glance.

Texas-style BBQ baby back ribs (for 4)

If you thought for one second that we Aussies were passionate about our barbies, you should travel to the southern states of America, where barbecuing is more of a religion than a pastime, and where the barbie sometimes takes up more room than the house. This is also where, during the summer months, barbecue contests are held with prizes of up to $50 000—an odd idea to Aussies, who regard the backyard barbie purely and simply as a social event which will only fail if the beer runs out (or is warm) and the missus has forgotten to order the tomato sauce.

Preheat BBQ.

300 ml tomato sauce
2 tbsp Worcestershire sauce
2 tbsp white vinegar
1 tbsp brown sugar
½ tbsp Dijon mustard
1 tbsp sambal oelek
2 garlic cloves, crushed

Whisk together.

4 slabs baby back pork ribs

Brush the above sauce generously all over and cook on moderate heat for 30–40 mins, brushing with more sauce regularly.

Serve with any remaining sauce on the side.

> **Serve with barbecued corn cobs (see page 101) or barbecued baby spuds (see page 103), or even with that good old favourite—jacket spuds cooked in foil around the edges of the barbie and topped with sour cream and chives.**

Tuscan barbecued rolled pork (for 8–10)

1 boned leg of pork, skin scored finely
6 tbsp chopped parsley
4 garlic cloves, crushed
freshly ground black pepper
¼ cup olive oil

½ cup olive oil
1½ cups dry white wine
2 bay leaves, crumbled
salt

Lay pork, skin-side down, on bench. Mix together parsley, garlic, pepper and oil, and rub all over the meat. Roll up as tightly as you can and tie up every 2 cm or so.

Mix these with any of the leftover garlic mix, and pour over the pork. Refrigerate overnight, turning two or three times.

Preheat kettle BBQ with indirect heat.

Place drip tray in middle, place pork on rack and barbecue, covered, basting with marinade at regular intervals until it reaches 75°C on meat thermometer. Rest for 10 mins in a warm spot and slice thickly, pouring any juices over the top.

Wolfgang Puck's marinated kangaroo with mint vinaigrette (for 4)

On a flying visit from the States, Wolfgang Puck, the American super-chef credited with, amongst other things, creating the gourmet pizza, made this for me in his Melbourne restaurant. It was brilliant and, like me, Wolfie was highly impressed by this delicious meat.

½ cup soy sauce ½ cup mirin (Japanese rice wine) ¼ cup chopped spring onions (green onions) ½ tbsp dried chilli flakes 2 garlic cloves, finely chopped	Mix well.
4 fillets of roo, trimmed of all fat and sinew	Add fillets to marinade and leave for 30 or 40 mins. Preheat BBQ.
½ cup chopped mint leaves ¼ cup chopped coriander ¼ cup chopped parsley ½ cup vegetable oil ¼ cup rice wine (or rice vinegar) 2 egg yolks freshly ground salt and pepper a dash of chilli oil	Whisk these vinaigrette ingredients together and set aside. Barbecue the roo on all sides (to no more than medium-rare as it will quickly dry out because it is so lean.)
rocket or salad leaves	When meat is ready, rest it for 5 mins, then slice and serve on the leaves with the vinaigrette sprinkled generously over the top.

Spatchcocked chicken with garlic butter and fresh basil (for 4)

Just a little useless information for your files—spatchcock is not the title of a small bird (which is, in fact, poussin or maybe even, to us Aussies, baby chook), but is instead the method by which a bird is split and flattened. The word itself comes from an eighteenth-century Irish dish called 'dispatch-cock', which referred to a split, grilled fowl (cock) which was prepared in this manner when time was short.

200 g soft butter **2 garlic cloves, crushed** **a squeeze of lemon juice** **1 tbsp chopped parsley**	Mix together.
4 baby chickens	Using kitchen scissors, cut through the back of the birds along both sides of the backbone. Discard this bone, lay chickens flesh-down on a surface, and whack very firmly with your hand to flatten.
basil leaves	Loosen skin along chicken breast and legs to make small pockets, and insert small amounts of the flavoured butter and the basil leaves under skin. Smooth with fingers then thread 2 bamboo skewers into each chicken criss-cross from wing to leg and leave for 30 mins to let flavours develop.
	Preheat BBQ.
freshly ground salt and pepper **wedges of lemon**	Season chickens, melt any leftover butter and brush all over, and then barbecue for 20–25 mins until golden-brown all over and the juices run clear when thigh is pierced with a skewer. Serve with lemon wedges.

Calypso chook (for 4)

A terrific herby-spicy marinade with citrus overtones.

½ cup soft herb (coriander, mint, parsley, etc.) 1 tbsp Dijon mustard 1 tsp ground allspice 2 garlic cloves 4 small chillies juice of 1 lime juice of 1 orange a splash of soy sauce freshly ground pepper	Whiz up.
8 boneless chicken thighs	Toss chicken in the marinade and leave for an hour or so. Preheat BBQ. Cook chicken, brushing with marinade and turning regularly, until golden all over.
wedges of lime rice pilaf (see page 226)	Serve with lime wedges and rice pilaf (or a green salad).

> **I like to serve this with honey-drenched bananas—cut 4 firm bananas, skin still on, in half lengthways then barbecue, skin-side down first, brushing with liquid honey as you do so.**

Real simple chicken breasts with a lemon-spiked herb marinade (for 4)

	Preheat BBQ.
½ cup olive oil juice of 1 lemon 2 tbsp chopped herbs (such as rosemary, parsley, thyme and coriander) 1 tsp fennel seeds freshly ground salt and pepper	Whisk together as a marinade.
4 chicken breasts, skin on	Put chicken in marinade and leave for 30 mins or so, turning a few times. Then cook on moderate part of barbie, brushing regularly with marinade, until skin is crispy and flesh is cooked through.

> **As an accompaniment, these need little more than a good green salad and, if you like, a dollop or two of my piquant BBQ mayo (see page 86).**

A piquant BBQ mayo

4 tbsp chopped flat-leaf parsley
2 tsp chopped tarragon
2 tsp chopped oregano
2 tsp chopped thyme
1 garlic clove, crushed
2 tbsp chopped onion
8 anchovies, chopped
2 tbsp capers, chopped
a splash of tarragon vinegar

Mix together in a bowl.

1 tbsp Dijon mustard
2 cups mayonnaise (see page 182)

Fold herb mixture and mustard gently into mayonnaise.

Glen Baxter's mexican tofu—serves 80 (from his 1999 Gourmet Guide)

1. Take one sombrero.
2. Invert.
3. Fill with tofu.
4. Allow to stand for 38 minutes.

A few tips for that successful barbie

- For extra flavour, add some woodchips which have been soaked in cold water (hardwood only). Prunings from grape vines or fruit trees also work well.
- Dipping a branch of rosemary in oil and brushing the food with it during cooking will also impart extra flavour.
- Before cooking, always rub the barbie down with an oiled cloth. Then wait until the flames subside. After cooking, scrub it down with a stiff brush to remove food particles and rub once again with an oiled cloth.
- Always be on the alert to move food that is browning too quickly to a more moderate part of the BBQ.
- Even the shortest dunk in a marinade (which can be as simple as oil, herbs, lemon and seasonings) will add zing to almost any barbecued food.
- And, most importantly, a good fire is essential. The coals or wood must be glowing rather than flaming, while even gas-fired barbies need to be preheated for about 20 minutes for a successful end product.

Kick-arse chicken tortilla with avocado salsa

(for 4)

One of our most popular dishes at my restaurant, this recipe shows that Tex Mex or Mexican food is not just about greasy mince, over-cooked beans and flavourless guacamole. In fact, if you have been to either Mexico or the States near the border, you will already have been surprised by the lightness, freshness and zing associated with such food—something that is certainly foreign to the majority of our Mexican cantinas.

	Preheat BBQ.
6–8 tbsp plain yoghurt **1–2 tbsp Indian mango chutney** **1 tbsp chopped coriander**	Mix together and set aside.
1 large ripe avocado, sliced **¼ red onion, finely sliced** **1 tbsp chopped coriander** **juice of 1 lime** **freshly ground pepper**	Mix together and lightly mash.
3 skinless chicken breasts, battened out and each cut into 4 even strips lengthways **BBQ sauce (see page 80)**	Brush chicken generously with sauce and then barbecue, brushing with more sauce as you do so, until firm to the touch.
8 flour tortillas	When chicken is almost ready, heat tortillas on barbie and place on 4 plates. Smear with yoghurt, top with salsa and chicken, and roll up.

> **Serve with icy-cold Mexican beer or, if you can find it, Lone Star (John Wayne's favourite brew).**

Salmon on a bed of charred radicchio with a tapenade butter (for 4)

½ cup olive oil
freshly ground black pepper
splash of soy sauce
4 x 160 g salmon cutlets

Mix olive oil, soy and pepper and marinate salmon for an hour or two.

3 anchovy fillets
10 pitted black olives
1–2 garlic cloves
1 tbsp chopped parsley
150 g soft unsalted butter

Whiz up anchovies, olives, garlic and parsley. Remove to bowl and mix in butter. Keep at room temperature.

Preheat BBQ.

2 small heads radicchio, washed well, dried and cut in half lengthwise

Toss radicchio with a little of the salmon marinade. Barbecue the salmon to the desired degree (it will always be better a little under-cooked), adding radicchio towards the end. Brush both with marinade as they cook.

chopped parsley

When radicchio is charred around the edges and salmon is ready, place radicchio on plates and top with salmon and a generous dollop of the tapenade butter. Sprinkle with parsley.

> **I often add a splash of soy to my marinades. I find this adds both the necessary salt content and some extra body as well.**

Whiting with an Italian herb relish (for 4)

Preheat BBQ.

1½ cups soft green herbs, such as basil, parsley and mint
¾ cup olive oil
8 capers
red-wine vinegar
Dijon mustard
freshly ground salt and pepper

Whiz up herbs, oil and capers. Then add vinegar, mustard and seasonings to taste (it should be quite tangy).

4 whole whiting (plate-sized), gutted, cleaned and scaled
olive oil
lemon juice
extra freshly ground salt and pepper

Take 4 pieces of foil, each large enough to loosely enclose one fish, and place on board. Brush all over with oil, place fish on top and add lemon juice and seasonings. Wrap up loosely, crimping the join, and place on barbie. Check fish after 8–10 mins by making a small cut behind the head. When ready, remove from foil and serve with all the juices poured over the top and herb relish alongside.

> **❝ Of course, you can use any baby fish for this recipe, or even fillets or cutlets, if you prefer. ❞**

Bahamian baby fish (for 4)

½ **cup olive oil** 2 fresh chillies, sliced finely 2 garlic cloves, crushed a 1 cm piece fresh ginger, minced juice of 2–3 limes freshly ground salt and pepper	Whisk together for a marinade.
4 baby fish, gutted, cleaned and scaled	Pour marinade over fish and leave for 45 mins, turning a couple of times.
	Preheat BBQ.
vegetable oil	Oil BBQ well and, when flames have died down, barbecue the fish until ready. (To check, make a small cut behind the head with a sharp knife.)
wedges of lime	Serve with wedges of lime and a simple salad.

> **In the Bahamas, this would be served with little more than a bottle of hot sauce alongside, but I also like it with a pile of sweetcorn salsa (see page 94).**

Stuffed squid (calamari) with Sicilian parsley, garlic and olive oil dressing

(for 4)

Preheat BBQ.

1½ cups breadcrumbs, made from day-old bread
1 spring onion (green onion), finely chopped
a squeeze of lemon
4 anchovies, chopped
¾ cup grated parmesan
a few chopped squid tentacles
1–2 eggs

Mix together, adding enough egg to moisten.

8 small squid tubes, cleaned
olive oil
freshly ground salt and pepper

To tenderise squid, plunge into boiling water for exactly 30 secs (it doesn't need to come back to the boil). Then drain well, stuff tubes and secure the openings with toothpicks. (Don't over-stuff, as they may burst during cooking.) Season, and cook on an oiled BBQ until golden all over.

2 garlic cloves, crushed
½ tsp salt
1 heaped tbsp Dijon mustard
2 tbsp chopped parsley
½ cup olive oil
lemon juice

While squid is cooking make the dressing. Whisk together the garlic, salt, mustard and parsley. Then add oil, little by little, and lemon juice to taste.

a handful of rocket leaves

Divide leaves between 4 plates, top with squid and sprinkle with dressing.

A bit of a clean

To clean squid, first of all separate head and tentacles from the body. Cut tentacles off in a V-shape just below the eyes, then remove and discard the hard ball at the top of the tentacles, and all the skin. From the tube peel away the body flaps and the outside membrane then put your finger inside and pull out the cartilage (it's like thin plastic). Wash and dry tubes and tentacles.

Barbecued sweetcorn salsa (for 4)

vegetable oil
4 corn cobs, husk and silk removed
2 seeded chillies, finely sliced
juice of 1–2 limes
½ red capsicum and ½ green capsicum, seeded, cored and finely diced
2 tbsp chopped coriander
freshly ground salt and pepper

Lightly oil and barbecue the corn until blistered in spots. Cool and cut off kernels. Add remaining ingredients to corn and toss well.

olive oil

Mix into corn mixture to taste.

Grilled marlin with roasted salsa (for 4)

Preheat oven to 225°C.

2 small chillies
2 red capsicums
1 onion

Toss with a little oil and roast until black-brown in spots. Remove, cover and, when cool, remove skins and seeds and dice.

5 ripe tomatoes
1 tsp chopped thyme
1 tsp chopped oregano
olive oil
balsamic vinegar
freshly ground salt and pepper

Peel, seed and dice (see below). Add to diced vegies, with herbs, oil, seasonings and vinegar to taste. Leave salsa for at least 1 hour to develop flavour.

Preheat BBQ.

4 x 180 g marlin steaks
vegetable oil
extra salt and pepper

Brush marlin with oil, season well and barbecue over a moderate heat, turning and brushing with oil frequently.

basil sprigs
wedges of lime

When fish is ready, scatter salsa over 4 plates, top with fish and garnish with basil and wedges of lime.

To peel and seed tomatoes

Remove cores and put in boiling water. Count to 10, then remove tomatoes and plunge into a bowl of iced water. Allow to cool, then peel and cut lengthways into quarters. Put each quarter on a board and cut away the pulp (reserve this for another use).

Sardines on toast with a twist (for 4)

Preheat BBQ.

4 large ripe tomatoes, peeled, seeded and diced (see page 95)
1 spring onion (green onion), finely chopped
4 basil leaves, sliced
3 tbsp olive oil
splash of balsamic vinegar
freshly ground salt and pepper

Mix together and set aside to develop flavours.

4 thick slices country-style bread
olive oil
12–16 sardine fillets
lemon
freshly ground salt and pepper
1–2 garlic cloves, cut in half
4 sprigs of basil

When ready to serve, brush bread with oil on both sides and barbecue until golden-brown. At same time, brush sardines with oil, season, sprinkle with lemon juice and barbecue briefly over high heat. Rub the barbecued bread vigorously with the cut side of the garlic. Then place on plates, top with tomato mixture and sardines, and garnish with basil.

❝ On cold wintry nights in New Zealand, we often sat in front of the fire and ate sardines on toast. But, unless my memory fails me, they were never quite like this. ❞

To oyster or not to oyster?

I have often wondered whether there is actually such a thing as an aphrodisiac. Because, while many of us believe that eating oysters somehow enhances our sexual appetite, their value as an aphrodisiac is actually disputed, with one nineteenth-century essayist, after much research, deciding that 'the oyster, when eaten, simply produced an inexplicable feeling of goodwill to one's fellow man'.

So, with that in mind, it appears that any improvement in sexual performance which occurs after eating oysters is more likely to be caused by these tasty bivalves' ability to stimulate a feeling of wellbeing, rather than by any magical component. A feeling that is borne out by famed American sex therapist Dr Ruth Westheimer, who declares that 'an aphrodisiac is anything you want it to be'.

This makes me truly thankful that I have an inherent leaning towards oysters. Because, in all honesty, I have never been too keen on the idea of sprinkling powdered deer antlers over my food, a supposed aphrodisiac so revered by our Asian neighbours. Or even the most ancient of love potions, that rather revolting drink made from fermented cocoa beans and hot chilli peppers on which the Aztecs were so keen.

Barbecued oysters with sausages (for 4)

8–12 small, spicy sausages, any variety	Beforehand, put the sausages in simmering water and gently simmer until firm to the touch. Drain and set aside.
	Preheat BBQ.
2 dozen or more oysters, unopened but shells scrubbed	Cook sausages on moderate part of the barbie until browned all over. Then place oysters on the hottest part and wait for them to open. (Have a knife ready just in case they need a little assistance—you can tell when they are ready, because the brine will begin to bubble around the edges. In that case, if the shells haven't opened, just slip in the knife and give it an upwards twist.)
lemon wedges	Serve oysters on the half shell, brine included, with the sausages, lemon wedges and a pepper grinder on the side.

> **I am told that this is a specialty of the Bordeaux region in France, although I am yet to find a restaurant which actually serves some. But, that aside, it is a delicious combination with the idea being that you eat an oyster, take a bite of the sausage and wash the lot down with icy-cold crisp white wine—a concept which certainly does promote feelings of wellbeing.**

Tolarno's bloody mary oyster shooters

(for 20 shooters)

And while we're on the subject of oysters—the perfect starter for any barbie.

---

500 ml V8 vegetable juice 60 ml vodka (Stoli preferably) 7 ml Worcestershire sauce 5 ml lemon juice Tabasco sauce to taste freshly ground salt and pepper, to taste	Combine well and keep cold.
20 oysters	Put oysters in individual shot glasses and top up with the above mix.

> **When fresh horseradish is available, to give your BM's even more kick, this idea from Melbourne's Gin Palace is a ripper—grate ½ cup of horseradish, add a bottle of vodka and leave for 3 days to infuse. Then use as above.**

And let's not forget the vegetarians

Vegies can also play a starring role at the barbie. Just the other day, I was invited to a friend's home where I enjoyed a vegetarian feast which was without parallel. (Both he and his wife are vegetarian.)

Thankfully, it was a beautiful day and he had fired up the big monster in the backyard, from which emerged large flat mushies sprinkled with tangy salsa verde, corn which had been cooked in its husk along with a good dollop of herb and lemon butter, and a sort of grilled ratatouille with a mound of roasted salsa on top. The bread had been brushed with a basil-infused oil before being given a brief run over the coals, and in the centre of the table there was a pile of the tiniest baby potatoes which had been simply cut in half before being rubbed generously with olive oil and sea salt and barbecued to a golden crusty brown. Accompanied by roasted-garlic aioli, these were so delicious I think I could have dined on them alone, but even they were overshadowed by large bowls of grilled Mediterranean vegies on couscous, served with yoghurt flavoured with that Moroccan staple, harissa (see page 26) – absolutely wonderful!

Barbecued corn on the cob with gremolata butter

(for 4–8)

Preheat BBQ.

1 lemon
½ orange
100 g soft unsalted butter
1 garlic clove, crushed
1 tbsp chopped parsley

With a zester, pare the zest of 1 lemon and ½ orange, and mix with the butter, garlic, parsley and lemon juice to taste.

4–8 corn cobs
freshly ground salt and pepper

Leave husk on cobs but remove silk, then cook in boiling, salted water until just tender. Drain, pull husk back and squeeze out any water. Neaten the husk with a sharp knife, season, and barbecue until corn is charred all over, brushing with a little of the butter as you do so. Serve with more butter and some extra orange and lemon zest on top.

Witloof in an Italian manner (for 4)

8 heads of witloof, outside and damaged leaves removed
vegetable oil
freshly ground salt and pepper

6 anchovies, chopped
extra virgin olive oil
balsamic or red-wine vinegar
chopped parsley

Cut witloof in half lengthways, wash well and drain. Brush on all sides with oil, then season and barbecue or grill until lightly browned all over (and slightly charred around the edges).

Arrange the witloof attractively on 4 plates and sprinkle with the anchovies, oil, a little vinegar and parsley.

> **This recipe also works brilliantly with small leeks. But in this case a brief dunk in a pot of boiling water is advisable before barbecuing.**

Barbecued potatoes with crispy bacon and sour cream

(for 4 as an accompaniment)

Preheat BBQ.

12 baby potatoes, scrubbed

Parboil potatoes in lightly salted water until almost tender. Drain well and allow to cool. Cut in half and place, cut side down, on oiled BBQ. Cook, turning frequently, until crisp and golden.

2–3 rashers of rindless bacon, sliced (optional)
vegetable oil

When potatoes are almost ready, heat a little oil in a pan on the barbie and fry bacon until crisp. Drain on kitchen towels.

sour cream
chives, snipped

Place spuds in bowl, sprinkle with bacon, then add a dollop of sour cream and some chives.

❝ Forget your fried American-style potato skins—these will beat them hands down any day. ❞

Some vegie quick picks

- Peel large flat mushrooms, remove stalks, brush with oil and season well. Then barbecue with a dollop of any herb butter in the centre, without turning, until cooked through.
- Butter a piece of foil. Top with just-cooked baby spuds, chopped spring onions, a squeeze of lemon and some seasonings. Wrap up and cook on a moderate part of the BBQ.
- Barbecue a selection of well oiled and seasoned Mediterranean vegies, such as peppers, eggplant and zucchini, and serve with a garlicky mayonnaise.
- Brush country or sourdough bread with flavoured oil (see page 125) and then grill. And, if you like, top that with a mixture of diced tomato, shredded basil, seasonings and a little olive oil.
- Blanch whole onions in boiling water for 10 mins, then drain and cut in 4. Brush with olive oil, season well and barbecue on the slowest part of the grill until browned all over and tender (about 30 mins).
- Barbecued radicchio with blue cheese is also a treat. Cut radicchio in half, brush with oil, season and cook until charred on the edges. Then top with some crumbled flavoursome blue cheese.
- When asparagus is at the height of its season, pick out the largest spears. Bend them until they break, discarding the bottom section and then peeling the rest. Blanch for 1 min. in lightly salted water, drain, brush with oil and throw on the barbie. Serve with a sprinkling of olive oil and a little balsamic vinegar.

Pumpkin with soy-honey caramel (for 4)

Preheat BBQ.

top half of a butternut pumpkin
olive oil

Peel and cut into even slices approx. 5 mm thick. Toss with olive oil and place on barbie.

3–4 tbsp honey
3–4 tbsp soy sauce
chopped parsley

Mix honey and soy together and brush on pumpkin as it cooks, until caramelised. Sprinkle with parsley.

> **Don't discard pumpkin seeds—they make a delicious snack. Clean them and toss in a hot, dry pan over moderate heat (or in a moderate oven) until golden. Then sprinkle generously with ground sea salt and serve.**

Big juicy mushrooms with basil oil (for 4–6)

Preheat BBQ.

12–16 large, flat mushrooms
salt and freshly ground pepper
basil oil (see page 125)

If need be, peel mushrooms and cut off stalks. (Reserve for another use.) Season well, brush with the basil oil and then barbecue, frequently turning and brushing with more oil.

sprigs of basil
freshly grated parmesan

Place mushrooms on platter, garnish with a little more oil and the basil sprigs, and sprinkle with freshly grated parmesan.

> **Mushrooms are very porous beings and if washed in water they will take up the most amazing amount of liquid, which will then leak out as they cook. So, instead of simply throwing them into a tub of water, wipe them individually with a damp cloth—the extra effort will pay off when it comes to the cooking.**

And on the sideline:

What about a few of the classic BBQ salads revisited?

We all remember the barbecue salads of our youth—tired old things with far too much vinegar, badly prepared ingredients and far too much sun. (For some reason, the salads and the bread were always put out on the table hours before the cooking even started.) Well, here are a few simple little variations that should be a little more appealing and not much more complicated to boot.

Almost a true blue Greek salad

Whiz up ½ cup olive oil, a good squeeze of lemon, ½ cup fresh herbs (parsley, mint, basil), a clove of garlic and some seasonings. Then toss in a bowl with tomato wedges, finely sliced red onion, pitted olives, frisée lettuce and plenty of crumbled fetta cheese.

Potato salad with a tangy lemon dressing

Whisk together 3 tbsp lemon juice, 8 tbsp olive oil, the zest of 1 lemon, 1 tsp Dijon mustard, 1 crushed clove of garlic and some seasonings. Then boil some well scrubbed baby potatoes until tender. Drain and, while still hot, toss with the dressing. Sprinkle with chopped chives and serve either hot or warm.

> **When making a potato salad, always use waxy potatoes such as southern golds, kipfler or bintje. And don't ever run them under cold water once they are cooked, as this will only make them waterlogged and almost impossible to dress.**

The return of the iceberg

Remove outer leaves from a small crisp iceberg lettuce, core and cut into 4 or 8 lengthways. Barbecue some bacon and chop coarsely. Then place the lettuce wedges in a bowl and sprinkle in the bacon and a mustard dressing (see page 210). (And if you are feeling really fancy, poach an egg for each person and place on top before sprinkling with the dressing.)

> A much-maligned salad ingredient, I believe this crisp and crunchy lettuce is about ready for another 15 minutes of fame.

Barbecued beetroot salad with spiced yoghurt

Scrub beetroot well, wrap them individually in foil and cook on barbie (or in a 190°C oven) until tender when pierced with a small knife. Cool a little, don your rubber gloves and peel beetroot under running water. Then cut into wedges and toss with a little olive oil, lemon and seasonings. Place in a bowl and top with yoghurt mixed with a little ground cumin and coriander and some chopped coriander leaves.

Me mum's coleslaw

Slice cabbage and gherkins. Add chopped hard-boiled egg, a good grinding of black pepper and a generous squeeze of lemon. Leave for 2 hours and then mix mayonnaise (see page 182) in.

An Australian revolution

FOR A NATION seemingly brought up on a diet of little apart from roasted meats and three veg, it was quite a surprise to finally realise that there were other cuisines which may better suit our climate and lifestyle.

The post-WWII Italian and Greek immigrants certainly gave us a taste of things to come. (Although I do remember that there was some resistance, in certain quarters, to their oil-based cuisine with my grandmother in particular complaining that the Barnaos across the road not only put garlic in their salad dressing, but didn't even use condensed milk as the base.)

But while it was not an overnight revolution, restaurateurs and an increasingly sophisticated Aussie public did eventually come to appreciate that the lighter, fresher fare from the

Mediterranean and surrounding regions was the ideal food for our sunburnt country. To the extent that now we even talk of an Aussie cuisine which, while it often has a touch of Asian associated with it, also always has lots of those zingy Mediterranean flavours which we have come to love and now try to claim as our very own.

- Mediterranean tuna steaks
- Slow-roasted tuna tonnata
- Roasted bugs with a red capsicum butter
- A fillet of roasted salmon on pesto mash with shavings of parmesan
- A minute steak in an Italian fashion
- A pot of Italian lamb chops
- Parmesan crumbed veal with roasted capsicum salad
- Twice-baked cheese soufflés with plumped oysters and blue mascarpone cream
- A flavoursome roasted tomato and basil soup
- Not even close to a minestrone
- For the true olive lover
- Microwave risotto with asparagus and peas
- Pasta with mussels and citrus crumble
- A pasta 'omelette' with the leftovers
- Eggplant almost parmigiano
- A brick-pressed Mediterranean sandwich
- A few almost-inspired pizza suggestions
- An onion and anchovy pizza from Provence (pissaladière)
- A Provençal seafood stew with a splash of Pernod
- A vegetarian lasagne from Provence
- A cheat's cassoulet from the south of France

Mediterranean tuna steaks (for 4)

2 zucchini, sliced on the diagonal
½ medium-sized eggplant, halved lengthways and then sliced
½ red and ½ green capsicum, cored, seeded and cut into even pieces
freshly ground salt and pepper
olive oil

Toss vegies and seasonings in oil and grill, roast or pan-fry until charred on the edges. Set aside in a warm spot.

4 x 160 g tuna steaks, all black removed
olive oil
freshly ground salt and pepper

Clean pan or grill, brush tuna with oil, season and cook to medium or less. (Don't overcook, or it will be dry.)

olive oil
balsamic vinegar

Place vegies on plates, top with tuna and sprinkle with olive oil and a little balsamic.

> **A dollop of roasted capsicum butter (see page 114) would be wonderful with these steaks.**

Bring on the real thing (and I don't mean Coca-Cola)

One of my mother's all-time favourites was her version of the ubiquitous tuna casserole—a dish she spent many hours slaving over. First of all, she would make a classical mornay sauce with plenty of top-quality cheese and thick country cream. Then a fresh tomato sauce of which any Italian Mama would be proud, into which she would fold butter-sautéed sliced onion, fresh herbs and chunks of canned tuna. Of course, herein lay the problem—canned tuna. And, while I love my mother dearly, this was not one of her greatest culinary creations, because the canned stuff overshadowed everything, including the lovingly made sauces.

Because of this, it was many, many years before I could bring myself to eat fresh tuna. For some strange reason, I had the misconception that it was going to have a similar flavour to the canned variety (which is strange, because I had discovered, years before, that canned salmon had as much to do with fresh as the Spice Girls have to do with good taste). But eventually, with much prodding, I plucked up enough courage, tasted the real thing and discovered one of the great culinary delights of the world.

Slow-roasted tuna tonnata (for 4)

Even after my tirade about canned tuna, here is a dish that includes—what else—canned tuna. It is modelled on that Italian classic, Vitello Tonnata (cold poached veal in tuna sauce) which, although it sounds strange, is delicious, and is actually the only time that I find the canned stuff palatable. But do keep in mind that we are not talking just any tuna here—it must be the classy little number preserved in olive oil.

Preheat oven to 135°C.

400 g fresh tuna, skin and all black removed
olive oil
freshly ground pepper

Cut tuna into 4 slices. Rub with oil and pepper, and place in oiled baking tray. Cook in oven for about 15 mins, turning once, until tuna is medium-rare. Remove and allow to cool, then flake into largish pieces.

100 g canned tuna in oil, drained
1 tbsp chopped anchovies
3 tbsp capers
1 tbsp Dijon mustard
1 garlic clove, crushed

Whiz everything up in a blender or processor.

2 egg yolks
½ cup olive oil
lemon juice
freshly ground pepper

Add yolks to the blended mixture and process for a few minutes again. Add oil through feeder tube, little by little. Then season, to taste, with lemon juice and pepper. Mix cooked tuna into the sauce, and refrigerate at least overnight.

crusty bread
rocket leaves
olive oil

Serve at room temperature with bread and some rocket dressed with a little oil.

Roasted bugs with a red capsicum butter

(for 4)

2 red capsicums, roasted and peeled (see page 245)
2 anchovies
1 tbsp chopped parsley
freshly ground pepper
200 g soft unsalted butter

8–12 bugs, cut in half lengthways and cleaned

In a blender or processor, whiz up everything but the butter. Put in a bowl and then mix in the butter and set aside at room temperature.

Put capsicum butter in a piping bag and pipe a generous amount onto the flesh of each bug. Put in the fridge for at least 1 hour.

Preheat oven to the maximum. Then place bugs in an oven tray, butter side up, and put in the oven. Check after 10–12 mins by making a cut in the thickest part and, when ready, place on plates and pour all the cooking juices over the top.

> **Because the butter is firm, it will melt gradually over the bugs as they cook, basting the meat continually.**

A fillet of roasted salmon on pesto mash with shavings of parmesan (for 4)

Another restaurant favourite—I could quite happily eat large bowls of the delicious pesto mash all by itself.

Preheat oven to 220°C.

4 large floury potatoes, peeled and cubed
hot milk
butter and cream
freshly ground salt and pepper

Boil the potatoes in salted water until tender. Drain well and then mash, adding hot milk little by little. Keep the mix fairly firm, then to finish add a little cream and butter, and seasonings to taste. Set aside.

15 basil leaves
1 garlic clove
2 tbsp grated parmesan
olive oil
freshly ground salt and pepper

Blend or process basil, garlic and parmesan with just enough oil to make a paste. Season to taste.

4 fresh salmon fillets (each 160–180 g), skin and bones removed
olive oil

Place salmon fillets on an oiled baking tray, season, brush with oil and bake in the oven for approx. 6–8 mins until opaque in the centre. Remove from tray.

shavings of parmesan
virgin olive oil

While fish is cooking, add some pesto to the mash, mix in well and then put in a microwave bowl. Cover and cook on High for 3–4 mins, then mound on 4 plates. Put salmon on top and sprinkle with parmesan and oil.

> **You could, of course, use olive oil in the mash instead of butter and cream, but although I'm crossing the barriers a little here I like the extra zing that these politically incorrect additions provide. And if you don't have a microwave, prepare the potatoes just before you cook the salmon, adding the pesto at the last minute.**

The perfect shave

Fine shavings of parmesan—or, in fact, any cheese—can be easily achieved with the aid of an inexpensive cheese shaver, which is available at almost any halfway-decent kitchen supplies store. (I always buy two!)

A minute steak in an Italian fashion (for 4)

I tasted a dish like this in Rome and couldn't wait to try cooking it for myself. So, the minute I got back to the hotel, I insisted that we set up the stove in my room. And the steak was delicious. But, unfortunately, the management was less than keen on the fact that I set off not only the fire alarm but the sprinkler system as well.

500 g beef porterhouse, trimmed of all fat and sinew	Cut beef into 4 slices and flatten a little with a steak hammer.
olive oil **freshly ground salt and pepper** **2 tbsp chopped basil** **2 tbsp chopped sage** **4 tbsp unsalted butter**	Lightly oil a large heavy-bottomed pan. Heat it and then sear steaks quickly on one side. Turn over, season and sprinkle with half the herbs. Cook for 30 secs and remove, leaving oil behind. Add butter to pan along with the remaining herbs. When melted, return steaks and cook to desired degree, turning once or twice.
2 handfuls mixed cress **balsamic vinegar**	Mound cress on 4 plates and sprinkle lightly with vinegar. Place steaks on top and pour cooking juices over.

A pot of Italian lamb chops (for 4)

Actually, this is almost like an Italian version of an Irish stew, with the addition of tomato and some savoury crumbs. But whatever its origins, it is certainly delicious and so easy to make.

	Preheat oven to 190°C.
1 cup breadcrumbs ½ **cup grated parmesan** **2 garlic cloves, crushed** ½ **cup chopped parsley**	Mix these together.
olive oil **10 baby potatoes, scrubbed and sliced** **1 large onion, finely sliced** **12 lamb chops (any variety), well trimmed** **white wine** **2 cups canned tomatoes, drained well and chopped** **freshly ground salt and pepper**	Brush the bottom of a Dutch oven or casserole with a little oil. Put in a layer of potatoes and onions, along with equal quantities of wine and water to just cover and season. Sprinkle some tomato over, and a fair quantity of the crumb mix, and top with 6 chops. Repeat layers of vegies, tomatoes, and crumbs, then more chops, finishing with a layer of crumbs. Sprinkle with olive oil and bake for approx. 1–1½ hours, until chops are tender.

Parmesan crumbed veal with roasted capsicum salad

(for 4)

One of the great delights in any halfway-decent Italian restaurant is Cotelette Milanese, a dish which one of my foodie friends described as a Wiener schnitzel with a bit of bone (the cutlet) and some parmesan thrown in. Well, he would be happy because this dish is even closer to the schnitzel as it doesn't have that troublesome bit of bone. But jokes aside, the parmesan does make a huge difference to the crumbing, and if you like you can add some fine strips of lemon zest and some chopped fresh herbs as well.

500–600 g veal fillet, cleaned of all fat and sinew
flour
2 eggs
½ cup milk
1 cup breadcrumbs, made from day-old bread
½ cup grated parmesan
salt and freshly ground pepper

vegetable oil
lemon wedges
roasted capsicum salad (see page 245)

Cut meat into approx. 7 cm lengths. Cut each piece through the middle parallel to the bench, leaving one edge attached. Spread open and gently batten out with a meat mallet. In separate bowls put seasoned flour, the beaten eggs and milk and the breadcrumbs mixed with parmesan. Dip the veal first into the flour, then into the eggwash and then firmly into the crumbs.

Heat oil in a non-stick pan and fry the veal in 2 or 3 lots until golden on both sides. Drain well on kitchen towels and serve with lemon wedges and roasted capsicum salad.

> **Crushed new potatoes would also go well with this. Boil scrubbed baby spuds until tender and then drain well. Gently heat a few tablespoons of olive oil, add it to the spuds and lightly mash with a fork. To finish, mix in a little chopped parsley, a squeeze of lemon and some freshly ground salt and pepper.**

Twice-baked cheese soufflés with plumped oysters and blue mascarpone cream

(for 4 soufflés)

Preheat oven to 180°C.

90 g butter
50 g flour
210 ml milk

Melt butter in a heavy-bottomed pot. Add flour and cook over a low heat for 2 mins. Heat milk on stove or in microwave and add gradually to flour mixture, whisking continually. Bring almost to the boil, reduce heat and simmer for 5 mins.

50 g gruyère, grated
25 g parmesan, grated
1 small garlic clove, crushed
½ tsp olive oil

Add to sauce and mix in well. Remove from heat, and cool slightly.

3 eggs, separated

Fold yolks into the sauce then beat whites to stiff peaks and fold them in gently too.

butter

Butter small soufflé moulds, spoon mix in and smooth the tops. Place folded newspaper in base of deep baking dishes, put moulds in and pour boiling water around them ⅔ way up the sides. Bake until firm to the touch and puffed (about 20 mins). Leave to rest for a few minutes and then remove from moulds. (They can be pre-prepared up to this point.)

1½ cups cream
blue cheese
mascarpone

When ready to serve, return soufflés upside-down to 220°C oven and cook until puffed. At same time, put cream in a pot with a couple of tablespoons each of the blue cheese and the mascarpone, and gently reduce (taste and add more cheese if necessary). Set aside.

1 tbsp chopped parsley
8 oysters

When soufflés are ready, bring cream back to the boil, add parsley and oysters, and simmer for a few seconds. Then place soufflés on plates, top with the oysters and pour sauce over and around.

> " I was asked for a suggestion for a St Valentine's Day supper. And this rather sexy dish was the one that I came up with because, purely and simply, it can be mostly pre-prepared. Which means that on this romantic occasion, little time needs to be spent in the kitchen, which is how it should be! "

A touch of class

I once read an interview with American food icon, Julia Child, in which she told of a very romantic St Valentine's Day spent in Paris with her husband, when they sat by the Seine in the middle of a snowstorm eating beluga caviar with their fingers from the jar and drinking Dom Perignon straight from the bottle—now that is definitely romantic.

A flavoursome roasted tomato and basil soup

(for 4)

I cooked this for 'A Cook's Journey' and the phones ran hot. And I'm sure everyone enjoyed it when they tried it at home, because the roasting accentuates the flavour of the tomatoes and gives the soup more flavour. (Actually, this works well with any vegie. So next time you're whipping up a parsnip, zucchini or even pumpkin soup, first roast the vegies until they are lightly caramelised, and notice the difference.)

Preheat oven to 200°C.

10 tomatoes, cored and halved
2 garlic cloves, coarsely chopped
8 basil leaves, sliced
6 tbsp olive oil
freshly ground salt and pepper

Place tomatoes in a baking tray, sprinkle with garlic, basil and seasonings. Then drizzle with oil, making sure that all the basil is moistened, and cook until tomatoes collapse and caramelise around the edges (approx. 50 mins).

1 large onion, chopped
1 large potato, chopped
vegetable stock (see page 237), or water and 2 vegie stock cubes

After tomatoes have been cooking for 30 mins, put onion and potato in a pot and cover with the stock. Cook until soft.

basil pesto (see page 115)

When tomatoes are ready, reserve the oil, drain them, add them to pot and bring back to the boil. Then whiz the whole lot in a blender or a processor. Serve in deep soup bowls with a dollop of pesto on top.

❝ **The leftover oil would be wonderful with bread or used in cooking. And for a terrific pasta sauce, forget the onions and potatoes and just blend the tomatoes along with most of the oil.** ❞

Not even close to a minestrone (for 6–8)

Minestrone is one of those recipes which, no matter how you make it, it is never right. And there is always someone who, of course, just happens to know all about the true-blue authentic version and what is missing from yours. So before you begin giving me a hard time, I would just like to state that this soup is definitely not supposed to be Huey's version of minestrone and that any similarities are purely coincidental.

olive oil
1 small onion, chopped
2 garlic cloves, crushed

Heat oil in large pot and cook onion and garlic until soft.

2 medium-sized carrots, sliced
2 small zucchini, sliced
10 green beans, cut into 3 cm lengths
½ medium-sized eggplant, diced

Add these vegies, with extra oil if necessary, and toss to coat.

2 cups finely sliced cabbage
2 cups canned tomatoes, drained and chopped
freshly ground salt and pepper

Add cabbage and cook it until it wilts a little. Then add tomatoes, seasonings and cover well with water. Put lid on and cook for 10 mins.

1 cup arborio or long-grain rice
½ cup canned red kidney beans, drained

Add rice and beans to the pot, cover and cook until rice is tender (about another 10 mins).

15 basil leaves
½ cup grated parmesan
olive oil

In a blender or processor, whiz up basil and parmesan and enough olive oil to moisten. Stir into soup, check seasoning and serve with plenty of crusty bread.

For the true olive lover

Marinated olives

Rinse black olives and place in clean jars. Add sprigs of fresh thyme, slivers of garlic and chilli, and very thin slices of lemon. Cover with olive oil and leave for a couple of weeks before using.

Tapenade olive oil

Purée equal quantities of olives and anchovies with enough olive oil to facilitate the blending. Push through a sieve and use to add extra zing to tomato-based sauces, in salad dressings, or even simply with good crusty bread. (As this will keep for weeks, I always make a fairly large quantity and store it in the fridge for when needed.)

Basil-infused olive oil

Wash and dry 2 cups basil leaves, add 2 cups olive oil and bring gently to the boil, stirring continually. Simmer for 5 mins, then cool and strain, pressing on the basil. Now strain again.

Microwave risotto with asparagus and peas

(for 4)

Now, I don't know about you, but when it comes to microwaves I've always been a bit of a culinary snob. To me, they invariably appeared the tool of the lazy chef and, on reflection, this feeling was most probably caused by their awful misuse—not only in our homes, but in our cafés and restaurants, as well.

Then I was given Barbara Kafka's *Microwave Gourmet*, a book which certainly opened my eyes to some microwave options. And while I would still not consider putting a whole chook or a chocolate cake anywhere near the thing, dishes like this risotto (which is a variation on one in Ms Kafka's book) certainly makes life very easy when you just don't have the time, or inclination, to slave over a hot stove.

16–20 baby asparagus, tips only **1 cup small fresh peas (or thawed frozen peas)**	Place vegies in a microwave bag and cook for 3 mins at 100°C. Then run under cold water, drain and set aside.
2 tbsp unsalted butter **2 tbsp olive oil** **1 medium-sized onion, finely chopped**	Put butter and oil in a deep microwave dish and cook at 100 per cent for 2 mins. Then add onion and cook, uncovered, for a further 4 mins.
1 cup arborio rice	Add rice, stir well and cook for 4 mins.
3 cups vegetable stock (see page 237 or water and stock cube)	Add stock, stir well and cook for 9 mins. Then remove dish from the microwave, give another good stir and return to cook for another 9 mins. Remove, add vegies and leave to stand for a few minutes.
¼ cup freshly grated parmesan **freshly ground salt and pepper** **1 tbsp chopped parsley**	Stir these in and serve the risotto with a simple salad.

> **Because microwave temperatures do vary, the first time you make this keep a careful eye to ensure that nothing burns or is overcooked.**

Caught out

A friend of mine once owned a café in the centre of Melbourne's theatre district. Realising that speed was of the essence, he installed a bank of microwaves rather than a kitchen, and arranged for one of the city's better caterers to pre-pack pasta and the like into microwave containers. The café was a huge success and the food was greatly appreciated. In fact, so much so that one day a customer requested to meet the chef so she could pass on her compliments. My friend quickly replied that 'chef' had left for the day—an answer which satisfied the customer at the time. But that simple excuse soon became a terrible cross to bear, because the lady became a regular and on almost every occasion asked to see the chef. About two years down the track, and after such imaginative excuses as 'he chopped his finger off and is at the hospital having it sewn back on' and 'his sister has been kidnapped and he's arranging for the ransom', my mate decided to 'fess up—only to be informed that one of the waitresses had told her the truth at the very beginning and she had enjoyed his bizarre excuses so much that she had just kept the game going.

Pasta with mussels and citrus crumble (for 4–6)

2–3 dozen mussels ½ small onion, finely chopped a few sprigs of parsley ½ cup white wine	Scrub the mussels well and de-beard (remove the beard or stringy bit issuing from between the shells by grasping it firmly and pulling it along towards the hinge). Then put the mussels in the pot with the onion, the parsley and wine. Put lid on and cook, giving the pot a good shake every now and then to redistribute the mussels. As they open, remove them from the pot and then from the shells. Set aside, and strain the cooking juices.
¾ cup strained juices ½ cup cream	Reduce over a high heat until the resulting mixture coats a finger lightly.
400 g pasta	At same time, cook the pasta and drain.
slivers of zest from 1 lemon slivers of zest from 1 orange 2 garlic cloves 4 tbsp chopped parsley	Chop all this together and then add half to the hot cream, mix with the pasta and mussels, and toss well to heat through. Put in bowls and sprinkle with the rest of the citrus crumble.

> Another of my favourite pastas involves the juices from the roast—any roast. Just de-grease the pan juices, put over heat and scrape up all those delicious brown bits. When bubbling, add ½ cup wine and reduce a little. Then add butter and seasonings and toss through the pasta, along with some grated parmesan and a little more butter.

A pasta 'omelette' with the leftovers (for 2–4)

Keeping in mind that you can use almost any variety of leftover pasta, this is great for a casual lunch, or even for that Sunday night snack in front of the TV.

2–3 eggs 2 tbsp cream 3 tbsp grated parmesan freshly ground salt and pepper 1 tbsp chopped parsley	Whisk these together.
400 g leftover cooked pasta and sauce olive oil	Mix pasta into the above. Heat a little oil in a non-stick pan, add pasta mix and cook gently until golden on the bottom. Slide onto a plate, put pan on top and turn over so that the top of the 'omelette' is now on the bottom. Add a little more oil around the sides and cook until golden on the second side too.
tomato purée (see page 236) 2 handfuls rocket leaves, well washed and dried virgin olive oil freshly ground salt and pepper balsamic vinegar	When omelette is ready, cut in wedges, top with the tomato purée and serve with a salad of the rocket leaves dressed with olive oil, seasonings and a little balsamic.

> **Balsamic, the king of vinegars, aged over a number of years in different sized wooden barrels, is expensive but fortunately it need only be used sparingly. A few drops will lift most salads. But if balsamic is not available (or out of your price bracket), then a good red-wine vinegar such as South Australia's Hill Smith will do almost as well.**

Eggplant almost parmigiano (for 4)

I think, at some stage in our life, all of us have eaten Veal Parmigiano—that bloody awful dish which is so popular in every second-rate Italian bistro. But the genuine article is actually not bad when it is made with tender, young veal, some good cheese, a freshly made tomato sauce and, if you are really lucky, a sprinkling of pesto to add that extra touch. And this, its vegetarian cousin, is also terrific—only needing a bit of care to make it rather special.

Preheat oven to 200°C.

4 medium-sized eggplant, sliced crossways into 7.5 mm slices
vegetable oil

Heat oil in a large pan until almost smoking and cook eggplant (in three or four lots) until golden on both sides. Drain well on kitchen towels.

mozzarella cheese, sliced
pesto (see page 115)
tomato purée (see page 236)

On a lightly oiled baking tray, re-form the eggplants into a stack, putting a little pesto, tomato purée and cheese between the slices. Rest for 15 mins to develop the flavours and then put in the oven for 15 mins.

virgin olive oil
balsamic vinegar
4 sprigs basil

Place eggplant on 4 plates, sprinkle with oil and balsamic, and garnish with basil.

> **If you're feeling a little fancy, put some pesto and tomato purée in a couple of squeezy bottles and make an attractive pattern, with a little of each, on the plates.**

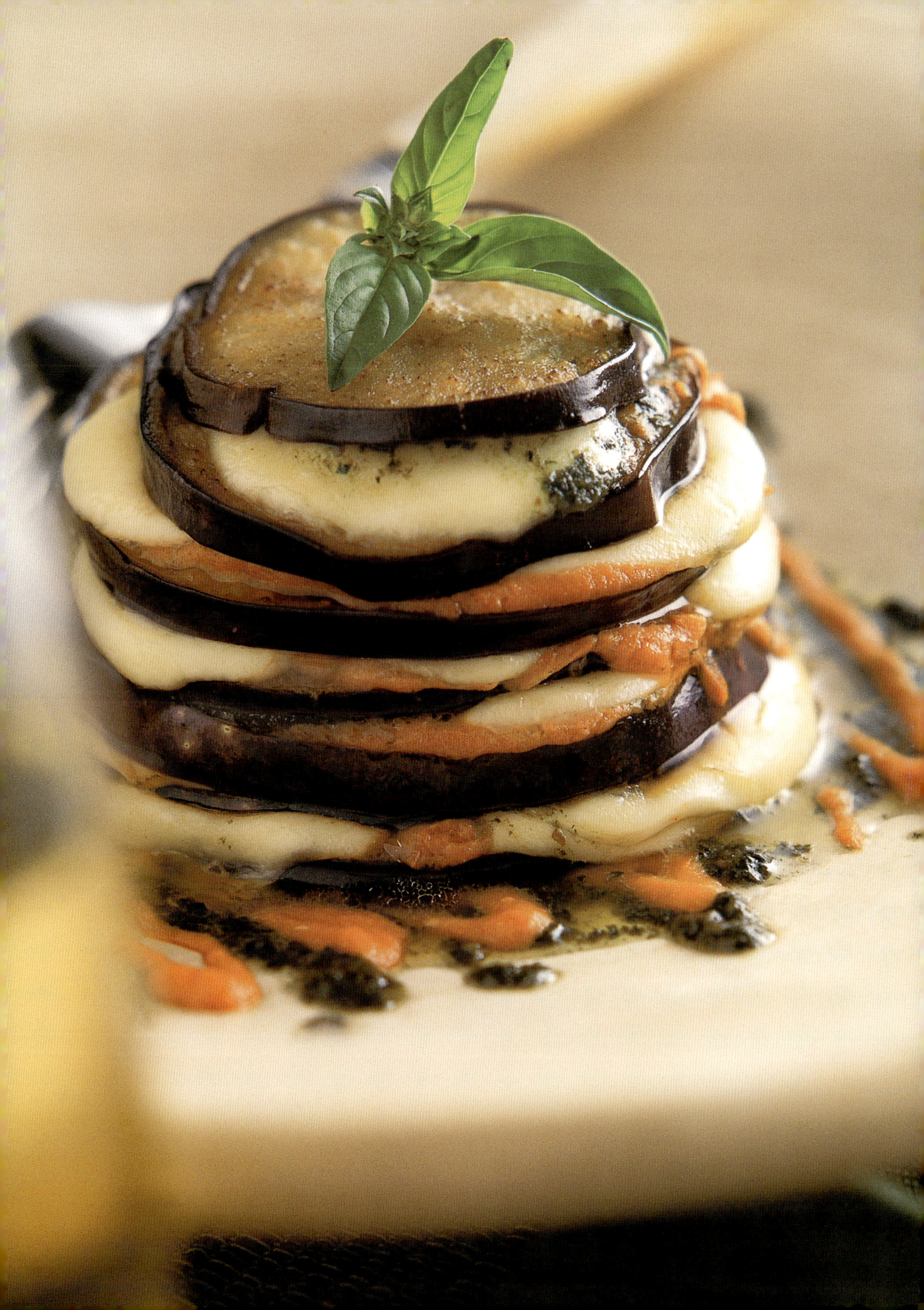

A brick-pressed Mediterranean sandwich (for 8)

Perfect for either a picnic or a casual lunch, this is that rare occasion when a sandwich actually improves with age. The secret is to use a robust bread such as a sourdough or ciabatta, and to remove and discard much of the soft centre.

---

1 medium-sized eggplant
2 garlic cloves
2 tbsp tahini
juice of 1 lemon
good pinch of ground cumin
freshly ground salt and pepper
2 tbsp chopped parsley
4 tbsp olive oil

Make baba ghanoush by cooking the eggplant in microwave for 8 mins, adding the garlic for the last 2 mins. Then peel and process with the remaining ingredients. (The eggplant could also, of course, be cooked on the BBQ or in the oven until tender.)

2 zucchini, sliced lengthways
2 capsicums, cored, seeded and cut into even pieces
olive oil
seasonings

Toss these vegies in oil and seasonings and grill or barbecue until golden and flecked with dark brown.

1 large loaf of bread
virgin olive oil
balsamic vinegar

Slice the loaf in half horizontally and remove a fair amount of the soft centre. Mix the oil with a little vinegar and sprinkle most of this all over the inside of the halved loaf. Then smear the bottom half generously with baba ghanoush (keep the remainder to use as a dip).

3 tomatoes, cored and sliced
6 bocconcini (fresh mozzarella balls) sliced
12–15 black olives, pitted and halved

rocket leaves

Next, top the spread bread with the grilled vegies and then the tomatoes, mozzarella and olives. Brush edges and under the lid with the remaining oil mix, place lid on firmly, wrap up in kitchen wrap and foil and, with brick on top, place in fridge overnight.

When ready to serve, open up, scatter some rocket leaves over and press lid back on firmly.

> **Use your imagination with this—almost any Mediterranean dip (bought or home-made) will work. Add other vegies, such as soft-dried tomatoes (see page 201), roasted capsicums (see page 245) and good bought marinated artichokes. And, if you like, slices of salami or prosciutto are also a terrific addition.**

A few almost-inspired pizza suggestions

- First of all, the main problem with commercial pizzas is the tomato sauce. This is either of a definite commercial bent, or simply whizzed-up canned tomatoes, but it's dead easy to improve on this. Just sauté some chopped onion, garlic and capsicum until soft, then add chopped drained canned tomatoes, seasonings and fresh herbs. Cook gently until thick, then whiz up or leave as is.
- If you can't be bothered with that, just slice some ripe tomatoes, place them on the pizza base and top with whatever you fancy.
- The classical tomato, basil and bocconcini salad also works well on a pizza. Toss tomato wedges, basil, olive oil and seasonings together. Place on base, scatter with some slices of bocconcini and sprinkle with any leftover oil.
- I also enjoy a real simple number made with finely sliced raw pumpkin, crushed garlic, seasonings, olive oil and the odd chunk of soft goat cheese.
- While I'm not the greatest fan of the trendy 'new' pizzas, I do enjoy this smoked salmon version, which is loosely based on a Wolfgang Puck number. Sauté some sliced red onion until tender, mix in a few capers and a splash of balsamic, and mound on a just-cooked pizza base. Top with some slices of smoked salmon, bung back in the oven for a minute and serve immediately sprinkled with sour cream (and chopped dill if you like).
- What about a pizza base with a real twist. Partly cook some spuds, grate them and then mix with egg, seasonings and chopped onions. Press in a flat layer into a large oiled pan and cook on both sides before adding your favourite topping and whacking under the grill.
- And for a crisp base, use an unglazed, clean terracotta tile as the base for individual pizzas.

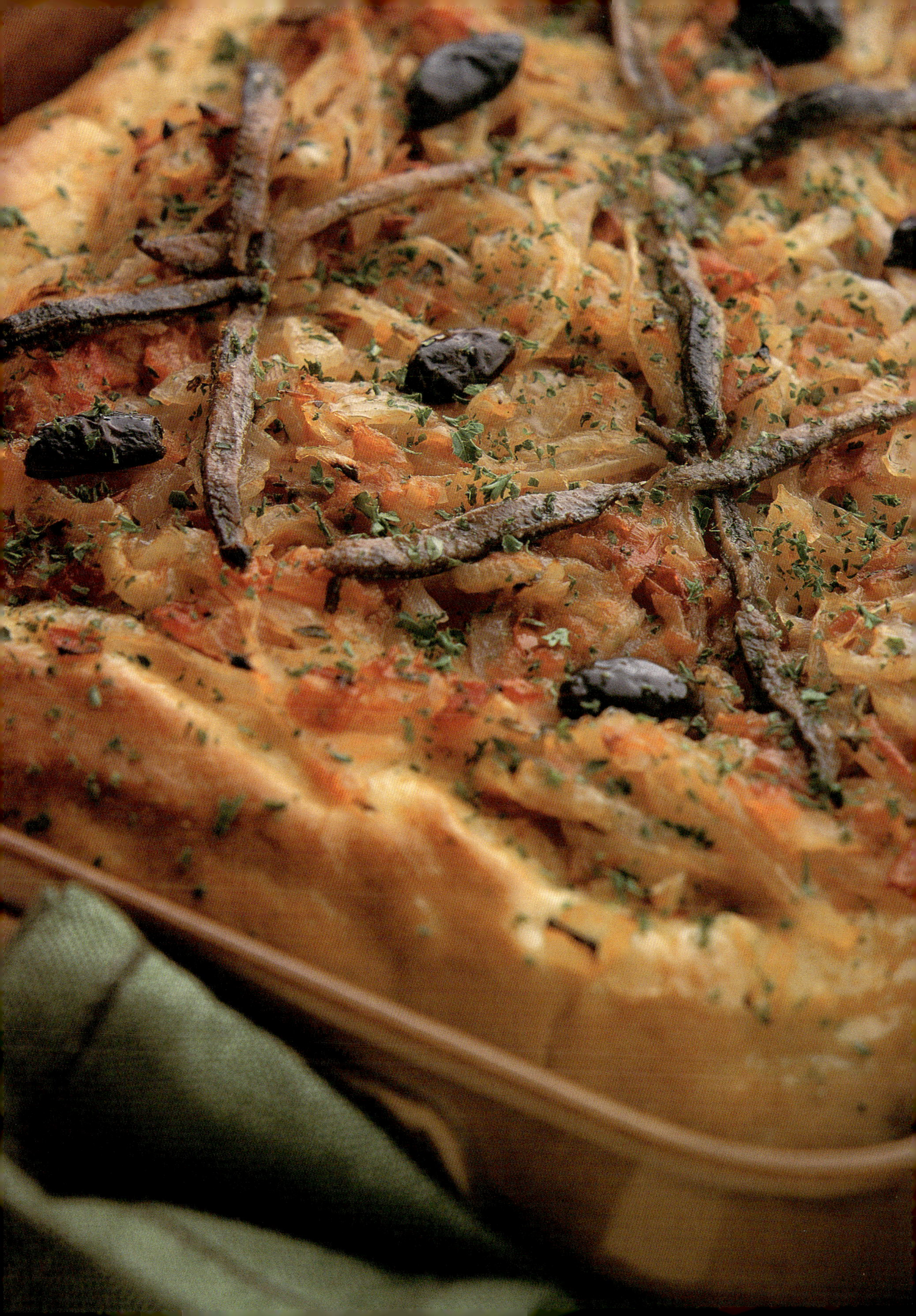

An onion and anchovy pizza from Provence (pissaladière)

(for 8–10)

The pizza began life as a way to use up leftover bread dough. Italian and Provençal bakers began by flattening the scraps before painting them with fresh tomato sauce or scattering them with sautéed onions, a few olives and an anchovy or two. And to this day the terrific pizzas of Italy and the south of France continue to be pretty basic affairs, with only a few ingredients on the top. (And I must tell you—surprise, surprise—they have never heard of the Hawaiian or Supreme versions, let alone Tandoori Chicken or Greek Lamb.)

---

1 cup lukewarm water
1 tbsp dry yeast
1 cup strong, bread flour
pinch of sugar

Make the dough. Combine the ingredients, stir until blended and leave for 5 or so minutes until foaming. (This is called proving and serves to ensure that the yeast is still active.)

1 tsp salt
1½ cups flour

Add salt to the dough and then up to 1½ cups flour, until the mix is no longer sticky. Knead until smooth and elastic. Put in large bowl, cover with kitchen wrap and leave for approx. 1 hour, until doubled.

Punch down the dough and let it rise again, covered, until once again doubled. (This can be done the day before, keeping it in a well-sealed container in the fridge.)

olive oil
6 medium-sized onions, sliced
2 garlic cloves, crushed
4 ripe red tomatoes, diced finely
a few sprigs of thyme
freshly ground salt and pepper

Heat oil in a pot and sauté onions and garlic until soft. Then add tomatoes, thyme and seasonings and cook gently for 15–20 mins.

some anchovies, cut in strips lengthways
pitted black olives

Roll out dough and spread it on an oiled baking tray to about 1–1.5 cm thick. Spread the onion–tomato mix on top and make diamond patterns with the anchovies, placing an olive in the centre of each diamond. Sprinkle with olive oil and bake in a very hot oven for 15–20 mins. Serve cut into squares or triangles.

> **To knead the dough, place it on a floured bench and push away from you with the palm and heel of the hand until smooth and elastic. And punching down is not a boxing term, but the process of pressing the dough down firmly to deflate the yeast's gases and allow fermentation to begin again.**

A Provençal seafood stew with a splash of Pernod (for 4)

vegetable oil ½ onion, chopped 1 garlic clove, chopped ½ tsp ground turmeric	Heat a little oil in a heavy-bottomed pan and sauté onion, garlic and turmeric until soft.
1 cup dry white wine	Add to pan and boil until reduced by half.
3 cups canned tomatoes, drained and chopped a pinch of red pepper flakes 2 bay leaves	Add these to the pan too, turn down heat and cook for 5–10 mins.
8 x 40 g pieces firm fish (such as groper, snapper, salmon, blue eye etc.)	Throw in, baste a little with the sauce, cover pan and simmer very gently for 3 mins.
8–12 mussels 1–2 calamari tubes, cleaned and sliced (see page 93) 8 large scallops, cleaned 8–12 large cooked prawns, peeled and deveined	Add these, mix in gently, cover and cook for another 2 mins. Then remove all seafood to a bowl, discarding any mussels that refuse to open.
1 tbsp Pernod or Ricard 2 tbsp chopped basil	Add to sauce in pan, mix in well and let bubble for a few seconds.
4 sprigs of basil	Pour sauce over the seafood and garnish with basil sprigs.

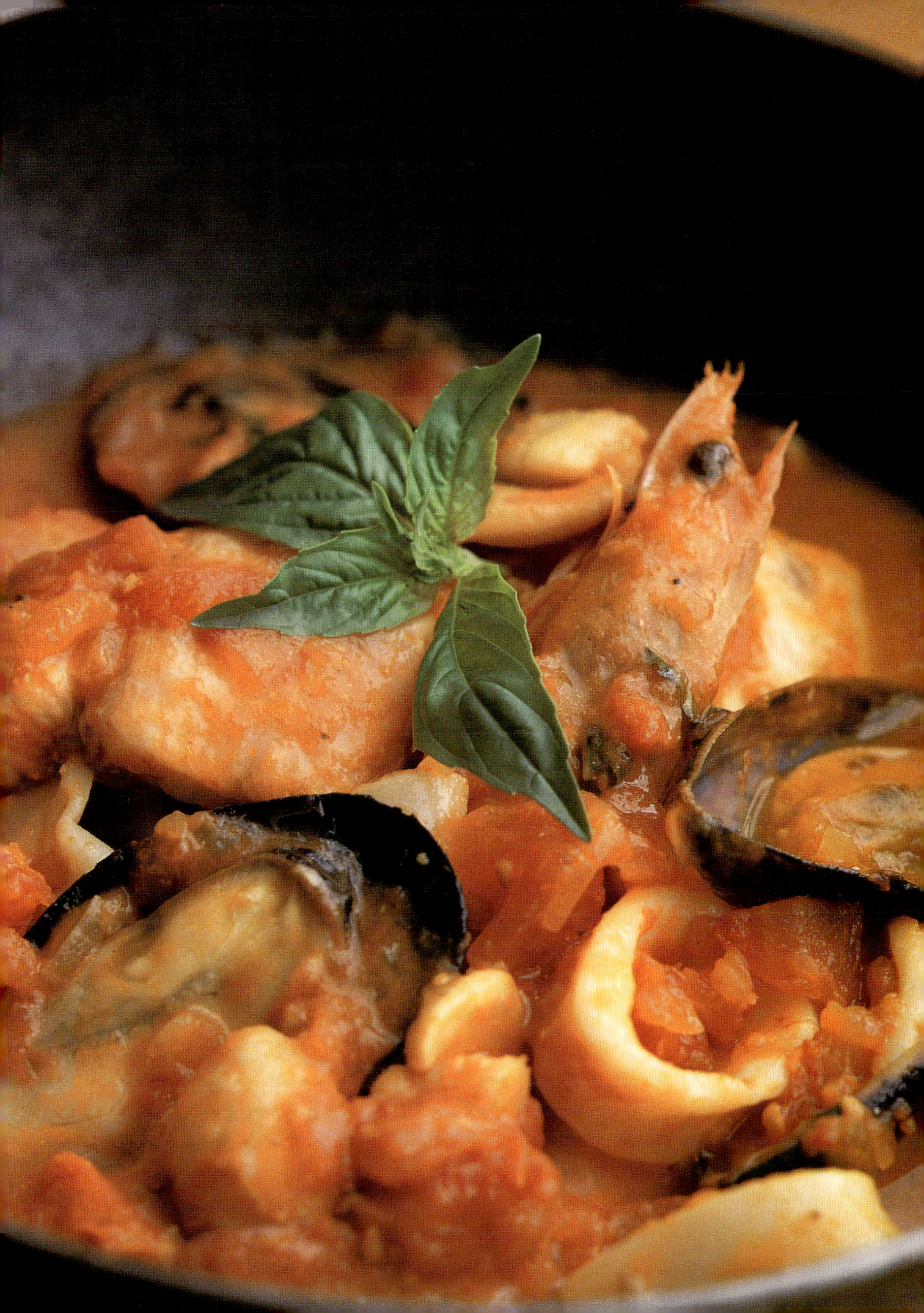

A vegetarian lasagne from Provence

(for 6–8)

For those of you who think that vegetable lasagne is boring—try this and think again.

---

4 tbsp unsalted butter
4 tbsp plain flour

Melt the butter in a heavy-bottomed pot and add the flour. Mix well and cook over very low heat for 4–5 mins.

3–4 cups hot milk

Add 2 cups of milk, little by little, whisking well. Then cook over moderate heat for 10 mins until reasonably thick, adding more milk as necessary.

grated tasty cheese
salt and freshly ground pepper

Add cheese and seasoning to sauce to taste, and set aside.

3 tbsp olive oil
1 garlic clove, crushed
1 medium-sized onion, peeled and chopped
6 zucchini, sliced into rounds
2 red capsicums, cored, seeded and chopped
1 large eggplant, cubed
2 cups canned, peeled tomatoes, drained and chopped
salt and freshly ground pepper

Heat oil in another heavy-bottomed pot and sauté garlic and onion for a few minutes. Then add zucchini, capsicum and eggplant, and toss for a few more minutes. Now add tomatoes and seasonings, turn down heat and cook until thick (approx. 15 mins).

Preheat oven to 200°C.

bought lasagne sheets
grated tasty cheese

Dip lasagne sheets one at a time in cold water, and cover bottom of a large square or rectangular lasagne dish. Top with the vegetable stew, then another layer of lasagne sheets. Cover generously with cheese sauce, sprinkle with grated tasty cheese and bake in oven for 30–35 mins, until golden.

A cheat's cassoulet from the south of France

(for 4)

Those of you who have spent hours and hours slaving over a hot stove whipping up an authentic cassoulet may not be overly impressed by this cheat's version. But it does have its advantages. First of all, it is a lot lighter and does not leave one feeling that he or she has just polished off an entire 18-course banquet. And secondly, it can be made almost at the drop of a hat without days of forward planning and the aforementioned hours at the stove face.

1½ cups haricot beans	Soak beans overnight in cold water. Then drain.
	Preheat oven to 160°C.
olive oil 4 duck legs 4 mid-loin lamb chops	In a large heavy-bottomed casserole, heat the oil and brown the duck and lamb in two or three lots. Set aside.
2 onions, sliced 2 celery stalks, diced 4 garlic cloves, chopped 2 thick spicy sausages, cut in thick slices freshly ground salt and pepper	Mix together the haricot beans and the vegies and layer into the casserole with the browned meats, sliced sausages and seasonings.
2 bay leaves 1½ cups canned tomatoes, drained and chopped 1¾ cups beef stock (packet is fine)	Put the bay leaves on top and cover the lot with the tomatoes. Pour the stock over, cover and cook for 2½ hours in the oven. Remove and mix well.
breadcrumbs made from day-old bread 1 tbsp chopped parsley	Mix crumbs and parsley together, sprinkle over the top of the cassoulet and return to the oven until you have a nice crisp top.

> **Nowhere has ever produced a canon of cookery as sybaritically lascivious … as Frenchly snoggable as the Gascons. It's like being massaged by a troupe of naked can-can dancers smeared in duck fat.**

English Restaurant Reviewer, A. A. Gill

The frugal cook

On regular occasions I (like almost everyone else) clean out my fridge and discover, at the very back, beautifully wrapped parcels containing leftover bits and pieces complete with mould growing in strange places. So, could I pass on a bit of advice that I once read in a book:

'Wrap all leftovers very carefully and neatly in a parcel and then unceremoniously dump them in the bin.'

Should east meet west?

Because I am not Asian, my Asian cooking will rarely be terribly authentic. Sure it will taste fine and will have a definite Asian bent, but because I have different skills to an Asian-born or -trained chef, it will definitely be different. I also can't help myself and tend to vary such recipes with a subtle use of Western ingredients or cooking methods. And this, to me, is what fusion or East-West cooking is about. Forget gimmicky dishes such as Peking Duck Lasagne or Char Siu Pork Risotto and think of a subtle marriage of flavours and tastes from both sides of the world. Which, with a little luck, may result in stunning dishes such as Ken Hom's Crispy Skinned Snapper, which is cooked in olive oil with Asian seasonings and has the flavours of both the East and West in every mouthful. Or

Adelaide chef Cheong Liew's Chilli Crab, which is braised in (what else) Cooper's very fine sparkling ale.

- Steamed salmon with a crackling dressing
- Char Siu rack of lamb
- Vietnamese chicken salad
- Malaysian noodle soup
- Whole baby fish, Cantonese-style
- Stir-fry of baby bok choy, snowpeas and shiitake mushrooms
- Chicken satays with macadamia nut sauce
- A crispy noodle cake with wok-fried beef and vegetables
- Chicken breast fillets in a fresh orange and soy marinade
- Red Emperor's twice-cooked spicy quail
- Mussels in a light green curry broth
- Malay chicken wings
- Thai garlic and chilli drumsticks
- Dead-easy duck
- Thai salmon patties
- An Asian oyster and vegetable 'omelette'
- A minute steak of kangaroo with a tangy apple salad
- Blue swimmer crabs with aromatics
- Japanese chicken 'sausage' with stirfried snowpeas
- Baby pumpkins stuffed with a Thai pumpkin and bean curry
- Vegetarian Hokkien noodles

Steamed salmon with a crackling dressing

(for 4)

	Fill wok about one-third full with water, put bamboo steamer in and bring to the boil.
1 medium-sized carrot, peeled 1 celery stalk ½ leek, well washed 1 small chilli 1 garlic clove	Cut vegies into julienne (thin strips about 5 cm long). Then finely slice the chilli and garlic, and mix everything together.
4 x 180 g salmon steaks or cutlets Japanese soy sauce leaves of ½ bunch coriander leaves 2 spring onions (green onions), sliced	When water is boiling, put salmon on a plate that will fit in the steamer, top with the vegetables and sprinkle generously with soy. Cover and steam until almost ready, add the coriander and spring onion, and cover again for a minute.
4 tbsp vegetable oil 4 tsp sesame oil	Place fish on 4 plates, along with any juices. Put the oils in a pan and heat until smoking. Then pour over the top of the fish.

> **Fish should smell like the tide. Once they smell like fish, it's too late.**
>
> Oscar Gizelt from famed New York Seafood Restaurant, Delmonico's

Char Siu rack of lamb (for 4)

4 tbsp honey
2 tbsp soy
2 tbsp dry sherry
3 tbsp hoisin sauce
1 tsp five spice powder

Combine well as a marinade.

4 racks of lamb, trimmed of all fat and sinew and chine bones removed

Pour marinade over lamb and leave for a few hours, turning two or three times.

stir-fry of bok choy, snowpeas and shiitakes (see page 154)

Preheat oven to its highest temperature. When it's hot, put lamb racks in a roasting tray, pour all of the marinade over the top and roast to the desired degree (approx. 10–12 mins for medium rare). Rest meat, loosely covered for 5 mins, slice into cutlets and pour cooking juices over the top. Serve with the stir-fry on the side.

A regret or two

There are few things that I regret about having spent most of my working life in restaurant kitchens. But one thing that does annoy the hell out of me is the fact that, because of this, I have developed a quite serious allergy to crustaceans. A fairly common problem amongst chefs, it means not only that I can't eat the blessed things but that I also sometimes have a problem even preparing them.

Fortunately, in recent times, this has not been so much of a problem because crayfish, mudcrabs and even prawns have almost priced themselves off our tables. And for some strange reason, the cheaper numbers such as blue swimmers, Moreton Bay bugs and yabbies just don't seem to have the same appeal. (Maybe purely and simply because they can be so bloody difficult to eat.)

Still, I suppose I should really count my lucky stars that it is only crustaceans that cause me such problems. And with other shellfish such as mussels, oysters and scallops freely available and still fairly inexpensive, I will hardly starve. Although I do remember the days when I could sit down to a whole cray with melted butter, which was not only affordable, but didn't try to kill me. Or piles of prawns pulled straight from the poaching stock and peeled the minute I could touch them. Or mudcrabs with black bean sauce in my local Asian restaurant which were so good, and cheap, that I invariably ordered two.

Vietnamese chicken salad (for 4–6)

When we had no gas in Melbourne a year or so back, I whipped this up for a group of friends by shredding the raw chicken fillet finely and pouring over it the liquid which I had boiled up in my kettle. It worked brilliantly and was a great success but, unfortunately, I must admit, my cups of tea have had a rather different flavour ever since. (See picture on page 150.)

6 dried shiitake mushrooms	Soak mushrooms in warm water for 15 mins. Drain, cut off and discard stalks, and slice caps finely.
2 skinless chicken breasts **½ tsp chicken stock powder** **1 parsley sprig** **1 star anise** **6 black peppercorns** **1 bay leaf**	At same time, put chicken in wok, with the rest of the ingredients and water to cover. Bring to boil, turn down until liquid just trembles, and cook until chicken is firm to the touch (approx. 7 mins). Turn off and leave in liquid for 15 mins. Remove meat and slice or shred.
vegetable oil **1 red onion, finely sliced** **2 celery stalks, finely sliced** **6 baby carrots, peeled and sliced** **1 tbsp whole raw peanuts** **a splash of soy sauce**	Wipe out wok, heat a little oil and stir-fry the mushies and vegies for a minute or two. Then add the peanuts and a splash of soy, and toss well. Turn off heat.
2 chillies, finely sliced **6 tbsp vegetable oil** **2 tbsp lime juice** **1 tbsp Asian fish sauce** **½ garlic clove** **a pinch of sugar**	Whisk together for the dressing.

8–10 Vietnamese mint leaves	Mix chicken and vegies together, and add above dressing to taste. Tear mint leaves and mix in gently.
½ iceberg lettuce, washed and outer and damaged leaves removed	Shred lettuce and place on plates or in bowls. Top with salad and sprinkle with a little more dressing.

> **Don't waste the chicken skin. Ken Hom, in his terrific book *East Meets West*, makes chicken crackling from the skin, which he then tosses through salads. Just cut the skins into 5 mm strips and put into hot oil. Turn the heat down and cook slowly until crispy. Drain very well on kitchen towels.**

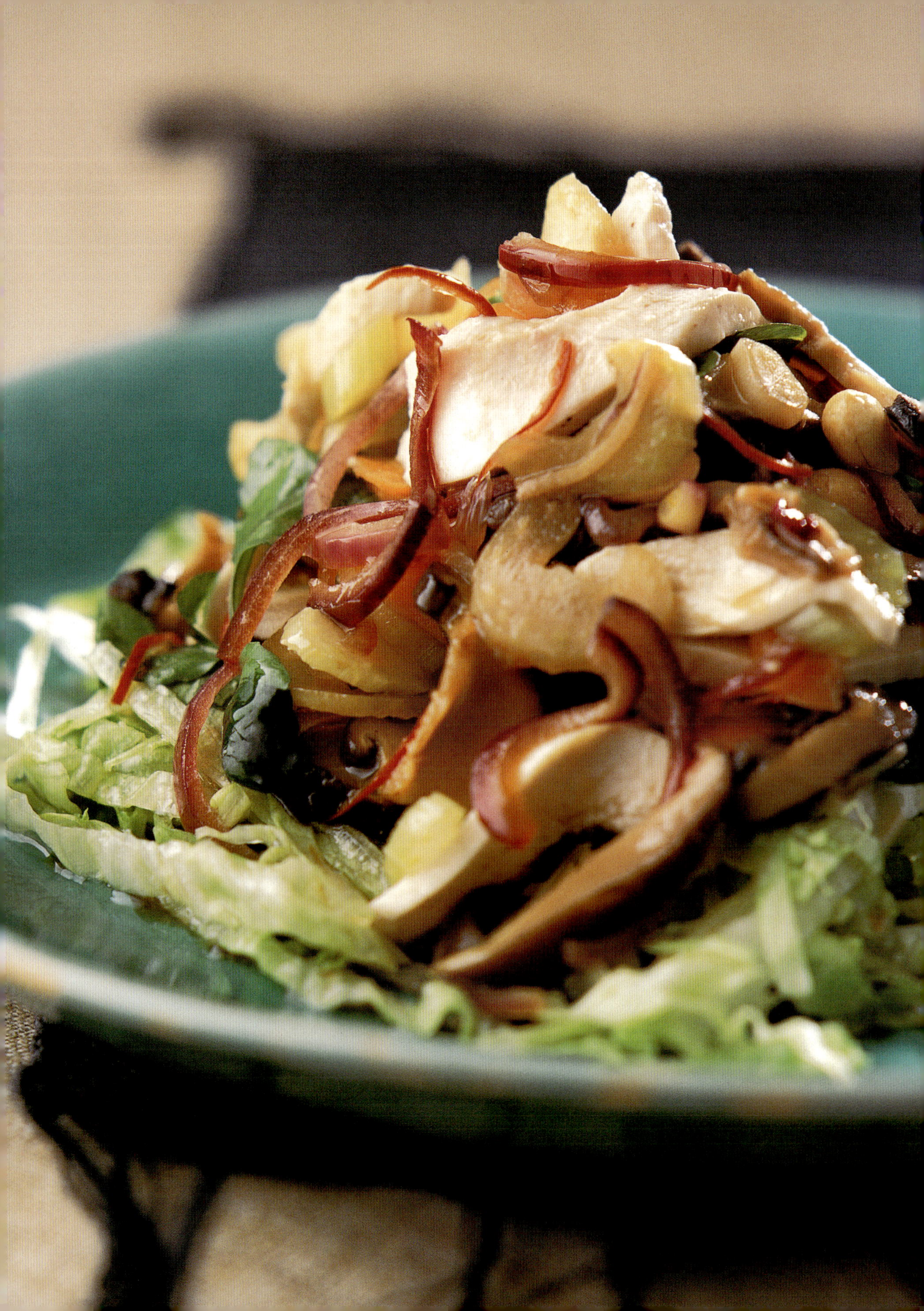

Malaysian noodle soup (for 6–8)

Soup plays an important role in any halfway-decent Asian banquet. This one, which is chockful of goodies, does the job well. And keep in mind you can make it hours or even days in advance, just throwing in the various bits and pieces at the last moment.

---

vegetable oil
1 large red capsicum, cored, seeded and chopped
½ red onion, sliced
1 stalk lemongrass, outer leaves removed and stem finely sliced
2 chillies, chopped

Heat a little oil in a large, heavy-bottomed pot and sauté everything until soft.

½ tbsp curry powder
½ tbsp sweet paprika
1 tsp sambal oelek

Add spices to pot and cook for a minute or two. Then add ½ cup of water and whiz up the mixture in a blender or processor.

1 litre chicken stock (packet is fine)
375 ml coconut cream

Return spicy paste to pot along with stock and coconut cream and simmer, uncovered, for 15–20 mins. Set aside until needed.

any Chinese greens, blanched briefly and well drained
cellophane noodles, soaked in hot water for a couple of minutes
shredded iceberg lettuce
roasted peanuts, coarsely chopped
bean or snowpea shoots
any poultry, pork or seafood, lightly cooked separately or in the broth itself

When ready to serve, bring back to the boil and add a combination of whatever takes your fancy from these suggestions (or, on a special occasion, the lot).

Whole baby fish, Cantonese-style (for 1 or 2 as a main, or 4–6 as part of a banquet)

It doesn't come much simpler than this Cantonese classic. But do remember that its success does depend heavily on the quality of the fish. And, if you like, make it into a one-pot (or one-wok) dish by also throwing in some Asian greens such as bok choy or snowpeas, towards the end.

1 whole plate-sized fish, scaled and cleaned
a 2 cm piece fresh ginger, peeled and finely sliced
Japanese soy sauce

Fill a wok to one-third with water and put a bamboo steamer on top. When water is boiling, put the fish on a plate which will fit in steamer and sprinkle with ginger and a generous amount of soy. Place in steamer, cover and cook until almost ready. (To check, make a small cut behind the head.)

2 spring onions (green onions), sliced

Throw onions on top of the fish, cover again and cook for a few seconds. Then place fish on platter and pour all the juices over the top. Serve with boiled rice on the side.

> **When buying fish, there are a few points to keep in mind. Look for a good bright colour, sparkling bulging eyes, a fresh sea smell and brightly coloured gills. This may be a little difficult when you're buying fillets or cutlets, but also keep in mind that the best fillets or cutlets will almost invariably come from a fish that is cut right there in front of you.**

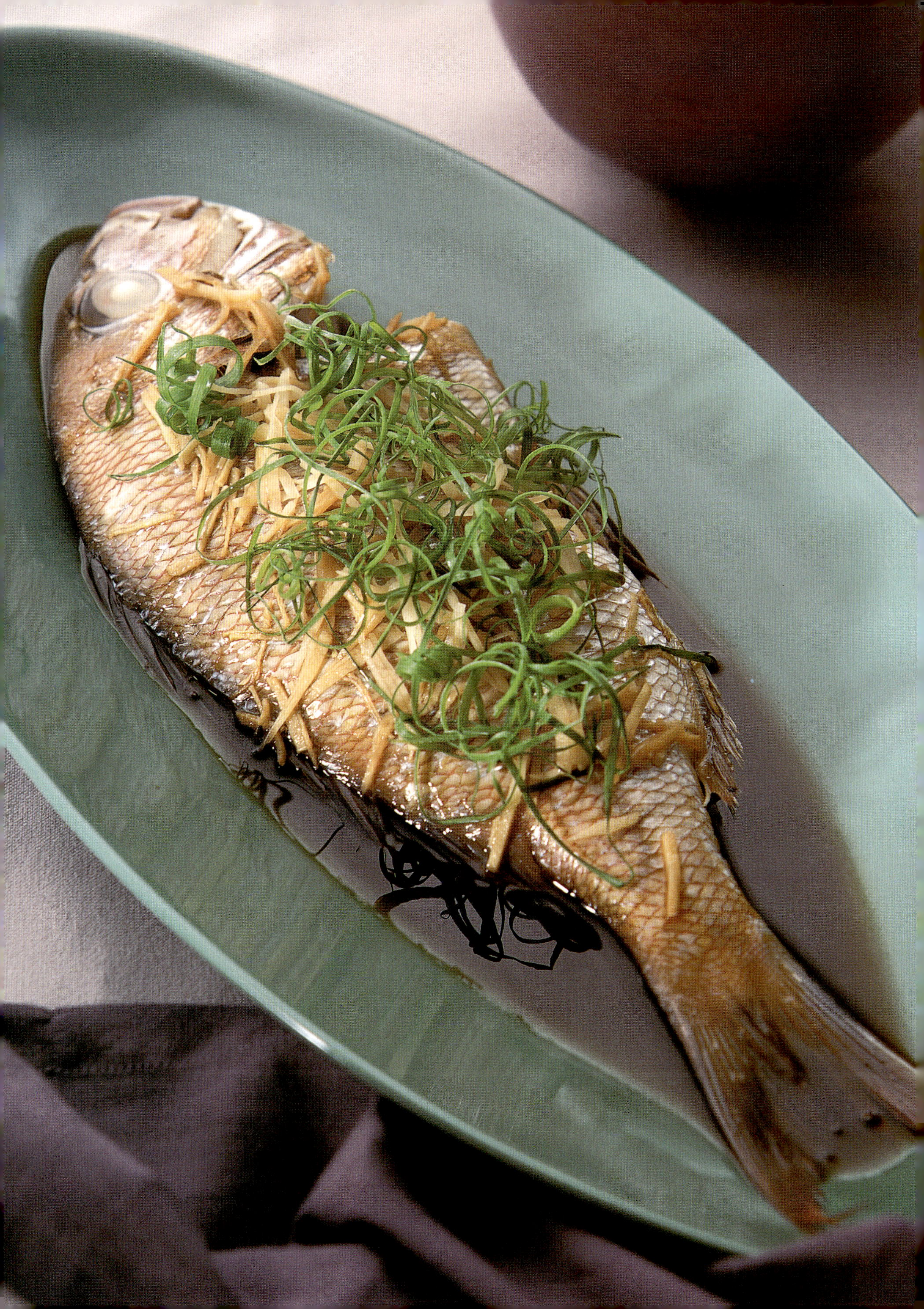

Stir-fry of baby bok choy, snowpeas and shiitake mushrooms (for 4)

8–12 dried shiitake mushrooms	Soak shiitakes in warm water for 10–15 mins. Then cut off and discard stalks, and slice the caps in two.
2 tsp oyster sauce **2 tsp soy sauce** **¼ cup chicken stock (packet is fine)**	Mix sauces and stock together.
vegetable oil **1 garlic clove, finely chopped** **a 5 mm piece of ginger, finely chopped** **4 heads baby bok choy, cut in half lengthways and washed well** **20–24 small snowpeas, topped and tailed**	Heat a little oil in a wok, add garlic and ginger and toss for a few seconds. Then add shiitakes and the sauce mix, and bring to the boil. Throw in the bok choy, cook for a minute or so, toss through the snowpeas, cook for another 30 secs and serve.

Chicken satays with macadamia nut sauce

(for 6–8)

½ cup macadamia nuts
½ tbsp macadamia oil (or peanut oil)

Toss nuts with the oil and roast in a moderate oven until golden-brown. Allow to cool, then chop coarsely.

2 tbsp macadamia or peanut oil
¼ red onion, finely chopped
1 garlic clove, finely chopped
2 tbsp lemongrass, finely sliced

Heat oil in a wok and sauté vegies over a moderate heat until soft.

1 tbsp Indian curry paste
1½ cups coconut milk

Add paste to wok and cook for a few minutes to release aroma, stirring constantly. Add the prepared nuts, turn up heat and add coconut milk, little by little, allowing it to reduce between each addition.

soy sauce
fresh lime juice
chopped coriander

When mixture is of a sauce-like consistency, add these flavourings to taste. Set aside.

4 skinless chicken breasts
bamboo skewers

Using a folded piece of cling wrap and a meat mallet, beat chicken until fairly thin and even. Then cut lengthways into 5 or 6 strips and thread these onto wooden skewers.

juice of 1 lime
2 tbsp soy sauce
2 tbsp coconut milk
1 chilli, finely sliced

Mix these with ½ cup of the sauce and pour over the skewered meat. Leave for at least 1 hour. Then BBQ or grill over high heat and serve with the warmed sauce and some wedges of tomato and cucumber, if you like.

" To prepare lemongrass, remove the rough outer leaves and give the bulb a good whack with the flat side of a meat mallet or large knife to break up the fibres, then slice it as finely as you can. "

A crispy noodle cake with wok-fried beef and vegetables (for 4)

100 g blade steak, well trimmed	Put beef in freezer for 2 hours.
1 x 200 g packet chow mein noodles **sesame oil**	Plunge noodles into a pot of boiling water for 1 min. Then run under cold water, drain very well and toss with a little sesame oil. Set aside.
3 cups vegetable oil	Remove steak from the freezer and slice thinly. Heat oil in wok to 190°C and, in two or three lots, put beef in and fry for 30 secs, reheating oil after each lot. Drain meat well and set aside. Strain oil and set aside for other use. Wipe out wok.
vegetable oil	When ready to serve, heat 2 tbsp oil in a large non-stick pan. Add cooked noodles and press down to form a cake. Fry for approx. 5 mins, adding a little more oil if necessary, until golden-brown. Turn out, re-oil pan and fry the cake on the other side.
vegetable oil **a 5 mm piece fresh ginger, finely chopped** **1 tbsp black beans, soaked in water, then drained and coarsely chopped** **1 garlic clove, finely chopped** **16 small snowpeas, topped, tailed and cut in half crossways** **2 baby bok choy, well washed and separated into leaves** **8 baby corn**	Heat a little oil in wok and sauté ginger, black beans and garlic for 30 secs. Then add vegies and stir-fry for 30 secs.
2 tbsp soy sauce	Add soy and beef to wok and toss until the beef is hot. Then place noodle cake on a large platter and mound the stir-fry in the centre.

❝ **Forget the beef and turn the noodle cake into a vegetarian treat—but, in this case, I often throw in some spicy sweet walnuts. Just melt a good knob of butter along with ½ tsp each of ground cinnamon and cardamom. Then add 1 cup walnut halves, mix in well and spread out on a baking tray. Bake until lightly browned and toss with a little melted honey to taste.** ❞

Chicken breast fillets in a fresh orange and soy marinade (for 4)

1 cup fresh orange juice
4 tbsp dry sherry
6 tbsp soy sauce
2 tbsp green peppercorns in brine, drained
2 garlic cloves, crushed
4 tbsp vegetable oil
2 tbsp honey

Whisk these marinade ingredients together.

4 chicken breast fillets, skin on

Pour half of the marinade over, cover and refrigerate overnight.

Preheat BBQ or grill.

Cook chicken over moderate heat, skin-down first, until golden, brushing with marinade as you do so. At same time, in a small pot reduce the reserved marinade to a glaze.

vegetable oil
freshly ground salt and pepper
4 baby bok choy, washed well and halved lengthways

When chicken is almost ready (check by making small cut), season and oil the bok choy and barbecue or grill it until tender and slightly charred around edges.

boiled rice

Mound rice on 4 plates, place chicken on it, drizzle with glaze and arrange bok choy on top.

Red Emperor's twice-cooked spicy quail

(for 4 as an entrée)

Maybe I like being spoilt, but my preferred yum-cha venue is the Red Emperor in Melbourne's Southgate, where not only is the food terrific, but the wine list is great and the staff knowledgeable and friendly—they even smile when I insist on ordering these quails from their à la carte menu (as if their huge yum-cha selection isn't enough).

1 tsp finely chopped garlic **1 tsp salt** **½ tsp sugar** **1 tbsp Chinese cooking wine** **½ tbsp soy sauce**	Mix marinade ingredients well in a large bowl.
4 large quails, cut in half	Add to marinade, stir well to coat and marinate for about an hour.
4–6 cups vegetable oil	Heat to 180°–190°C in a wok. Drain quails well and deep-fry for 7 or 8 mins until golden.
1 chilli, finely sliced **½ garlic clove, finely sliced** **½ tbsp spicy salt.** **1 tbsp Chinese cooking wine** **½ tbsp ground ginger**	To make spicy salt, mix 5 tbsp salt with 1 tbsp five spice powder. Heat pan and lightly fry ½ tbsp spicy salt mix with the other ingredients. Then add quail and toss well to coat.

> **I love defenceless animals, especially in a good sauce.**
>
> Anon. (I wonder why)

Missed by that much

I don't know whether you remember the Charles Atlas body building courses which were heavily advertised in our newspapers during the forties, fifties and early sixties. They invariably featured a muscle-bound thug kicking sand in the face of a puny little fellow who, after enrolling in the Charles Atlas course, returned the favour. Although not every participant benefited in such a manner, with one in particular writing to say that he had 'followed the course in its entirety—now could you please send me the mussels'. I wonder if they sent him a large bag of mussels (fresh from the sea, of course).

Mussels in a light green curry broth (for 2)

vegetable oil 2 tbsp lemongrass, very finely sliced 2 garlic cloves, finely chopped	Heat a little oil in wok and sauté lemongrass and garlic for a few minutes.
1 heaped tbsp Thai green curry paste ½ cup coconut milk 2 tbsp water	Add curry paste to wok and cook for a minute to release flavour. Then add liquids and whisk well.
3 dozen mussels, scrubbed and bearded. (To beard the mussels, grasp the string-like substance coming out of the shell, run it towards the hinge and then pull off.)	Add to wok, then cover and cook. Remove mussels as they open, placing them in 2 large bowls (discard any that do not open).
2 tbsp chopped basil a splash of Asian fish sauce a squeeze of fresh lime	Add these to liquid in wok, bring to boil and pour over the mussels.
sliced spring onion (green onion)	Sprinkle over the top before serving.

Wild mussels

If the mussels are dredged, not farmed, get rid of sand and grit by immersing the mussels in salted water for an hour or so, along with a sprinkling of flour. This mix encourages live mussels to expel all foreign substances.

Malay chicken wings (for 4–6)

1 cup coconut milk
2 tsp Indian curry paste
2 garlic cloves, crushed
1 finely sliced fresh chilli
1 tsp ground coriander
1 tsp ground turmeric
1 tbsp chopped basil
squeeze of lemon

Whisk these marinade ingredients together.

24–30 chicken wings

Cut off wingtips and reserve for stock. Cut wings in half at joint and mix into marinade. Leave for 3–4 hours in fridge.

Preheat BBQ.

wedges of tomato
thick slices of telegraph (continental) cucumber, skin on
chopped coriander

Barbecue the wings over a moderate-high heat, frequently turning and brushing with marinade. Serve with tomatoes, cucumbers and a sprinkling of coriander.

Thai garlic and chilli drumsticks (for 4)

1 bunch coriander, including roots
4 garlic cloves
3 chillies
2 tsp castor sugar
2 tsp rock salt
freshly ground black pepper
juice of 2–3 limes (or lemons)

Wash coriander very well and chop the lot coarsely. Whiz up with the remaining ingredients.

16 chicken drumsticks, skin on

Pour the above marinade over the drumsticks, rub in well and leave for 1–2 hours, turning once or twice.

Preheat BBQ.

lime wedges
1 cup plain yoghurt
1–2 tbsp chopped coriander

Barbecue the drumsticks over moderate heat, turning and brushing with marinade frequently. When ready, serve with lime wedges and the yoghurt mixed with coriander.

> **To check if chicken is ready, cheat a little by making a small cut along the bone with a sharp knife.**

A culinary disaster

One of my favourite restaurant dishes is Cantonese Roast Duck. So, rather foolishly, I decided that for my next dinner party I would attempt this rather complicated little number. But I must admit, it wasn't quite the culinary triumph I had hoped for.

For a start, the recipe involved drying the duck either by hanging it in a well ventilated spot overnight or using a hairdryer to speed the process up. Of course, impatient sod that I am, the hairdryer method appealed, but after burning out my girlfriend's rather expensive little number I decided to give this step a miss and move on. The instructions then had me whipping up an aromatic broth to be poured into the duck's cavity, which was then sewn up tightly.

Well, the whipping was fine, but seamstress I'm not and the next few hours were spent attempting to sew up the bloody cavity so that the liquid wouldn't run out. The less said about the end result the better, but at least some good came out of the whole episode—next time, I'll just take my guests to the best Chinese restaurant, where they do such dishes seemingly with ease and where taking into account the cost of my girlfriend's hairdryer, it will most probably cost far less. (And if I do insist on cooking at home, I'll cheat a little and buy my duck from Chinatown, which will also be a darn sight cheaper.)

Dead-easy duck (for 6–8)

1 bought Chinese barbecued duck	Ask the Chinese grocer or restaurant to cut the duck into pieces—the Chinese way, bones and all.
6–8 dried shiitake mushrooms	Soak shiitakes in warm water for 10–15 mins. Then remove and discard stalks before slicing the caps.
1 tbsp hoisin sauce 1 tbsp soy sauce ¾ cup chicken stock (packet is fine)	Whisk these together.
vegetable oil 1 garlic clove, finely chopped a 1 cm piece fresh ginger, finely chopped 10 baby corn ½ red capsicum, cored, seeded and sliced 4 baby carrots, peeled and diagonally sliced 2 celery stalks, sliced 8–12 baby green beans, topped and tailed and cut into 3 crossways	Heat a little oil in a wok and toss garlic and ginger for a few seconds. Add vegies and the prepared shiitakes and toss for a few minutes. Then add the stock mix and the duck, turn down heat and simmer, very gently, until duck is heated through.
2 spring onions (green onions), sliced	Share wok contents between deep bowls, sprinkle with spring onion and serve with boiled rice on the side.

Thai salmon patties (for 8)

Certainly in the tradition of Thai fish cakes, but a lot lighter and fluffier and, because they are cooked in the oven rather than in tonnes of oil, a lot healthier too.

Preheat oven to 220°C.

2 garlic cloves, chopped
2 coriander roots, well washed and finely chopped
1 tsp rock salt
1 tsp castor sugar
4 chillies, chopped
2 tbsp fish sauce

Make a Thai-style vinaigrette by whizzing these ingredients up in a blender or processor.

4–6 tbsp lime juice
3 tbsp coriander leaves, chopped

Mix these into the dressing, keeping in mind that the sauce should hit you in the face. Set aside.

½ large red capsicum, seeded, cored and coarsely chopped
a 1 cm piece of fresh ginger, finely sliced
2 garlic cloves, finely sliced
3 tbsp Asian chilli sauce

Whiz up in a processor.

500 g fresh salmon offcuts or scraps
100 ml coconut cream

Add these to capsicum paste and process until smooth.

1 egg
pinch of salt

Add and whiz for a few more seconds.

6 spring onions (green onions), chopped
leaves from ½ bunch coriander leaves, well washed and chopped

Put spicy fish mixture in a bowl, mix in these greens and form into patties approx. 7 cm in diameter.

vegetable oil plain flour	Heat a little oil in a pan, which can go into the oven. Flour and cook the patties on both sides. Then place in oven until firm to the touch, turning over once.
1 telegraph (continental) cucumber, skin on and sliced	Arrange cucumber on plates, top with patties and sprinkle dressing over.

> **I have also made these patties with other fish varieties and, for that special occasion, chunks of fresh crab folded through—delicious.**

An Asian oyster and vegetable 'omelette' (for 4)

vegetable oil 1 small chilli, finely sliced 1 garlic clove, finely chopped a 5 mm piece of fresh ginger, finely chopped	In a large non-stick pan, heat a little oil and sauté chilli, garlic and ginger for 2–3 mins.
½ cup shredded Chinese white cabbage (wonga bok) 2 small spring onions (green onions), sliced 6 small snowpeas, topped, tailed and halved crossways 2 baby carrots, peeled and sliced ¼ cup bean shoots 2–3 tbsp soy sauce	Add vegies to the pan and toss for about 2 mins. Add soy and toss well. Remove from heat and cool. Wipe out pan.
8 eggs vegetable oil	Beat eggs well and mix into vegies. Heat a little oil in pan, pour in egg mixture, turn down heat to very low, cover and cook until just set.
8–12 oysters, freshly shucked, then drained	Scatter oysters on top of omelette, cover and leave for 30 secs more. Then cut into wedges and place on 4 plates.
Thai vinaigrette (optional—see page 166)	Sprinkle omelette with a little Thai vinaigrette and, if you like, serve more on the side.

❝ I remember, in the mid-seventies, when we first began opening oysters to order, a common customer complaint was that they were too salty. Sadly, many of us had become accustomed to the flavour of oysters which had often been opened up to two days beforehand and had been washed under tap water (sometimes two or three times). And we had most probably, up until then, rarely tasted the wonderful briny, salty flavour of a 'real' oyster. Thankfully, these complaints soon petered out as customers came to realise that this succulent bivalve should actually taste of the sea, not chlorine. ❞

A minute steak of kangaroo with a tangy apple salad (for 4)

4 small fillets of roo, trimmed of all fat and sinew

Cut lengthways two-thirds of the way through each fillet, lay on bench and flatten slightly to an even thickness.

½ cup olive oil
1 tsp sambal oelek
1 tsp soy sauce
freshly ground pepper

Mix these marinade ingredients together, pour over roo and leave for at least 30 mins.

2 small chillies
½ tsp sugar
1 tbsp white vinegar
1 tbsp fish sauce
1 garlic clove
2 tbsp honey
a good squeeze of lemon juice

Whiz up to make the Asian-style dressing.

1 Granny Smith apple, cored and sliced
a handful of baby cress
8 mint leaves, torn
½ medium-sized red onion, sliced
½ cup bean shoots
2 tbsp coarsely chopped roasted peanuts

Toss these with the dressing, to taste, and mound on 4 plates. Sprinkle a little more dressing over the top.

Quickly sear the kangaroo on a very hot grill or BBQ (to no more than medium-rare, or it will be dry) and place on the salads.

Blue swimmer crabs with aromatics

(for 2)

2 blue swimmer crabs	Lift top shell away from each crab and set aside. Clean crabs by washing body under cold water, then cut into 4 pieces in the shape of a cross. Blanch tops in boiling water to use as a garnish.
vegetable oil 2 garlic cloves, finely sliced a 1 cm piece of fresh ginger, finely sliced 2 small chillies, finely sliced	In a large wok, heat a little oil. Add the crabs and the garlic, ginger and chillies and cook, tossing, for 3–4 mins.
1 cup white wine a splash of soy sauce ½ carrot, peeled and cut into julienne ½ leek, well washed and cut into julienne	Add wine, soy and vegies to wok and bring to the boil. Cover and simmer until crab is cooked (approx. 12–15 mins), tossing at regular intervals.
a handful of snowpea shoots	Toss these through mixture in wok and serve in large bowls with all the juices poured over the top.

> **The blue swimmer crab is one of the unsung gastronomic heroes of Australia. Tender and succulent, these delicious crustaceans are ignored by the majority, who seemingly find them a bit of a bugger to eat. But please don't be deterred by this fact. Roll up your sleeves, tuck your napkin into the collar and dive into the bowl—I promise you won't be disappointed.**

The admirable wok

I sometimes wonder how I survived without a wok in my kitchen. The perfect vehicle for everything from a simple stir-fry to an Italian ragu, the wok is about on a par with the great Ian Botham, whose skills as an all-rounder are well documented. Sure, it may not be able to bowl, bat or even catch as well as the big boy, but when it comes to sautéing, steaming, smoking and deep-frying it is almost without equal.

And, even better, the wok is about the most inexpensive piece of culinary equipment to be found. Admittedly, at present I'm in love with a slightly more up-market number, but I have also over many years had great success with those wonderful cheapies to be found by the dozen in every Asian grocery.

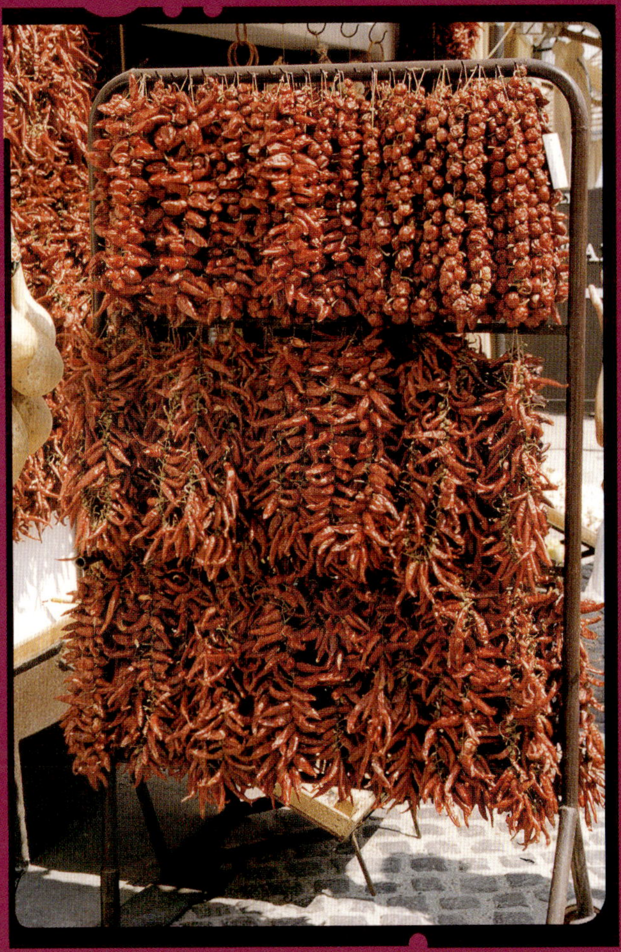

Japanese chicken 'sausage' with stirfried snowpeas (for 4)

4 skinless chicken breasts
⅓ cup Japanese soy sauce
⅓ cup mirin (Japanese rice wine)
⅓ cup sake

½ carrot, peeled
1 celery stalk
½ red capsicum, cored and seeded
½ leek, well washed
vegetable oil

2–3 dozen small snowpeas, topped and tailed
vegetable oil

Flatten chicken breasts to an even thickness. Mix together the other ingredients and pour most of this over the top. Leave for 15–30 mins.

Cut all these vegies into fine long strips (julienne). Heat a little oil in a wok and toss vegies until softened. Add the remaining soy marinade mix, toss well and remove from wok.

Lay chicken breasts on bench and arrange julienned vegies crossways in the centre of each. Roll up separately and place each on a square of kitchen wrap, rolling up and tying the ends as you would a bonbon. Repeat this process with a square of foil and then poach sausages in simmering water until firm when squeezed. Remove, rest for 5 mins, then unwrap and slice into rounds.

Heat a little oil in wok and sauté the snowpeas briefly. Place on 4 plates and top with the sliced chicken.

> **I won't eat anything that has intelligent life, but I'd gladly eat a television executive or a politician.**
>
> Marty Feldman

Baby pumpkins stuffed with a Thai pumpkin and bean curry

(for 4)

Preheat oven to 200°C.

4 baby pumpkins
vegetable oil

Cut a small slice from bottom of each pumpkin and a slightly larger one from the top. With a knife and spoon, hollow out seeds and fibre from each pumpkin. Brush flesh of lids and the pumpkin with a little oil, and bake in the oven until flesh is tender when pierced with a small knife. (Obviously, the lids will be ready before body.)

vegetable oil
2 garlic cloves, finely sliced
a 1 cm piece of fresh ginger, finely sliced
1 tbsp lemongrass, finely sliced

Heat oil in a wok and sauté briefly.

1 heaped tbsp Thai red curry paste

Add paste to wok and stir to release aromas, for 2 mins.

1 cup coconut cream
1 butternut pumpkin, peeled, seeded and cubed
16–20 green beans, topped, tailed and cut into 3
2 curry leaves

Add half the coconut cream to the wok, whisk well and then add the vegies and curry leaves. Turn down heat and simmer until pumpkin is tender, adding more coconut cream, little by little, as it reduces (plus a little water if need be).

2 tbsp chopped basil
lime juice

Mix basil into curry and add lime juice to taste. Set aside.

When baby pumpkins are ready, reheat curry and mound into pumpkins. Put lids on top and serve with boiled rice on the side.

Vegetarian Hokkien noodles (for 2–4)

1 packet Hokkien noodles	Soak noodles in hot water for 10 mins. Then drain.
vegetable oil a 1 cm piece of fresh ginger, chopped 2 garlic cloves, chopped 1 tsp sambal oelek	Heat a little oil in a wok. Briefly toss the garlic and ginger in it, then add the sambal and mix for a few seconds.
1 red capsicum, cored, seeded and sliced 1 medium-sized carrot, peeled and sliced 2 celery stalks, sliced 6 mushrooms, sliced	Add vegies to wok and toss for 2–3 mins.
½ cup Japanese soy sauce ½ cup chicken stock (packet is fine)	Add liquids to wok and cook for another 2–3 mins.
18 snowpeas, topped and tailed a small handful of shredded Chinese cabbage a small handful of snowpea shoots	Add these vegies to wok with the noodles, and toss until vegies are lightly wilted and noodles are hot.
soy sauce wedges of lime sweet chilli sauce sliced fresh chilli Asian fish sauce	Serve noodles in deep bowls with these condiments on the side.

> **The waiter in the Chinese restaurant was so friendly that, when I waved at him, trying to attract his attention, he simply smiled and waved back.**

The English *Good Food Guide 1972*

Salads of all shapes and sizes

THESE REALLY ARE great times for the true salad believer, because our shops and markets are full to overflowing with a huge variety of salad ingredients, many of which were unheard of even a few short years ago. But when making those purchases do keep in mind that a creation using the most mundane of ingredients which are at their peak will always beat, hands down, one using even the most exotic produce that is past its seasonal prime.

- BLT salad with avocado and a poached egg
- My ever-changing warm salad
- A salad of raw vegies with a garlic and herb mayo
- Lemon and basil crusted chicken salad
- Fidel Castro's favourite Cuban beef salad
- Thai beef and cranberry salad

- A salad of pink livers and spinach in a Dubonnet, orange and cranberry dressing
- Peppered beef salad with rocket, balsamic and parmesan
- Barbecued octopus salad with olive oil roasted vegies
- Spicy fresh salmon tartare in witloof boats
- A ripper warm salmon salad with anchovy mayo
- A calamari salad with eastern flavours
- Carpaccio of mushrooms with rocket, parmesan and virgin olive oil
- Pasta insalata
- Iain's salad in the style of Caesar
- My very own Caesar pasta
- The simplest of tomato salads
- Roasted capsicum, anchovy and soft-dried tomato salad
- Green beans with soft-dried tomatoes and crispy prosciutto
- Tea-smoked tomatoes
- Further thoughts on tomato salads
- A mozzarella salad with gazpacho overtones
- A trio of salads
- And while we're on the subject of salads—a dressing or two

BLT salad with avocado and a poached egg

(for 4)

After many nights spent in hotels all over the world, I decided that I must be able to improve on the ubiquitous BLT (bacon, lettuce and tomato) sandwich, which is seemingly an essential item on every hotel-room service menu. So here is what I came up with, and it's a terrific lunch or brunch dish which can also double as a late-night snack between slices of baguette (and, by the way, it was a huge hit on my show 'A Cook's Journey'; so much so that I have always felt that the Egg Board could have, at the very least, given me a knighthood for services to the industry).

2 slices day-old bread **vegetable oil**	Cut crusts off bread and cut into 1 cm cubes. Heat oil in pan and fry bread until golden on all sides. Drain well on kitchen paper towels.
3 bacon rashers, cut crossways into 3	Grill or pan-fry until crisp. Drain well.
6 tbsp olive oil **1 tbsp lemon juice** **1 tbsp chopped chives** **freshly ground salt and pepper**	Whisk these together for a dressing.
8 cherry tomatoes, cored and halved **1 handful salad leaves**	Toss bacon and croutons with the tomatoes, leaves and dressing to taste.
4 eggs **white vinegar** **1 avocado, peeled and sliced** **chopped parsley**	Poach the eggs in lightly vinegared water. Mound salad on 4 plates, top with slices of avocado and a poached egg, and sprinkle with parsley.

> **An easy way to poach an egg perfectly is to bring a pan of water to a simmer, add a little vinegar and then break in the eggs. Simmer for exactly 1 minute, cover, turn off heat and leave for exactly 10 minutes.**

Oops!

While I am loath to admit that I have ever made a mistake in the kitchen, I must confess that my first-ever warm salad came about because of a monumental gastronomic blunder.

It was my first dinner party and, having invited six to dine—inexperienced as I then was—I decided it was the perfect opportunity to attempt cassoulet; that delicious, yet oh-so-complicated dish from the Toulouse region of France.

Actually it started rather well, although maybe I could have portioned the duck a little more carefully. (It looked like the dog had been at it—which interestingly enough is where it ended up.) But for the first half hour or so the cassoulet bubbled along quite merrily, filling the house with the wonderful aromas of tomatoes, herbs and garlic. Then disaster struck, in the form of a young Huey. Realising that my guests were almost on the doorstep, I turned the stove to its highest setting and, within 15 minutes those wonderful odours had turned sour, as the beans caught on the bottom of the pot. And when my guests arrived a few minutes later, they did so to a smoke-filled house and the sounds of loud curses emanating from the kitchen and a smoke filled house.

But all was not lost, as the day before I had received my weekly vegie delivery from home and the fridge was full to overflowing with my father's just-picked lettuces, tomatoes, beans, and the like. So with the help of the takeaway chicken shop next door and the mustardy salad dressing I had already whipped up (and the odd rasher of bacon), I created a terrific warm salad—a concept which I had only read about the day before—but which was, fortunately for all and sundry, a huge hit.

My ever-changing warm salad

A salad which can be thrown together just as easily for ten as it can be for two—with the added advantage that the components can, with ease, be varied to suit your larder, your taste buds or even your budget.

So, let your imagination run wild and adjust the dressing by adding fresh herbs, toasted Middle Eastern spices or maybe a dollop of Indian pickle or chutney. Throw in some roasted capsicums, roasted tomatoes or even some steamed Asian greens. And to top it all off, feature anything from BBQ quail, a mixture of seafood, Cajun blackened fish or, as they do in France, various strange parts of a cow or chicken.

	Preheat BBQ.
1 cup vegetable oil 1 tsp sambal oelek 1 garlic clove, crushed a splash of soy sauce 2 tsp Dijon mustard freshly ground pepper	Whisk together marinade ingredients and set half aside.
chicken, quail, seafood, or whatever takes your fancy	Marinate your chosen meat in half of the marinade for 30 mins.
8 baby potatoes, scrubbed and halved	While meat or seafood is marinating, boil the potatoes until crisp-tender, then drain. Barbecue the meat or seafood and baby potatoes, brushing with marinade as you do so.
4 rindless bacon rashers, halved 2 handfuls salad leaves 2 tomatoes, cored and cut into quarters chopped parsley	Meanwhile, cook the bacon until crisp. Toss together in a large bowl, along with reserved marinade to taste, and sprinkle with parsley.

" If using a bought mayonnaise, add a little Dijon mustard and lemon juice to enliven its flavour. "

A salad of raw vegies with a garlic and herb mayo

a selection of vegies, such as radishes, celery, tomatoes, mushrooms, witloof, carrots, beans, etc.

Wash vegies well (just wipe the mushrooms with a damp cloth) and peel if necessary. Either leave whole or slice, depending on size. Arrange neatly, in separate piles, on a large platter.

1 cup mayonnaise (bought or home-made)
2 tbsp chopped fresh herbs
1 crushed garlic clove

Mix together, place in a bowl and serve alongside the vegies.

The real stuff

It doesn't come much simpler than this. To whiz up home-made mayonnaise in the food processor, simply throw in 1 egg, 1 extra yolk, ½ tbsp mustard and a pinch of salt. Process for a minute, then add 250 ml of any oil, little by little through the feeder tube. When all is added, flavour to taste with lemon juice and seasonings.

Lemon and basil crusted chicken salad

(for 4 as a main course)

Preheat BBQ or ridged grill pan.

¾ cup olive oil
zest of 1 lemon
¾ cup fresh basil leaves
a generous squeeze of lemon juice
1 garlic clove, crushed
freshly ground salt and pepper

Whiz up marinade ingredients.

4 skinless chicken breasts

Pour half the marinade over the chicken breasts and leave for 20–30 mins, turning once or twice. Then barbecue or grill until firm to the touch.

inner leaves from 1 cos lettuce, washed and dried
shavings of parmesan

Divide leaves between 4 plates. Slice chicken breasts lengthways, place on top of the leaves and sprinkle with reserved marinade and some parmesan shavings.

> **I love this as a sandwich filling, too—but watch out for the drips.**

Fidel Castro's favourite Cuban beef salad

(for 4)

Rumour has it that Fidel, on that balcony where he spends so much of his time, has a small barbie where at every opportunity he whips up this salad to keep his energy levels high as he harangues the crowd.

2 x 200 g porterhouse steaks, trimmed well
vegetable oil
freshly ground salt and pepper

Brush steaks all over with oil and season well.

½ cup olive oil
juice of 1 lime
1–2 chillies, finely sliced
dash of Tabasco
2 tbsp chopped basil
2 tbsp chopped parsley

Whisk dressing ingredients.

½ red onion, sliced
1 red capsicum, cored, seeded and finely sliced
4 radishes, washed well and sliced into rounds
4 small spring onions (green onions), cut into 4 cm lengths
1 avocado, diced

Mix vegies in a bowl. Then pan-fry or grill the steaks to the desired degree. Rest steaks in a warm spot for 5 mins, cut into cubes and toss with vegies and dressing to taste.

wedges of lime

Toss everything in a large bowl, along with reserved dressing. Place salad in bowls, sprinkle a little more dressing over the top and serve with lime wedges.

> As the majority of a chilli's heat lies in the seeds, if you want a milder dish simply whip them out. But do be careful as, having once smeared these seeds in my eyes, I can tell you that not only is the experience painful, but it is also embarrassing as you sit at the table with eyes streaming for at least the next few hours.

Thai beef and cranberry salad (for 4 as a main)

I must say that until recently I knew very little about cranberries, except for the fact that the jelly is the perfect accompaniment to the good old Christmas turkey and the juice goes very well with a generous slug of vodka.

But a recent visit to Ocean Spray, the world's largest producer of cranberries, near Boston happily coincided with their harvest, so I got the chance to whip up a few different recipes using both fresh cranberries (delicious, but very tart) and their various bottled preparations as the base. With a certain degree of bias, I would have to say they all worked rather well!

A purée of fresh berries sweetened with a small amount of the jelly proved to be a terrific accompaniment to a fresh shellfish salad, while a sauce of Dubonnet, orange and cranberry juice highlighted some sautéed duck livers perfectly (see page 186). But the star of the show was definitely a Thai-style beef salad where I used cranberry jelly as the sweet component of a reasonably traditional sauce (which worked particularly well because the jelly added not only the essential sweetness, but extra oomph as well).

---

2 x 200 g porterhouse steaks, trimmed of all fat and sinew

Grill or pan-fry to the desired degree and set aside in a warm spot to rest.

1 tbsp cranberry jelly
1 tbsp Asian fish sauce
2 tbsp chopped mint
coriander
1 green chilli, seeded and sliced
juice of 2 limes
1 garlic clove, crushed
4 tbsp peanut oil

At same time, whisk these dressing ingredients together.

peanut or safflower oil
¼ red onion, finely sliced
3 baby bok choy, washed, cleaned and separated into leaves
3 tbsp roasted, unsalted peanuts, chopped

Heat a little oil in a wok or pan, add all the other ingredients and toss until leaves are lightly wilted. Add a little of the dressing and mound salad on 4 plates. Then slice beef, place on top and sprinkle more dressing over the lot.

alfalfa sprouts

Scatter the sprouts over the top.

A salad of pink livers and spinach in a Dubonnet, orange and cranberry dressing

(for 4 as a starter)

olive oil 16–20 chicken or duck livers, cleaned	Heat a little oil in a large pan and seal the livers quickly on both sides over high heat. Drain and set aside. (Do this in two or three lots.)
olive oil 2 tbsp finely chopped onion ¼ cup Dubonnet (a French apéritif) ¼ cup cranberry juice ¼ cup orange juice 1 tbsp chopped parsley 2 tbsp butter 1 handful baby spinach, well washed and dried	Add a little more oil to pan and sauté onion until soft. Add Dubonnet and juices, and boil until reduced by two-thirds. Then add parsley, butter and livers, simmer for a few seconds and toss in a bowl with the raw spinach leaves.
4 thick slices country-style bread freshly ground salt and pepper chopped parsley	Grill or barbecue bread on both sides and place on 4 plates. Check sauce seasoning, mound livers on bread, spoon sauce over and sprinkle with more parsley.

❝ **Most of the world's cranberries are grown around Boston, purely and simply because they need great temperature extremes—in summer lots of hot sun, and in the winter freezing temperatures which ensure that the cranberry bogs will freeze when flooded, allowing the bushes to lie dormant during this period.** ❞

> **I ate his liver with fava beans and a nice chianti.**
>
> Dr Hannibal Lecter, *Silence of the Lambs*

Peppered beef salad with rocket, balsamic and parmesan

(for 4)

2 x 200 g porterhouse steaks, trimmed of all fat and sinew
cracked black pepper

Press steaks on both sides into the pepper. Then grill or pan-fry to the desired degree. Rest in a warm spot for 5 mins, then slice finely and place in a circle on 4 plates, along with any juices.

1 handful rocket leaves, washed and dried
extra virgin olive oil
balsamic vinegar
parmesan shavings
freshly ground salt

Dress rocket with oil, balsamic and seasoning. Place in centre of the beef circles and sprinkle with parmesan.

Barbecued octopus salad with olive oil roasted vegetables (for 8 as an entrée, 4 as a main)

Preheat BBQ and oven to 210°C.

1 sweet potato
2 parsnips
¼ butternut pumpkin
2 carrots
6 baby potatoes
1 corn cob
olive oil
freshly ground salt and pepper

Peel sweet potato, parsnip, pumpkin and carrots, and cut into even pieces. Scrub spuds and cut in half. Remove husk and silk from corn and cut cob into 5 mm slices. Then toss the vegies with oil and seasonings, put in baking dish and roast in hot oven, tossing two or three times.

600 g baby octopus, cleaned
olive oil

When vegies are almost ready, brush octopus with oil and barbecue for about 3–4 mins on the hottest part.

extra virgin olive oil
balsamic vinegar
chopped parsley

Place roasted vegies on 4 plates, top with octopus and sprinkle with oil, vinegar and chopped parsley.

> If you've ever been to the Sydney Fish Market, I'm sure you will have been fascinated (as I was) by the continually churning cement mixers with white foam at their mouths. This is actually how they tenderise the octopus but, if you don't happen to have a clean cement mixer nearby, you can always tenderise the blessed stuff by beating it, in a more traditional manner, on the rocks. But, no matter what, for this recipe, the octopus does need to be treated in one of these ways, because otherwise it will be as tough as old boots.

Spicy fresh salmon tartare in witloof boats

(for 8 as a starter)

400 g fresh salmon, skin and bones removed
freshly ground salt and pepper

Brush fish with oil and season well. Heat oil in pan until almost smoking, then sear salmon quickly on all sides. Set aside to cool.

vegetable oil
1 chilli, finely chopped
1 garlic clove, finely chopped
4 tbsp olive oil
a good splash of soy sauce

Dice the salmon fairly finely and mix with these ingredients.

2 witloof, well washed and leaves separated
chopped parsley

Place a small mound of the salmon mix at the base of each leaf, place attractively on platter and sprinkle with parsley.

" Serve these on your very best platter. "

Silver service with the lot

The Banquet Manager was, to say the least, a little bit up himself. But, to the delight of the staff on one particular night, he came out looking like a real fool. It was a very special party and the client had requested that it be silver service (meaning that the waiters served the food onto the plates at the table).

Our superstar manager decided that, while three staff were needed to serve one side of the table, Mr Efficiency, with the aid of one apprentice to place the plates, could serve the other side by himself.

All went swimmingly, with both sides finishing at almost the same time, but can you imagine the look on his face when the manager looked up to discover that in his haste he had not noticed that the apprentice had not got all the plates down and half the diners on his side of the table had their meat and three veg arranged oh-so-perfectly on the white tablecloth itself.

A ripper warm salmon salad with anchovy mayo (for 4)

Preheat BBQ or grill.

400 g fresh salmon in one piece, skin and bones removed
olive oil
freshly ground salt and pepper

Sprinkle salmon on both sides with the oil and seasonings.

½–¾ cup mayonnaise (see page 182)
3–4 anchovies
splash of hot water

Whiz up and set aside.

4 eggs
6 ripe red tomatoes, cored and cut in wedges
16 or so black olives, pitted
a handful of rocket leaves

Hard-boil, peel and quarter the eggs. Put in a bowl with the other ingredients.

6 baby potatoes, scrubbed and halved
16 green beans, topped and tailed

Boil the spuds in salted water until tender. Add beans towards the end, for 3–4 mins. Drain vegies and add to bowl.

olive oil
chopped parsley

At the same time, barbecue or grill the salmon for 3–4 mins on each side. Then remove and, when cool enough to handle, flake and toss carefully with the vegies along with a little oil. Place in a large bowl and sprinkle with the mayonnaise and chopped parsley.

> **Before you start, check that the salmon pin bones have been removed: run your fingers, against the grain, along the top of the fillet and, if need be, remove the bones with tweezers or small pliers.**
>
> **And to successfully hard-boil an egg, start in cold water, boil for 6–7 minutes and instantly run under cold water.**

A calamari salad with eastern flavours

(for 4–6 as a starter)

5 tbsp plain flour 1 tsp ground cayenne 1 tsp freshly ground black pepper 1 tsp salt 1 tsp onion powder 1 tsp garlic powder	Mix together.
6 tbsp vegetable oil juice of 1–2 limes a splash of Asian fish sauce 1–2 chillies, seeded and finely sliced	Whisk dressing and set aside.
10 snowpeas, finely sliced ½ red capsicum, cored, seeded and finely sliced ¼ red onion, finely sliced ¼ cup bean shoots, washed 1 handful baby salad leaves ½ avocado, peeled and cubed	Combine vegies in a large bowl.
5 cups vegetable oil or shortening 2–3 calamari tubes, cleaned (see page 93)	Heat oil to 180°C in a deep-sided pot or wok. (To check if the temperature is right, drop in a cube of bread: when it sizzles gently and turns golden in about a minute, the oil is ready.) Cut calamari into rings and toss in flour mix. Fry in two or three lots, drain well and add to vegies in bowl. Dress salad to taste and mound on plates, drizzling a little extra sauce over and around.

❝ **This also works well with prawns which can be either sautéed or, if you prefer, gently poached in a courtbouillon of water, white wine, a few whole star anise, a couple of bay leaves and 3 or 4 sprigs of parsley.** ❞

Oils ain't oils

Research has recently discovered that those inhabitants of the Mediterranean who survive purely on an olive-oil based diet have far fewer heart problems and almost invariably live to a ripe old age. But before we grasp such a diet as the cure-all of the twenty-first century (and begin quaffing litres of the blessed stuff), I must point out that what wasn't highlighted in these studies was the fact that they were conducted in rural areas where there was little or no chemical enhancement of crops, canned and packet foods were almost unheard of and there wasn't an American fast-food chain in sight.

As well, the oil these peasants live on was not just any old oil and was, almost without exception, from the first or second pressing, which is achieved using only natural means and, because of that, has a low percentage of acidity as well as a large quantity of anti-oxidants—both of which are essential components in the fight against heart disease—properties often missing in the more common, less expensive products.

So, while not wishing to put a damper on the theory that simply substituting olive oil for butter and cream will result in a far healthier life, I must point out that the better (and sadly, the more expensive) the oil, the better it will be for you.

Carpaccio of mushrooms with rocket, parmesan and virgin olive oil

(for 4 as a starter, 8 as a side dish)

I first sampled a dish like this in a trattoria in Rome, where the waiters created it at the table, somehow making it seem very complicated (which it is not) through exaggerated flourishes with the oil bottle and parmesan shaver. But even without the theatrical approach it tastes damned good and is simple to boot.

18 very firm, white button mushrooms
extra virgin olive oil
freshly ground salt and pepper
1 handful rocket leaves, well washed and dried
shavings of parmesan
chopped parsley

Wipe mushrooms with a damp cloth, slice finely and arrange flat on 4 plates. Sprinkle with oil and seasonings, and then top with the rocket leaves. Once again, sprinkle with oil and seasonings, then top with parmesan shavings and chopped parsley.

The buying of the parmesan

Where possible, buy parmesan in the piece. It is ten times better than the pre-grated muck which has almost invariably lost its zing. But, as it is expensive, look after it by wrapping it in oiled cheesecloth before placing it in the fridge. And, when required, use a potato peeler or cheese shaver to make fine slices (or just freshly grate it). Also, by the way, cheese and household refrigeration is not the happiest mix: the best spot, surprisingly, is your fridge's vegetable drawer.

Pasta insalata (pasta with salad) (for 4)

This is an unusual recipe based on a dish I enjoyed in Positano. I like it because of its fresh, light flavours and the fact that you can easily vary the salad ingredients, depending on the season, without compromising the taste.

½ **celery stalk, sliced**
¼ **red onion, sliced finely**
3 ripe red tomatoes, cored and diced
1 garlic clove, crushed
2 tbsp chopped parsley
2 tbsp chopped basil
freshly ground salt and pepper
¼ **cup olive oil**

Combine vegies with garlic and herbs. Season well and then mix in the oil.

400 g spaghetti
freshly grated parmesan

Cook pasta to al dente (which means firm to the bite), drain well and toss with the salad. Place in bowls and sprinkle with parmesan.

Real simple pasta

When cooking pasta, you can follow the directions on the packet or box and, if cooking beforehand, drain the pasta well and toss in a little oil to keep strands separate. But, for an even simpler method, put the pasta in a large pot of boiling salted water, along with a little oil, for exactly 2 minutes. Then give it a good stir, turn the heat off, cover it and leave for exactly 4 minutes. Drain well and use. (These timings are for spaghetti—other varieties will take a little more.)

Iain's salad in the style of Caesar

(for 4 as a starter)

It appears almost certain that today's most popular restaurant dish goes something along the lines of 'our very own Caesar Salad.' And, with those few rather insignificant words every chef or restaurateur is immediately given carte blanche to create absolute mayhem within the poor old salad bowl. But, for the edification of these culinary cowboys, I would like to point out that Caesar Cardini's original little number (created in Tijuana in 1924) was a rather simple affair which contained neither avocado, bean shoots nor even bacon or anchovies. Although, I must come clean and admit that my version doesn't quite come out smelling of roses either, because I also can't resist the temptation to muck around with this classic.

3 slices day-old bread
olive oil
1 garlic clove, crushed

Trim crusts and cut bread into 5-mm cubes. Heat oil and garlic in a pan and fry bread cubes until golden on all sides. Drain well, on kitchen paper towels.

8 thin slices pancetta (or 4 slices lean bacon)

Pour most of the oil from the pan and then cook the pancetta or bacon until crisp. Drain well and crumble.

1 cup mayonnaise (see page 182)
1 tsp Dijon mustard
3 anchovies, chopped finely
hot water

Mix mayonnaise with mustard and anchovies and then add enough water to give a dressing consistency.

inner leaves of 2 cos lettuces, washed and dried
shavings of parmesan
snipped chives

Place leaves in one large or 4 smaller bowls. Toss gently with the croutons, pancetta and dressing. Then sprinkle with parmesan and chives.

My very own Caesar pasta (for 4)

Just to show I too am a bit of a culinary cowboy.

olive oil
2 rashers bacon, sliced
2 garlic cloves, crushed

400 g cooked fettuccini
4 leaves cos lettuce, finely sliced
freshly ground salt and pepper
4 egg yolks
freshly grated parmesan

Heat a little oil in a large pot, add bacon and garlic and cook until bacon is crisp.

Add pasta to pot and toss until it is hot adding more oil if necessary. Then mix in the lettuce until just wilted. Season pasta mix well and place in 4 bowls. Top each with an egg yolk and sprinkle with plenty of parmesan.

> **Before eating the pasta, mix the egg yolk in—the heat of the pasta will lightly cook it and form a delicate light sauce.**

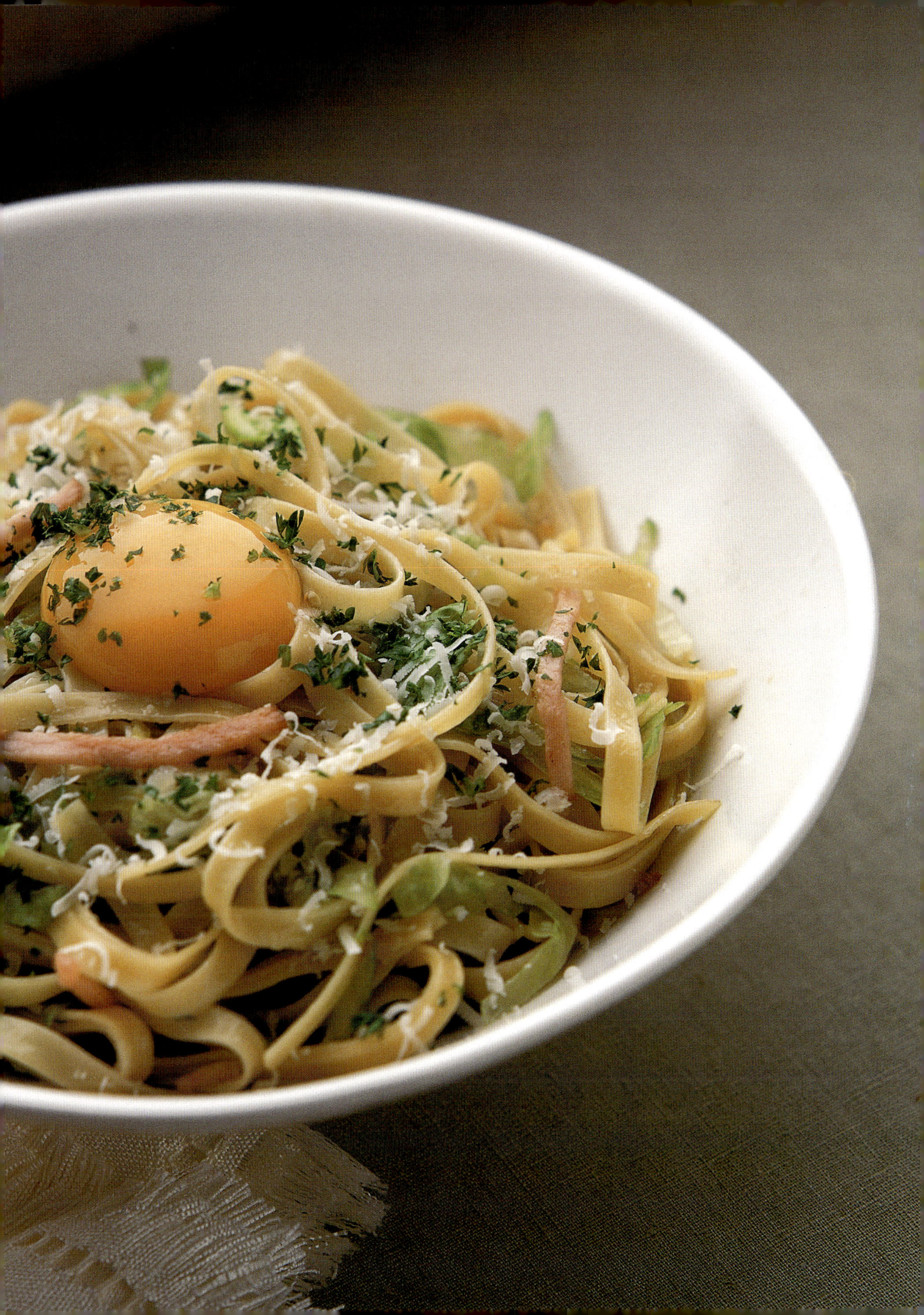

The simplest of tomato salads

(for 6–8 as an accompaniment)

6–8 ripe red tomatoes
1 red onion, finely sliced
12 basil leaves, finely sliced

freshly ground salt and pepper
extra virgin olive oil
balsamic or red-wine vinegar

Core tomatoes and slice thickly. Then place in one layer on a large platter. Scatter onion and basil over the top.

Season salad well, sprinkle generously with oil and add a small amount of vinegar to taste.

Roasted capsicum, anchovy and soft-dried tomato salad

(for 4–6 as an accompaniment)

4 roasted capsicums, peeled and sliced (see page 245)
6 anchovies, chopped
12 soft-dried tomatoes in oil, sliced
freshly ground pepper

basil leaves

Layer capsicums, anchovies and tomatoes in a dish, seasoning each layer with pepper. Mix some of the tomato oil with a little oil from the anchovies, to taste, and sprinkle generously over the top. Refrigerate overnight.

Tear basil and sprinkle over the salad. Serve with plenty of crusty bread, to mop up the juices.

Soft-drying tomatoes at home

You can easily soft-dry your own tomatoes. It takes a bit of time, but once you have bunged them in the oven, they almost look after themselves. Just cut roma tomatoes in half lengthways, season with freshly ground salt and pepper, and put them on a mesh rack over a tray in a 100°C oven (with the door ajar) until they are dry yet still soft. (You will have to experiment with the timing, as ovens do vary, but they will take at least 6–8 hours.) Remove, allow to cool, put in jar, cover with olive oil and refrigerate. They will keep for at least a month and any leftover oil can be used either with bread or in a salad dressing.

In search of a 'real' tomato

The first recipe book I ever read was Elizabeth David's wonderful ode to French provincial cooking. And, to a young Iain whose culinary highlights had, up until then, revolved around me Mum's lamb roast and the mixed grill at the local greasy spoon, it was quite a revelation.

But I couldn't for the life of me understand all the fuss she made about a visit to a small country bistro where the proprietor simply served a bowl of freshly picked tomatoes (with stalks intact) which tasted of the sun. The reason I couldn't comprehend her excitement was purely and simply because living with a father who was a wonderful gardener I had this rather quaint notion that all tomatoes were like that. And it wasn't until I left home that I discovered no, not all tomatoes were picked straight from the garden and served seconds later, perfectly ripe and ready to eat. In fact, most were pale, insipid and tasted of nothing in particular.

Thankfully, this to a certain extent has changed. We can now buy, admittedly for only a couple of months of the year, tomatoes which are not half bad. Sure, they may not as yet be quite in Ms David's class, but when slapped between some country bread with a generous grinding of salt and pepper, or simply thrown on a plate with a sprinkling of olive oil and a few drops of balsamic, they are certainly an improvement on the past.

Green beans with soft-dried tomatoes and crispy prosciutto

(for 4 as an accompaniment)

24–30 small green beans, topped and tailed

a little olive oil
8–12 thin slices of prosciutto (or 4 slices of bacon)

12 soft-dried tomatoes in oil
freshly ground salt and pepper

Blanch beans in a large pot of boiling salted water until crisp-tender. Remove, and dunk in a bowl of iced water. Drain well.

Heat a little olive oil in a pan and fry the prosciutto or bacon until crispy. Drain on paper towels, and crumble when cold.

Remove tomatoes from oil and slice. Place beans neatly down the centre of a large platter. Top with tomatoes and prosciutto, season and sprinkle with oil from the tomatoes.

Tea-smoked tomatoes (for 4–6 as an accompaniment)

One particularly stupid friend followed my instructions for this to the T, except for the fact that he used tea-bags. I must tell you, it wasn't the greatest success and in fact, he almost burnt down the kitchen. Needless to say, he has since been barred from the kitchen unless accompanied by his six-year-old daughter, who can actually read and follow recipes.

120 g rice **120 g brown sugar** **60 g Lapsang Souchong tea leaves**	Mix well.
2 punnets large cherry tomatoes	Core, blanch and peel the tomatoes (see page 95).
½ cup rosemary sprigs	Line a large wok with two layers of foil. Put in 1 cup of the rice mix plus the rosemary. Put a round cake rack on top and place the tomatoes on this. Cover with foil, sealing the edges, and cook over a high heat for 5 mins. Remove from heat and leave to stand for 5 mins.
olive oil **rosemary sprigs**	Toss the tomatoes with oil and the rosemary sprigs, and put in a large bowl.

Further thoughts on tomato salads

- Tomatoes and fresh basil pesto (see page 115) have a natural affinity. Serve on grilled country bread, or add some chunks of Aussie goat cheese, a few olives and some baby cress for a great starter or light lunch.
- Place whole, cored tomatoes and wedges of red onion in an oven tray. Sprinkle generously with olive oil and seasonings and roast slowly (150°C) until blistered and lightly charred. Dress with the oil from the tray along with a few drops of vinegar and sprinkle with sliced spring onion (green onion).
- Replace the onion, in the simple tomato salad (see page 200) with slices of bocconcini for a true Italian classic.
- For a great tomato vinaigrette, blend some soft-dried tomatoes along with a little of their oil, a spoon of Dijon mustard and seasonings. Then sprinkle this over salad leaves, an avocado or two, or even thick slices of fresh tomato.
- Make a mixed tomato salad by using different varieties and colours. Slice or cut tomatoes into wedges and sprinkle with freshly ground salt and pepper, and a little sugar. Leave for 2 hours and then dress with olive oil and a splash of wine vinegar.
- Any of the aforementioned salads will work well between slices of bread. But my favourite involves garlic-rubbed bread, tomatoes, rocket and slivers of parmesan, along with a generous quantity of olive oil and seasonings.

A dangerous love affair

When first introduced into Europe from Peru, the tomato or 'love apple', as it was then known, was regarded with great suspicion. Of course, this could have had something to do with its close relationship to the deadly nightshade, but it was regarded more as a decorative plant than as something you ate. And if you were crazy enough to imbibe, it was advised that you cooked them for at least three hours, adding vinegar and spices to ward off any poisonous side effects (obviously, our earliest relishes and chutneys).

A mozzarella salad with gazpacho overtones

(for 6–8 as an accompaniment)

This is a salad that deserves the finest ingredients you can get your hands on. And the buffalo-milk mozzarella from Lake Purrumbete in Victoria is just such an ingredient. It is made from the milk of buffalo which were flown in from Europe especially for this purpose (in their own specially chartered 747, would you believe): you should be able to find it in gourmet delis or cheese shops.

---

8 buffalo-milk bocconcini
1 red capsicum, cored, seeded and diced
a 6-cm piece telegraph (continental) cucumber, diced
1 green capsicum, cored, seeded and diced
6 green olives, pitted and halved
6 black olives, pitted and halved
¼ red onion, diced
3 large ripe tomatoes, cored, seeded and diced (see page 95)

Cut the bocconcini into 4. Toss with the vegies.

virgin olive oil
balsamic vinegar
freshly ground salt and pepper
6 basil leaves, finely sliced
flat-leaf parsley sprigs

Toss the salad with oil, seasonings and vinegar to taste. Then gently fold in the herbs.

A trio of salads (for 4–8)

This trio of refreshing, tangy salads is definitely one of my favourite starters for any posh dinner party (but would work equally well for an al fresco lunch). You can place them attractively on individual plates, or even on your very best platter in the centre of the table allowing your guests to help themselves. Which is not a bad idea, because I always find that any dinner party perks up the minute the first guest drops a bit of food while attempting to serve themselves (but, then again, maybe I've just got a strange sense of humour).

Olive oil braised artichoke salad

8 globe artichokes	Cut artichoke stems to within 2 cm of the bulb and peel them down to their soft centre. Remove tough outermost leaves from the bulb and cut off top.
1 lemon, halved **olive oil**	Remove hairy inner chokes with a spoon and rub lemon all over the cut sides of the artichokes. Then place in a large pot, cover with olive oil, weight down with a plate and cook slowly until the bases of the outer leaves are soft when pierced with a small knife. Remove from heat and allow to cool in the oil.
chopped parsley	Drain artichokes and serve sprinkled with parsley and, if need be, a little of the cooking oil.

> **The oil used to cook the artichokes is wonderful in salad dressings or for cooking.**

Middle eastern chickpea, date and carrot salad

4 medium carrots, peeled	Cut on the bias, blanch briefly in lightly salted water and plunge into iced water. When cool, drain well.
1 cup cooked chickpeas (see page 39) 3 dates, pitted and sliced into slivers	Toss these in a bowl with the carrots.
2 tsp ground paprika 1½ tsp ground cinnamon ½ tsp ground cayenne 2 tsp ground cumin ½ cup lemon juice 2 tbsp liquid honey ½ cup olive oil	Whisk ingredients together and dress the vegies to taste.

Minted zucchini salad

6 zucchini, washed and dried	Cut on the diagonal into 2 mm slices.
olive oil 3 garlic cloves	Slice garlic finely. Heat a little oil in a pan, add garlic and zucchini, and cook until lightly browned.
olive oil 10 fresh mint leaves freshly ground salt and pepper mint vinegar (available from delis or some supermarkets)	Drain vegies and put in a bowl along with fresh oil, seasonings, finely sliced mint and vinegar to taste.

And while we're on the subject of salads—a dressing or two

- A terrific mustardy all-round dressing can be easily made by whisking up 2 tbsp Dijon mustard with 1 crushed garlic clove until mixture thickens slightly. Then add 300 ml of any vegetable oil and, to follow, 50 ml white vinegar—both little by little as you would when making a mayonnaise. To finish, season with freshly ground salt and pepper.
- Add to the above mustard dressing other flavourings such as roasted and peeled capsicums (see page 245), soft-dried tomatoes (see page 201), blanched spring onions (green onions), a handful of fresh herbs or even some cubes of blue cheese. Then whiz up the lot in a blender or food processor.
- A terrific idea from English super-chef Alastair Little: for any barbecued seafood salad, mix a little taramasalata with some olive oil, a squeeze of lemon and chopped parsley.
- A delightful, delicate dressing when the tomatoes are juicy and ripe. Peel, seed and dice the tomatoes and then mix them with olive oil, shredded basil and seasonings. And this is not only great on almost any salad (with some freshly grated parmesan), but on freshly cooked pasta as well.
- And what about this one for the true anchovy lover. Cook some anchovies very slowly in olive oil until they almost melt and then add lemon juice, more oil if necessary and some freshly ground pepper. Perfect with robust vegies such as green beans, broccoli, cauliflower and carrots.
- Or you can even whip up an Indian-flavoured salad dressing by combining any Indian chutney or pickle with plain yoghurt, a squeeze of lemon and some freshly chopped coriander leaves.

An Indian sojourn

WHEN I VISITED INDIA with 'A Cook's Journey', I must admit I was surprised by the sheer diversity of the food. Because in my ignorance I had expected to dine on little apart from hot curries and tandoori chicken, with the odd bit of naan thrown in. Instead I found myself sampling the most amazing variety of food which seemed to vary greatly not only from region to region but almost from town to town.

Actually I shouldn't really have been surprised because, as my research quickly showed, the reason for such diversity is the diversity of the nation itself. Almost 80 per cent of the population are Hindu, many of them strictly vegetarian, and India is the world's second-largest Muslim country. So, taking into account the dietary restrictions imposed by these faiths, and the past Mughal, Arabic, Persian, Portuguese and even English influences, it is no wonder the food is so varied.

- Cochin prawns in a spiced coconut sauce
- Snapper steamed in banana leaves
- A stack of northern Indian vegetable cutlets
- Potato and green pea pastries in the style of samosas
- Curried root vegetable soup with a purée of roasted capsicum
- A lamb, sweet potato and coconut curry
- Mint and cucumber raita
- Meena Pathak's chicken korma
- Lamb koftas in rogan josh sauce
- Chicken with dates and a lemon yoghurt
- Tandoori swordfish
- Madhur Jaffrey's perfect rice pilaf
- An Indian cucumber, tomato and onion salad with mint yoghurt
- Sudhakaran Meetinay's dahl makhani

Cochin prawns in a spiced coconut sauce (for 4)

Cochin, a very pretty seaside city in the south, was until recently the largest prawn fishing port in the world. It is also home to the St Francis Church where Vasco de Gama was once buried (his remains have since been moved to Portugal) and the amazing Chinese fishing nets which work, to this day, with a series of different-sized rocks as weights and which were erected centuries ago by traders from the Chinese court.

16–20 large green prawns **½ tsp ground turmeric** **½ tsp ground cayenne** **freshly ground salt**	Peel and devein the prawns, but leave the tails on. Mix spices together and massage into the prawns.
ghee	Whack a little ghee in a wok or large pan and seal prawns on both sides. Remove and set aside. Wipe out pan.
a 5 mm piece of fresh ginger, chopped **1 garlic clove, crushed** **2 chillies, sliced** **1 medium onion, chopped**	Throw a little more ghee into pan, heat and then sauté these ingredients until golden.
4 cardamom pods, lightly crushed **½ tsp garam masala** **½ tsp ground turmeric** **2 cloves** **a pinch of ground cumin**	Add spices to pan, and cook, stirring continually, for 30 secs or so.
330 ml can of coconut cream **¼ cup water** **4 canned tomatoes, drained and chopped** **1 tbsp Dijon mustard**	Add half of the coconut cream with the other ingredients. Then simmer until of a sauce-like consistency, adding rest of the coconut cream, little by little.
freshly ground salt **lemon juice**	Add these to taste, return prawns to pan and simmer gently until just cooked. Serve with a simple salad or even some steamed spinach.

Snapper steamed in banana leaves (for 4)

2 tbsp lemongrass, very finely chopped 2 garlic cloves, chopped a 1 cm piece fresh ginger, chopped 1 cup coconut cream 2 cups desiccated coconut 2 tsp ground turmeric 1 tbsp Indian lime pickle 1 cup mint leaves 2 chillies, chopped juice of 1 lime	Whiz to a paste in a processor or blender.
4 x 180 g boneless snapper steaks 4 large squares of banana leaf freshly ground salt and pepper lemon juice	Lay each piece of fish on a banana leaf and sprinkle with seasonings and lemon juice. Spread prepared spice paste on top, fold banana leaf around and under, and put in freezer for 10–15 mins.
mint yoghurt (see page 228) 4 extra squares banana leaf	Put fish parcels on a plate in a steamer and steam until cooked (about 8–10 mins). Unwrap, place each fish steak on fresh banana leaf and sprinkle with yoghurt.

> ❝ I also whipped this up in Cochin using a fish which the chef told me was very similar to our slapper. I presumed he meant snapper, but didn't have the heart to tell him because he was so proud of both his English and his knowledge of our ingredients and produce. ❞

A stack of northern Indian vegetable cutlets (for 4)

This is one of those Anglo-Indian recipes created by Indian cooks during the days of the Raj, in an attempt to satisfy the British craving for familiar dishes. Originally formed into the shape of a meat cutlet, these days the patties are more commonly round and are served either as an entrée as part of a banquet or as a vegetarian main course.

---

2 large potatoes, chopped

Cook spuds in plenty of salted water until almost cooked.

1 medium-sized carrot, chopped
1 medium-sized onion, chopped
kernels from 1 corn cob
½ cup thawed frozen peas

Add vegies to potatoes and cook until soft. Then drain well, return to pot and place over low heat to dry out. Mash coarsely.

1 chilli, seeds removed and very finely sliced
a good pinch ground coriander
1 tsp garam masala
freshly ground salt and pepper
2 tbsp chopped coriander
2 tbsp yoghurt, drained in a sieve for 15 mins

Mix these into the mash and form into 8 patties, adding a little flour if sloppy.

flour
vegetable oil

Flour patties lightly and shallow-fry in hot oil until golden on both sides. Drain well on paper towels.

½ telegraph (continental) cucumber, sliced
3 ripe red tomatoes, cored and sliced
onion relish (see page 228)
raita (see page 220)
2 tbsp chopped coriander leaves

Make stacks by placing a vegetable patty on each plate and topping with cucumber and tomato slices, then another patty and finally the onion relish. Sprinkle with raita and chopped coriander.

Potato and green pea pastries in the style of samosas

2 large potatoes

ghee
1 small onion, finely chopped
½ tsp finely chopped fresh ginger
1 garlic clove, crushed

½ chilli, sliced
a good pinch each of ground turmeric, cumin and coriander
freshly ground salt and pepper
½ cup thawed frozen peas
3 tbsp chopped coriander
lemon juice

6 or so sheets frozen puff pastry
1 egg, mixed with a little milk

Peel spuds, boil until tender and then grate.

Heat a little ghee in a wok or pot, and sauté these ingredients until soft.

Add chilli, spices and seasoning to wok and cook for a few seconds. Then add grated potatoes with the peas and coriander and lemon juice to taste. Mix in well and allow to cool.

Separate pastry sheets and cut into small rounds with a pastry cutter. Brush pastry with eggwash. Place a little potato mix in centre of pastry, fold pastry over and crimp edges.

Preheat oven to 220°C.

When ready to serve, brush pastries with more eggwash and bake until golden.

Curried root vegetable soup with a purée of roasted capsicum (for 4–6)

1 tbsp each of coriander, mustard and cumin seeds
1 tbsp ground turmeric
½ tsp fenugreek seeds
2 fresh chillies, chopped
a 2 cm piece cinnamon stick
½ tsp black peppercorns
a pinch of ground ginger

Whiz spices up in a processor to a fine powder.

2 roasted and peeled capsicums (see page 245)
olive oil
freshly ground salt and pepper

Purée the capsicums with a little oil and seasonings. Set aside.

vegetable oil
1 large swede, peeled and chopped
2 large onions, peeled and chopped
1 large sweet potato, peeled and chopped
2 large parsnips, peeled and chopped
vegetable stock (see page 237)

Heat a little oil in a large, heavy-bottomed pot. Add 2 tbsp of the spice mix (keep the rest in a tightly covered container for later use). Sauté for 1 min, then add vegies with stock to cover. Bring to boil and simmer until tender.

unsalted butter
cream
freshly ground salt

Add a good dollop of butter and a splash of cream to the cooked vegies, and blend. Check for salt and serve in bowls with a dollop of the capsicum purée on top.

The developing palate (part 2)

My first experience of fairly authentic Indian food was when I went to London in the early seventies. (A city which to this day, because of its former strong ties with the sub-continent, still serves pretty decent Indian food.)

I must admit I was at first rather unwilling to dine at our local cheapie 'The Curry Inn' although, to be honest, I could afford little else. My reluctance was, in the main, caused by my mother's so-called curries, which had always been a treat to be avoided at all costs. Normally made up of leftovers, they were invariably bright yellow and spiked with such exotica as two fruits, desiccated coconut and, on very special occasions, Auntie Zelda's rather unusual rhubarb pickles which were optimistically deemed to be Indian. Still, after a couple of close encounters of the poisoning kind at my local London pub, I was finally tempted to enter The Curry Inn's doors, where my eyes opened to a whole new culinary experience. Not only was there not a bowl of bright-yellow muck in sight, but the food was delicious and ranged from the very hot–sour flavours of vindaloo to the almost sweetish rogan josh to the wonderful smokey aromas of food emanating from the tandoori oven right there in the middle of the dining room. Needless to say, I was quickly hooked.

A lamb, sweet potato and coconut curry

(for 4–6)

vegetable oil or ghee
1 kilo well trimmed lamb, cut into 1.5 cm cubes

Heat a little oil in a large heavy-bottomed pot and brown the meat in 3 or 4 lots, adding more oil as necessary.

1 large onion, sliced
a 5 mm piece ginger, chopped
2 garlic cloves, chopped

Add a little more oil to the pot and sauté onion, ginger and garlic until soft.

2 tbsp of Indian curry paste
6 canned tomatoes, drained and chopped
½ cinnamon stick
6 cardamom pods, lightly crushed
1 bay leaf
2 cups coconut cream
1 cup water

Add curry paste to pot, mix in well and cook, stirring, for 1 min. Add remaining ingredients, mix in and bring to the boil. Return lamb to pot and simmer, very gently, for half an hour.

2 sweet potatoes, peeled and cut into 1.5 cm cubes

Add sweet spuds to curry and simmer until lamb is tender (about another 45 mins), adding more water if necessary.

rice pilaf (see page 226)
raita (see next page)

Serve with pilaf and, if you like, raita on the side.

> **Adding a spoon of Indian curry paste to almost any stew or braise will add that extra bit of oomph that is so often missing. But it will certainly not turn it into a curry or even, in fact, add any great degree of spice.**

Mint and cucumber raita

2 cups plain yoghurt
¼ telegraph (continental) cucumber, grated and then drained for 10 mins in a sieve
1 heaped tbsp chopped mint
2 tomatoes, peeled, seeded and diced (see page 95)
generous pinch of ground cayenne
freshly ground salt and pepper

Mix everything together.

Meena Pathak's chicken korma (for 4)

Meena, who I cooked with a number of times on 'Healthy, Wealthy & Wise', was our guide in India, where her advice was invaluable. She is, of course, better known as the genius behind the Patak's range of Indian ingredients and just happens to be a bloody good cook as well.

4 tbsp ghee **1 onion, finely chopped** **4 skinless, boned chicken thighs, cubed**	Heat ghee in a wok or heavy-bottomed pan and brown onion. Add chicken and toss until it changes colour.
2 tbsp chopped coriander **2 heaped tbsp Patak's korma paste**	Add these to wok and cook, stirring, for 2 mins.
¼ cup water **2 tbsp plain yoghurt** **1 tbsp slivered almonds**	Add water and simmer gently for 15 mins. Add yoghurt and almonds, and mix in well.
rice pilaf (see page 226) **extra slivered almonds** **chopped coriander**	Serve korma on the pilaf, with a sprinkling of almonds and coriander.

Lamb koftas in rogan josh sauce (for 4–6)

500 g lean minced lamb
a 2 cm piece of fresh ginger, peeled and grated
2 garlic cloves, crushed
2 tbsp rogan josh curry paste
2 tbsp plain yoghurt

Mix meat well with flavourings, then wet hands and shape into balls approx. 3 cm in diameter.

ghee

Heat a little ghee in a large pan, add koftas in three or four lots and brown on all sides, adding more ghee as necessary. Remove koftas as they cook and set aside.

1 medium-sized onion, finely chopped
½ cinnamon stick
6 cardamom pods, lightly crushed
1 bay leaf
3 cloves
extra 2 tbsp rogan josh curry paste
at least 1 cup coconut cream
½ cup water
6 canned tomatoes, drained and chopped

Wipe out pan, heat a little more ghee and sauté onion until soft and lightly browned. Add remaining ingredients and mix in well. Bring to the boil, add koftas and simmer gently for 15–20 mins, adding more coconut cream if necessary.

plain yoghurt

Serve koftas sprinkled with extra yoghurt.

> **Now I know this has absolutely nothing to do with Indian food but, in extolling the virtues of garlic in anything that moves, an Indian informed me that in Ancient Egypt garlic was so prized that 15 lbs would buy a male slave—so there.**

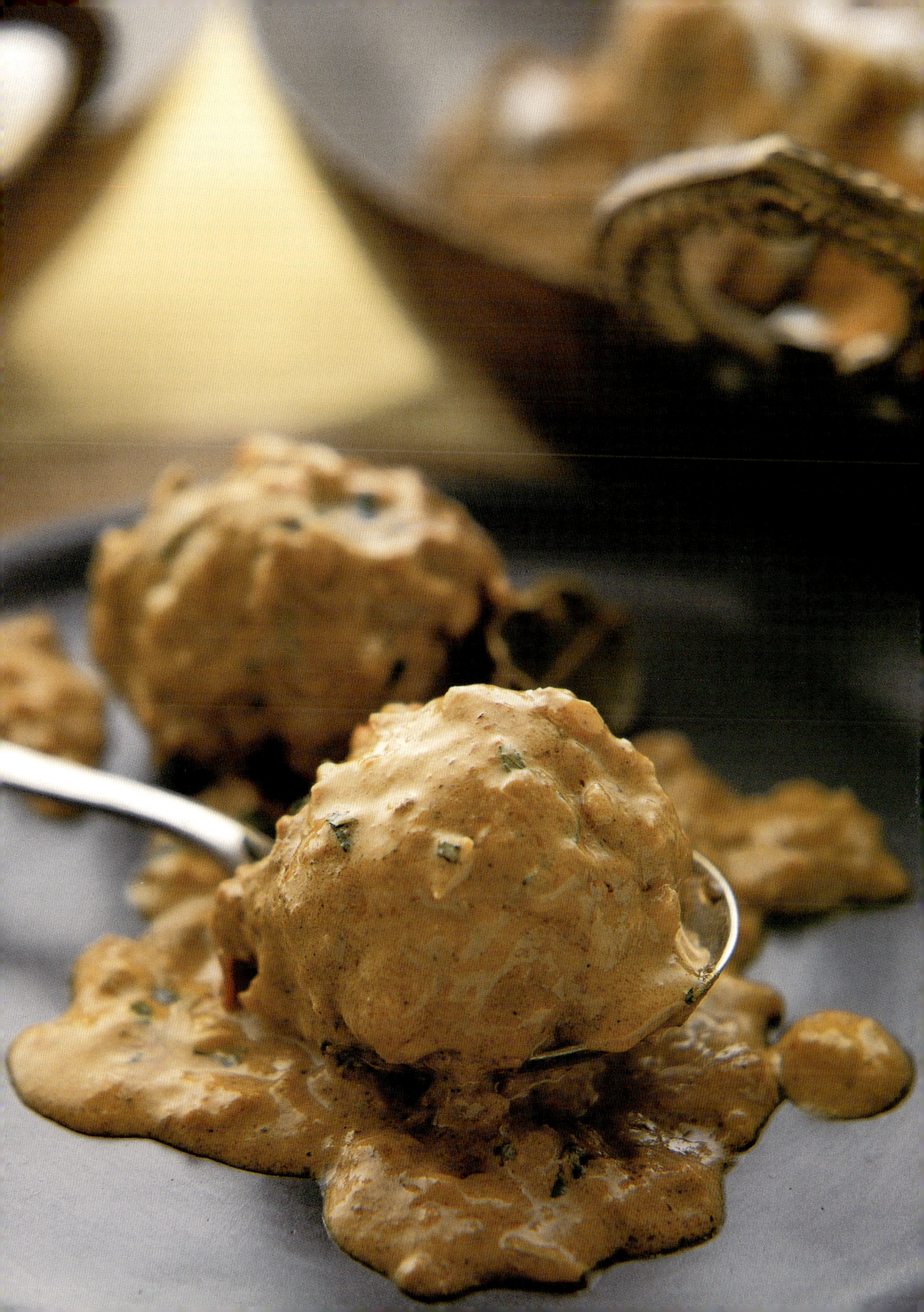

Chicken with dates and a lemon yoghurt (for 4)

¼ cup vegetable oil
8–12 boneless chicken thighs, skin on

Heat oil in a large pan and fry the chicken in two or three lots until skin is crisp. Remove chicken and most of the oil.

2 chillies, sliced
1 large onion, chopped
a 2 cm piece of fresh ginger, chopped

Add these to the pan and fry until onions are golden.

1 tsp ground turmeric
1 tsp ground coriander powder
½ tsp ground cayenne
½ tsp ground cumin

Add spices to pan and cook, stirring, for 2 mins.

1 cup chicken stock (packet is fine)
juice of 2 lemons

Add liquids and mix well. Put chicken back into pan and simmer, very gently, for 15 mins.

12 dates

Now add dates to pan and continue to simmer for another 5 mins or so, until chicken is cooked.

¼ cup yoghurt
3 tbsp chopped coriander
freshly ground salt
lemon juice
rice pilaf (see page 226)

Finally add yoghurt and coriander, mix in well and season to taste with salt and, if necessary, a little more lemon juice. Bring to a simmer and serve with rice pilaf.

Tandoori swordfish (for 4)

½ cup yoghurt
2 tbsp lemon juice
2 garlic cloves, chopped
a 1 cm piece of fresh ginger, chopped
1 chilli, sliced
1 tsp garam masala
1 tsp ground turmeric
1 tsp ground coriander
1 tsp tandoori paste
freshly ground salt

Whiz everything up in a processor or blender.

4 x 180 g swordfish steaks

Pour most of the above mixture over the swordfish and leave for 30–45 mins.

vegetable oil
rice pilaf (see page 226)

Heat a large non-stick pan and cook swordfish over medium heat, adding a little oil if necessary. Serve on rice with a little of the marinade sprinkled over the top.

Madhur Jaffrey's perfect rice pilaf

Until I tried this recipe, I must admit that, on many occasions, I cooked rice badly. Once in a while, I hit the jackpot and came up with tender, perfumed grains with each almost completely separate. But, just as regularly, my rice was gluggy, waterlogged and closer to rice pudding (but without the charm) than it was to pilaf. Fortunately, I then tried this recipe from talented Indian superstar Madhur Jaffrey and I have not had a failure since.

basmati rice to the 450 ml level in measuring jug	Pick over rice and put in a bowl. Wash under running water until water runs clear, then drain. Cover with 1.25 litres of water and leave for 30 mins. Then drain in a sieve or colander and leave for 20 mins.
3 tbsp vegetable oil **50 g finely chopped onion** **½ chilli, finely sliced** **½ tsp finely chopped garlic** **½ tsp garam masala** **1 tsp salt**	Heat oil in a heavy-bottomed pot and gently sauté onion until soft. Add rice and rest of ingredients and cook, gently stirring, for 3–4 mins until grains are well covered with oil.
600 ml chicken stock (packet is fine)	Add stock to pot and bring to boil. Cover with foil and a tight-fitting lid, turn heat down to very, very low and cook for 15 mins.

❝ **And, do me a favour—while the rice is cooking, DON'T PEEK!** ❞

Food at the movies

We all, I'm sure, have our favourite food scenes from the movies. Being a romantic sort of fellow, to me the fruit-eating scene from *Tom Jones* certainly stands out. And I do remember being the only member of the audience who saw the humour in the situation as Robert Morley (that sensibly proportioned gentleman) dispatched a number of chefs in *Who's Killing the Great Chefs of Europe* in the manner of their specialities, e.g. one was pressed in the same way as the famed pressed duck of La Tour d'Argent. There was also that great tantrum by Jack Nicholson when he was refused toast in *Five Easy Pieces*: 'All right, if you won't give me toast, just give me a chicken salad sandwich. Hold the chicken, hold the salad and then can I just have my f...ing toast'—or words to that effect.

But my favourite of all time would have to be from that terrific Aussie movie *Sunday Too Far Away*, when Jack Thompson told of the wonderful meatballs made by a particular one-armed shearer's cook. After unsuccessfully trying to persuade him to divulge his secret, a rival spied on the cook only to discover that the extra flavour came about because of his disability, which forced him to form the meatballs with his one good hand and then roll them—where else, but under his armpit.

An Indian cucumber, tomato and onion salad with mint yoghurt (for 4–8)

1 cup plain yoghurt 2 tbsp chopped mint a pinch of cayenne a squeeze of lemon freshly ground salt and pepper	Mix together.
2 medium-sized onions, finely sliced a squeeze of lemon ground sweet paprika freshly ground salt and pepper 2 tbsp chopped coriander	Make onion relish by putting sliced onions in a bowl with the rest of the ingredients and massage well with your fingers. Then leave for 15 mins.
1 telegraph (continental) cucumber, cut into thick slices 4 large ripe red tomatoes, cored and cut into thick slices	Arrange cucumber and tomato around outside of individual plates or on one platter. Mound onion in centre and sprinkle the lot with some of the minted yoghurt (serve the rest on the side).

Sudhakaran Meetinay's dahl makhani

1 cup black lentils (available from any Indian grocer)

Place lentils in a bowl and put under running water until the water runs clear. Then simmer in 3 litres of water until just tender. Drain well.

100 g ghee
1 medium-sized onion
1 tsp cumin seeds

Heat ghee and sauté onion and cumin until light brown.

2 medium-sized ripe tomatoes, cored and chopped
1 tbsp ground turmeric
2 tbsp ground chilli powder
5 tbsp tomato purée (see page 236)

Add these to the onion, along with the lentils, and cook for 10 mins.

2 tbsp cream
1 tbsp chopped coriander
freshly ground salt and pepper

Add to pan and cook for another 2 mins or so. Serve as an accompaniment to any Indian dishes.

Some more advice for our airlines

Something our airlines need to discover is that 'wet' food reheats perfectly and, in many cases, improves with age. So stews, braises, ragouts and curries work brilliantly when reheated, unlike the steaks, chicken breasts, fish fillets and the like which are so beloved by the majority of the world's airline operators.

So, keeping this in mind, it was not surprising that in the majority of cases the food on the Indian airlines was terrific, well suited to reheating and, in deference to the majority, not overly spiced. But there was one notable exception: travelling from Goa to Delhi, I was handed a lunch box which contained not only a piece of fruit cake of indeterminate age but also a cheese sandwich from which someone had already taken a bite—and, not that I'm difficult, but if it wasn't good enough for the last recipient I was damned if it was good enough for me.

Spanish fusion

AT A TIME IN Australia when we constantly talk of 'fusion' food, Spain is a country whose food style is just that. Roman invaders began the process when they introduced wheat, wine and olive oil. Christopher Columbus certainly added his two pennies' worth when he came back from the New World with tomatoes, peppers and potatoes. And the Moors from North Africa introduced to the cuisine not only their love of sweet-sour flavours, but spices such as saffron, nutmeg and pepper and another Spanish staple—rice.

- Lamb chops in the style of Catalonia
- Tuna steaks with a Spanish green-olive relish
- Spanish vegetable pilaf
- A flavoursome vegetable stock
- Chicken in cava

- Chicken with sherry vinegar and cloves of garlic
- Spanish pork kebabs (pinchos morunos)
- A warm rabbit, orange and chorizo salad
- Potato and anchovy tortilla
- A mousse of home-salted cod
- Sardines with sea salt and alioli

Lamb chops in the style of Catalonia (for 4–6)

I cooked this dish for TV in a Spanish street, where I not only stopped the traffic (admittedly only a few cars who all stopped to have a squiz) but interrupted the town's siesta. Because within minutes I had a large audience all keen to discover what this madman from Australia was up to. Happily, the dish wasn't half-bad and my newfound friends quickly lapped it up.

olive oil
12 mid-loin lamb chops
1 large onion, sliced
1 large red capsicum, cored, seeded and sliced
1 large green capsicum, cored, seeded and sliced
2 garlic cloves, crushed

20 black or green olives, pitted
2 cups canned, peeled tomatoes, drained and chopped
10 baby spuds, scrubbed and halved, or quartered
freshly ground salt and pepper

liquid honey
sherry or (red-wine) vinegar
chopped parsley

Preheat oven to 190°C.

Heat a little oil in a large heavy-bottomed pot. Seal chops in two or three lots, and remove. Add a little more oil, if necessary, then add the rest of the ingredients and sauté for 5 mins or so.

Add all this to the pot along with seasonings to taste. Cook for a few minutes, return chops to pot, cover tightly and put in the oven. Cook for 50 mins or so, until potatoes and lamb are tender.

Remove lamb and place in a large bowl or on 4-6 plates. Add honey and vinegar to the sauce (to taste—enough to add a slightly sweet-sour finish), pour over the lamb and sprinkle with parsley. Serve with steamed green beans.

Where, oh where, is Basil when you need him?

Manuel from Faulty Towers is alive and well and back living in Spain.

Well, at least I think he is, though these days he has forsaken his career as a waiter and is instead working in the laundry of one of Costa Brava's leading hotels. Because it was here that, after three days of asking, I was informed that the reason my shirts hadn't been returned was that the laundry supervisor (Manuel?) had lost the key to the laundry door. I, of course, offered to kick the door in (this was politely declined), but it would have been a waste of time anyway, because when the shirts did eventually turn up, two or three hotels down the track, they had faded and shrunk with sleeves which, interestingly, were still rolled up.

Needless to say, I am now the proud owner of a fair number of two-toned shirts ready for the 'After' shot in a Weight Watcher's commercial.

Tuna steaks with a Spanish green-olive relish (for 4)

If overcooked, tuna will be dry and tasteless. So, always regard this delicious fish as the steak of the sea and cook it as you would a piece of beef—crusty on the outside and, at the most, medium within.

2 dozen, or so, green olives, pitted and finely chopped
2 tbsp chopped parsley
4 anchovies, finely chopped
juice of 1 lemon
freshly ground salt and pepper
virgin olive oil

Combine olives, parsley, anchovies, lemon juice and seasonings with enough oil to moisten.

4 x 160 g tuna steaks, all black removed
freshly ground salt and pepper
olive oil

Brush tuna with oil, sprinkle with seasoning and grill or panfry over high heat to the desired degree. Then place on plates, top with the olive relish and sprinkle a little oil around the plate.

> ❝ **This dish goes perfectly with double-peeled broad beans. Pod them and then plunge into boiling water for 5 or 6 seconds. Remove, peel off outer shell and set aside. When ready to use, either plunge back into boiling water briefly or toss in a little hot oil.** ❞

Spanish vegetable pilaf (for 6-8)

This is a bit of a bastardised dish, which started off as a vegetable paella but ended up more like a pilaf because, purely and simply, I hadn't made quite enough tomato purée. But it was delicious nonetheless and, if you must, also works well with some chunks of chicken thrown in at about the same time as the carrot and capsicum.

---

olive oil
1 medium-sized onion, chopped finely
2 garlic cloves, chopped finely
3 red chillies, sliced finely

Heat a little oil in a large heavy-bottomed pot and sauté onion, garlic and chillies until soft.

1 small carrot, diced
1 red capsicum, cored, seeded and diced
2 corn cobs, kernels removed

Add vegies to pot and toss well.

500 g well-washed basmati rice
1 litre vegetable stock (see page 237)
a pinch of saffron threads, soaked in a little hot stock

Add these to pot also, cover tightly with foil and a lid, and cook over gentle heat until rice is tender and liquid is absorbed (about 15 mins).

8 green beans, topped and tailed and cut in 2
¼ head broccoli, cut into small florets
2 zucchini, cut into thickish slices
6 baby squash, cut in 4

Add these vegies to salted boiling water and cook until crisp-tender and then drain well.

1 cup tomato purée, hot

Add purée to the rice, along with the boiled vegies, mix in well and check seasoning. Serve with salad.

❝ **To make a simple tomato purée, sauté some chopped onion, capsicum and garlic in a little hot oil until soft, then add some well drained, chopped canned tomatoes. Season with salt, pepper and a pinch of sugar and cook gently until thickened. Either use as is, or whiz up in a blender or processor.** ❞

A flavoursome vegetable stock

1 leek, washed well and sliced
1 stalk celery, sliced
1 medium-sized onion, sliced
2 cloves garlic, skin on, but crushed lightly
1 tsp salt
2 small carrots, diced
6 whole black peppercorns
2 bay leaves
6 parsley sprigs
6 celery leaves
a few sprigs of fresh thyme
a few sage leaves
any mushroom trimmings

Put leek, celery, onion, garlic and salt in a large pot. Add ½ cup water, cover and cook very gently for 15 mins. Then add the rest of the ingredients, cover with cold water and simmer for 45 mins. Strain, pressing down hard on the vegies as you do so.

Chicken in cava (for 4)

This is a recipe from my Spanish 'brother' Jaume (Hymie) Dominech, who is PR director of Freixenet, the world's largest producer of sparkling wines (or Cava, as they are known in Spain). Hymie is also the man who, to my detriment, introduced me to the Cuba Libra, which in true generous Spanish style consists of at least a third of a bottle of Havana Gold Cuban Rum and, at the most, a splash of Coke.

Preheat oven to 200°C.

olive oil
1 chicken, portioned
freshly ground salt and pepper

Heat oil in a large heavy-bottomed pot. Season and brown chicken on all sides. Remove and set aside.

1 large onion, chopped
8 button mushrooms, sliced
1 leek, well washed and sliced

Add a little more oil, if necessary, and sauté these vegies over gentle heat until soft.

12–15 baby shallots (or tiny baby onions), peeled
½ bottle Freixenet Cordon Negro (or, dare I say it, any good sparkling)
½ cup chicken stock (packet is fine)

Mix these ingredients in with the vegies, bring to the boil and return chicken to the pot. Reduce to a gentle simmer, cover and then cook in oven for 30–40 mins.

3 tbsp cream
1 tbsp chopped parsley

When chicken is cooked (make a small cut near the bone to check), remove and place in large bowl. Add cream and parsley to the sauce in the pot, bring to the boil, pour over chicken and sprinkle with more parsley.

> **Obviously, this should be served with copious quantities of Cordon Negro, but definitely not after even one Cuba Libra.**

❝ **You are definitely not drunk if you can lie on the floor without holding on.** ❞

Dean Martin

Chicken with sherry vinegar and cloves of garlic (for 4)

vegetable oil
plain flour
freshly ground salt and pepper
4 Maryland chicken portions, cut in 2 at the joint

olive oil
½ medium-sized onion, finely chopped
12 garlic cloves, peeled but left whole
½ cup sherry vinegar
½ cup sherry
1 cup chicken stock (packet is fine)
1 cup canned, peeled tomatoes, drained and chopped

12 sprigs fresh tarragon
rice pilaf (see page 226)

Heat a little oil in a large heavy-bottomed pot. Flour and season the chicken, and brown all over in two or three lots, adding more oil as necessary.

Discard oil, put a little olive oil in the same pot and sauté the onion and garlic gently. Then add the rest, bring to the boil, return chicken and simmer gently for 20–30 mins.

Remove chicken from pot, add tarragon and, if necessary, boil sauce to reduce. Put chicken back in and serve in bowls, with pilaf on the side.

> **Now, I know this seems like a lot of garlic, but when it is slowly cooked like this it's pretty mellow stuff.**

Spanish pork kebabs (pinchos morunos)

(for 6–8)

2 tbsp honey 6 tbsp olive oil 2 tbsp lemon juice 2 garlic cloves, crushed 2 tbsp chopped parsley 1 tsp ground cumin 3 tsp ground paprika 1 chilli, finely sliced freshly ground pepper and salt	Whisk well.
1 kilo lean pork, cut into 1.5 cm cubes	Thread pork onto skewers, pour marinade over and leave overnight in refrigerator, mixing up every now and then. Preheat BBQ.
1 cup yoghurt 2 garlic cloves, crushed 1 tsp paprika 1 tbsp chopped mint a squeeze of lemon	Mix these ingredients together and set aside. BBQ skewers on the hottest part of the grill, brushing with marinade as you do so.
rice pilaf (see page 226) lemon wedges	Serve kebabs on rice pilaf, sprinkled with the yoghurt mixture and served with lemon wedges on the side.

> **A Spanish dish which shows that country's strong Moorish influences.**

A warm rabbit, orange and chorizo salad

(for 4 as a main)

Chorizo, a wonderful hearty Spanish sausage, is available in delis and many large supermarkets. But if it is not available, instead use any coarse, well-flavoured snag. Also, while searching for that sausage, buy a bottle of sherry vinegar, which is great in any salad dressing (and is also now available in many delis and supermarkets).

vegetable oil
8 rabbit fillets, trimmed of all sinew
4 chorizo sausages

½ red onion, finely sliced
2–3 juicy oranges, cut into segments
2–3 large tomatoes, quartered
12 green olives, pitted
1 handful frisée lettuce (or mixed cresses)

olive oil
sherry vinegar (or red wine vinegar)
12 leaves flat-leaf parsley

Preheat ridged grill.

Oil the grill and cook the rabbit and sausages, removing the rabbit while it is still pink in the centre. Rest meats in a warm spot on the side.

Toss salad ingredients in bowl, along with a little of the juice from the oranges.

Slice rabbit and sausage, and add to bowl along with parsley leaves. Add oil and a little vinegar to taste, and mound in one large bowl or on 4 plates.

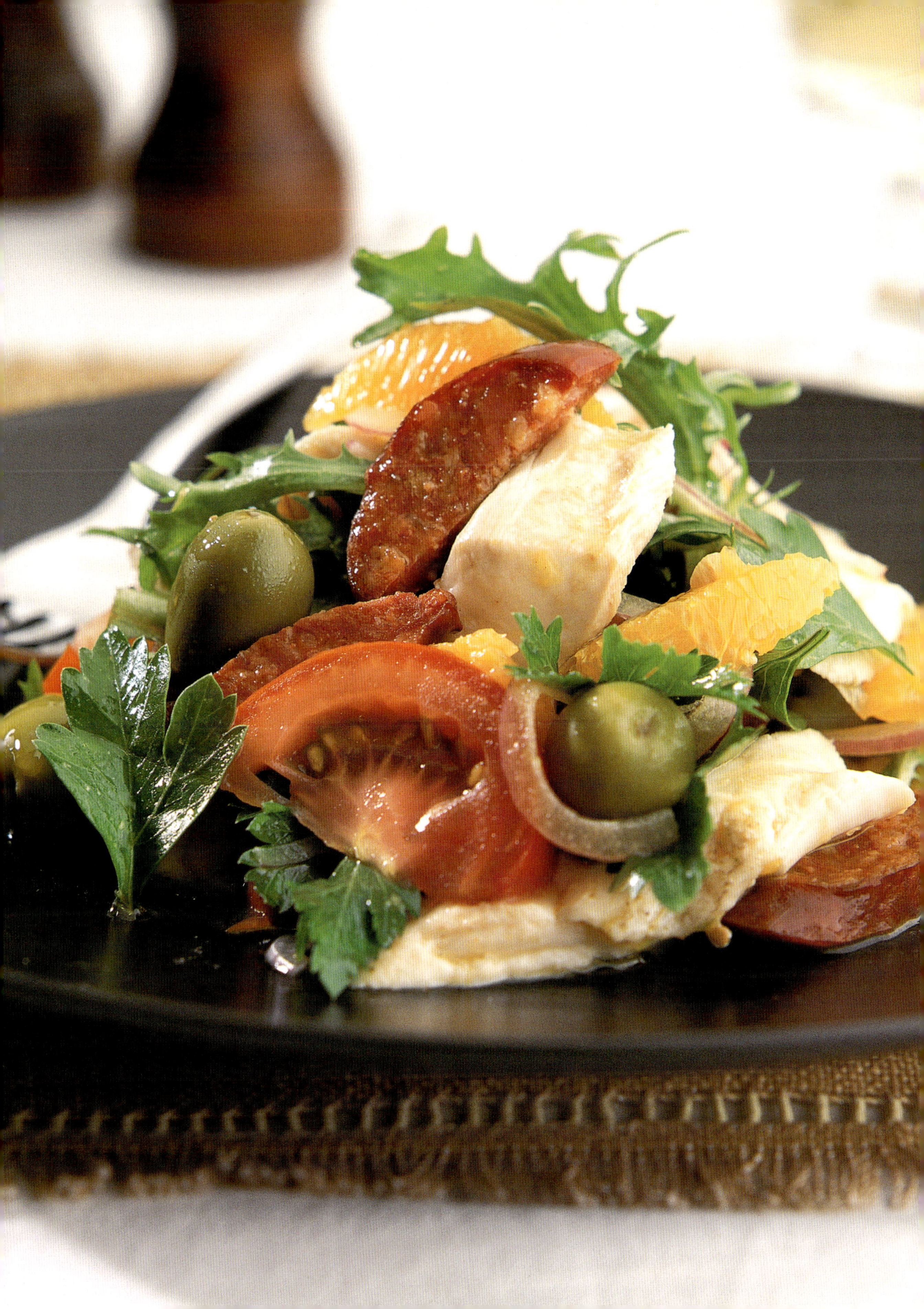

Potato and anchovy tortilla

(for 4 as an entrée, 8 as a Tapas)

Don't be confused. This true Spanish flat omelette has absolutely nothing to do with the tortilla of Mexico. And there is only one secret when whipping it up—the potatoes and onion must be slowly simmered in plenty of olive oil, rather than sautéed, and must not brown at all.

¾ cup olive oil
4 large spuds, peeled and sliced into 5 mm slices
1 medium-sized onion, finely chopped
freshly ground salt and pepper

5 large eggs, beaten
6–8 anchovies, cut in slices, lengthways
chopped parsley

Gently heat oil in a large non-stick pan and add potatoes and onion. Season and cook very slowly for 20 mins until tender, lifting and turning as they cook. Remove vegies, pour off oil and reserve a few teaspoons.

Mix eggs into the potato mix and season. Wipe out pan, add reserved oil and heat to almost smoking. Tip in egg mixture, lower heat, cover and cook gently, shaking at regular intervals to ensure that it doesn't stick. When bottom is golden, place a plate over the pan and turn out. Slide back into pan (adding a little more oil if necessary), arrange the anchovies in a lattice pattern and cook until other side is golden too. Slide out onto a plate, sprinkle with parsley and serve either warm or at room temperature, cut into wedges.

> **A dollop of alioli (Spanish garlic mayo—see page 246) would be brilliant with this.**

A mousse of home-salted cod (for 8 as a Tapas)

Salt cod is one of the stars of Mediterranean cuisine. In almost every market, there are stalls devoted to nothing else. But it can be a bit of an acquired taste to the novice so, instead of using a commercial variety, try this home-salted version, which is a bit milder but still delicious.

a 400 g piece of blue eye cod, skin on **rock salt**	The day before, cover the fish with a generous amount of salt and leave overnight in the fridge. Next day, brush off the salt and run fish under cold water for 15 mins.
milk **¼ small onion, sliced** **1 bay leaf** **2 sprigs of thyme** **4 whole peppercorns**	Put fish in a tray or pan, cover with milk and add other ingredients. Poach, very gently, for about 15–20 mins, until cooked. Then remove fish, discarding the cooking liquid. When cool remove skin and any bones.
plain boiled potatoes, drained very well and mashed	Blend or process the fish with about two-thirds its quantity of mash.

> **Serve this, as is, with crusty bread and a green salad, or with a roasted capsicum salad. Make this salad by roasting or grilling capsicums until skin is blistered and brown-black: cover with roasting tray (or put in a sealed paper bag), allow to cool and then peel. Cut flesh into strips and toss with olive oil, a splash of balsamic vinegar and some capers.**

Sardines with sea salt and alioli

(for 4 or 8 as a Tapas)

The Spanish certainly love garlic and this garlic mayonnaise is served with almost everything. In fact, one night when I felt that I just had to have an Asian fix, my chosen Cantonese restaurant in Barcelona even added a generous slurp of alioli on top of my Beef in Black Bean Sauce—an interesting combination, to say the least.

½–¾ cup mayonnaise (see page 182) 1 tsp Dijon mustard 3 garlic cloves, crushed lemon juice to taste	Mix together and set aside.
20 whole sardines, gutted and cleaned sea salt olive oil	Sprinkle sardines generously with salt, pressing it firmly into the skin. Then sprinkle them lightly with oil and pan-fry, grill or barbecue for 2 mins on each side. Serve with the alioli on the side.

Keeping the flies away

A visit to Spain must include at least one night in the tapas bars, where the varied, interesting small courses easily build into a terrific food experience. And at the same time you can listen to the many exotic explanations as to their origins.

Actually, to set the record straight, tapas were originally created as a means of keeping flies away from the patrons' wine. To achieve this, barmen began placing pieces of bread on top of the glasses. When the customers began snacking on these hats (*tapas*) they began adding small tastes, such as olives, anchovies and the like, and the tradition began.

More than just a slice of bread

A specialty of Catalonia, *pa amb tomaquet* (bread and tomato) is a delicious starter, but it must be made only with tomatoes that are very ripe and full of flavour. Actually, it is so much a part of Catalan life that entire books have been written on the subject of making it.

But don't be scared off by that—it's really rather simple. Just grill some thick slices of a country-style loaf and vigorously rub some cut cloves of garlic all over them. Then cut tomatoes in half and also rub them all over the grilled bread, gently squeezing the tomato as you do so. Finally sprinkle with olive oil and freshly ground salt and pepper, and serve.

Good old Aussie tucker

I REMEMBER MARGARET FULTON ONCE telling me about travelling into Wollongong at 11 a.m. on a Sunday morning to find that the whole town smelt of roasting lamb. Admittedly, it was in the early 50s when our obsession with Anglo-Saxon cooking was at its very strongest. But I think if today you went into any country town at a similar time you would be far more likely to find it smelling of pesto, soy sauce, coriander and, seemingly, a thousand other exotic flavours.

Because, while our politicians continually talk of the necessity of Australia becoming a multicultural society, our food has already done just that. To the extent that even when we talk of good old Aussie tucker, very few of those dishes are actually really Australian. Because even in those early days we were borrowing from the rest of the world (although, unlike today, we were rarely improving on the originals).

And then again we, of course, have the Hewitson factor, which involves bringing those old (and some not so old) favourites kicking and screaming into the new millennium. Maybe we should just call this section Good New Aussie Tucker—now there's a good idea.

- Shepherd's pie
- Devilled lamb's kidneys on toast
- Lamb's fry and crispy bacon with apple stew and a mustard and thyme butter
- Lamb brains with a brown lemon and caper butter
- Tripe and onions
- Bangers and mash with golden onions
- Baked beans and sausages
- The perfect roast chook
- And let's not forget some crispy, crunchy roast spuds
- Roast chicken and crudités in lettuce cups
- Chicken schnitzel with pesto mash
- Chicken Maryland with crispy bacon and sauce béarnaise
- Chateaubriand of beef fillet with a mustard, soy and fresh herb crust and roasted kumara mash
- Peppered steak casserole
- Huey's true blue Aussie burger
- Steak diane
- Spag bog with a beef and chicken liver ragu
- Crumbed cutlets with a blue-cheese stuffing
- Braised lamb shanks with osso buco sauce and gremolata
- Roast leg of lamb with olive oil roasted vegetables
- Lamb-shank hotch-potch

- Canned salmon patties for Mavis
- Fish fingers with home-made tomato sauce
- Johnny Hewitson's fish and chips
- Yabby and cheese crepes
- Kippers with a Lyonnaise potato salad
- Pork stroganoff
- A modern-day pea and ham soup
- Asparagus soup with a touch of orange
- Corned beef bubble and squeak
- Country sausages with bashed neeps
- Beer damper

Shepherd's pie (for 4–6)

This is about the most popular dish on the Tolarno menu, and summer or winter, there are many regulars who order nothing else. Which is fine by me, because I also have favourite restaurants where I go when I feel like particular dishes. But there was one couple who got my goat. Constantly enquiring when we were due to change our menu, no matter what we featured, they both invariably ordered, what else, the Shepherd's Pie. So, being a perverse sort of fellow, I decided to fix them right up by taking the pie off the next menu (but offering it as a special). The staff, of course, knew of my little game and most were nearby when the menus arrived at the couple's table. Great expectation was on their face as they discovered that, finally, there was a new menu. But, just as quickly, that look of anticipation was replaced by one of sheer dismay as they discovered the absence of their favourite dish. The waiter politely enquired whether there was anything wrong and, after a moment's hesitation, they asked what had happened to the pie, whereupon he took pity on them and explained that it had been left off by mistake and was still available.

To this day they still come in regularly, still both have the Shepherd's Pie but no longer, thank God, enquire as to any change in menu.

---

vegetable oil **2 rindless bacon rashers, diced** **1 large onion, finely chopped** **½ carrot, peeled and diced** **½ celery stalk, diced** **2 garlic cloves, chopped**	In a large heavy-bottomed pot heat a little oil and sauté bacon and vegies gently for 5 mins.
750 g lean minced lamb	Add to pot and stir until lamb changes colour.
½ cup white wine **¼ cup canned tomato purée** **3 tbsp tomato chutney** **½ cup beef stock (packet is fine)** **freshly ground pepper and salt** **1 bay leaf**	Add these to the pot, mix well and cook for 45 mins, stirring regularly, adding more stock and tomato purée if necessary. Check seasoning and then place meat mixture in a large ovenproof dish. Preheat oven to 220°C.

mashed potato (see page 260)
a mixture of grated tasty cheese and grated parmesan (3 parts tasty to 1 parmesan)

Mound mash over meat, sprinkle generously with the cheeses and bake in oven until top is golden.

Awful offal

My mate Charlie is a pretty terrific cook and invitations to dine at his place are much sought after.

So I was pretty pleased to score one for a recent Sunday lunch. And what a lunch it was too. Because not only did the sun shine and the wine flow freely, but a surprise was in hand with a delicious course of an almost-forgotten delicacy—lamb kidneys. They were served in a creamy devilled sauce atop a generous chunk of grilled country bread, and I was instantly reminded of palmier days when rarely a week went by without at least one plate of awful offal gracing the Hewitson table. When everything from tripe to tongue to liver was regarded as a special treat, and when mums prided themselves on their ability to transform these cheap cuts into tasty meals.

Devilled lamb's kidneys on toast (for 4)

10–12 lamb kidneys vegetable oil	Remove membrane, cut kidneys in half lengthways and, with a sharp knife or kitchen scissors, cut out all the sinew. Then cut each half into 4 even pieces. Heat oil in a large pan and brown the kidneys quickly on all sides, in three or four lots. Remove and set aside.
½ medium-sized onion, finely chopped 6 button mushrooms, sliced 1 garlic clove, crushed	Wipe out pan, heat a little more oil and sauté vegies until soft.
⅓ cup cream ¼ cup chicken stock (packet is fine) 1 tbsp Dijon mustard splash of Worcestershire sauce freshly ground pepper	Mix these well into mixture in pan and reduce over high heat until thickened.
freshly ground salt Tabasco sauce	Add salt and Tabasco to taste, return kidneys to pan and simmer, very gently, for about 3 mins.
4 thick slices country-style bread chopped parsley	Grill or toast the bread, place on plates, spoon kidneys over and sprinkle with chopped parsley.

> **Kidneys, to be tender, should be cooked no more than medium—so, pink in the centre, please.**

Lamb's fry and crispy bacon with apple stew and a mustard and thyme butter

(for 4)

150 g soft unsalted butter 1 heaped tbsp Dijon mustard 2 tbsp chopped thyme	Mix together and leave aside at room temperature.
vegetable oil 1 medium-sized onion, finely sliced 3 Granny Smith apples, cored, peeled and finely sliced ½ cup water 1 tbsp chopped parsley freshly ground salt and pepper	Heat a little oil in a pot and sauté onion until soft. Then add the apples and cook until lightly browned. Add water, parsley and seasonings, and simmer until water has almost evaporated. Cover and keep warm.
vegetable oil 4 rashers rindless bacon 8 thick slices lamb liver, all sinews removed flour freshly ground salt and pepper	Heat a little oil in a large pan and fry bacon until crisp. Push to the side. Dust the liver with flour and seasonings, and cook until crusty on the outside but pink within, adding more oil if necessary.
chopped parsley	Place apple stew on individual plates, top with 2 pieces of liver, a rasher of bacon and a good dollop of butter. Then sprinkle with parsley.

❝ **I would hate to think that in future years Australians will become like their American counterparts—a race known more for their ability to reheat, rather than for any ability with frying pan, wok or skillet.** ❞

Melbourne movie man, Chris Ryan

Lamb brains with a brown lemon and caper butter (for 4 as an entrée, 2 as a main)

8 sets of brains
lemon juice
1 parsley sprig
¼ onion, sliced
splash of white vinegar
water

flour
freshly ground salt and pepper
vegetable oil

50 g butter
1–2 lemons, peeled and diced, pips removed
2 tbsp capers, drained

chopped parsley

Soak brains for a few hours (or overnight) in water with a little lemon juice. Drain and put in a pot with parsley, onion and vinegar, and water to cover. Bring to the boil, turn off and allow to cool in the water. Then remove the brains, drain well and separate into two, removing any lobes or membrane.

Flour and season the brains. Heat a little oil in a large pan and fry in two or three lots, adding more oil as necessary, until golden-brown on all sides. Drain well and keep warm in the oven.

Pour off the oil, wipe out the pan and add butter, lemon and capers. Cook until butter is light brown (not burnt).

Arrange brains in a circle on individual plates, pour butter over and sprinkle with parsley.

> **There is only one secret when cooking brains—take time and care with their preparation.**

Tripe and onions

(for 4–6)

olive oil
3 onions, finely sliced
1 garlic clove, crushed

Heat a little oil in a large, heavy-bottomed pan and sauté onion and garlic over a medium heat until golden-brown, stirring frequently.

¾–1 kilo pre-cooked honeycomb tripe
freshly ground salt and pepper
olive oil
1 tbsp butter

Slice tripe into strips about 5 mm thick by 6 cm long and season. In another large pan, heat oil and butter until almost smoking. Sauté the tripe until golden and crisp, add to sautéed onion mix and stir well for a minute or two.

2 tbsp red-wine vinegar
3 tbsp chopped parsley

Add vinegar to tripe mixture to taste along with the parsley, and cook for another minute. Serve with a simple salad and plenty of crusty bread.

> Well cooked tripe is rare. Perhaps it's because perfection of ingredients and cooking just isn't enough. Because, you also need a certain atmosphere and you don't eat tripe just anywhere or anyhow and, even less, with just anyone. First of all, you need a suitable partner to enter into your communion of tripe. Then you need plenty of time and appetite. And, last but not least, a certain intellectual comfort too.

French author and gourmet, Robert Courtine

Bangers and mash with golden onions

(for 4)

12 sausages of any variety	Blanch bangers in simmering water until just firm when squeezed. Drain well and set aside until needed.
4–6 large floury potatoes **up to ¾ cup milk** **freshly ground salt and pepper**	Peel and cut spuds into even pieces and cook in lightly salted water until tender and drain well. Bring milk to boil and mash the spuds, adding the hot milk little by little as you do so. Season mash and set aside.
3 tbsp olive oil **a knob of butter** **2 onions, finely sliced** **freshly ground salt and pepper**	Heat oil and butter in a large pan and sauté onions until golden and crispy on some of the ends. Season.
cream **butter**	Pan-fry or grill the sausages until browned all over. At same time, put mash in microwave with a good slurp of cream and a generous dollop of butter on top. Heat until piping-hot, then mix in the butter and cream.
mustard (Dijon or English)	Place mash on plates, top with sausages, scatter with onions and serve mustard on the side.

> **Blanching the sausages beforehand may be frowned on by the purists, but it is guaranteed to stop them bursting.**

Baked beans and sausages (for 4)

I am sure many of us remember Shane Warne's SOS from India, because his favourite food—baked beans—didn't make it onto the hotel menu. Well, I'm certainly not going to make any comments on his taste (or lack of), but this recipe is dedicated to him with the suggestion that, the next time he visits the sub-continent, he takes along copies of this book and slips one to each hotel chef along the way.

1½ cups dried haricot beans	Soak beans overnight in cold water, then drain well.
vegetable oil ½ medium onion, chopped ½ red capsicum, cored and diced	In a large heavy-bottomed pot, heat oil and sauté onion and capsicum until soft.
½ tsp ground cumin ¼ cup white wine ½ cup canned tomato purée ¼ cup American-style BBQ sauce (bought or see page 80) a good ½ tbsp brown sugar 1 tbsp molasses 1 level tbsp mustard salt and freshly ground pepper	Add cumin to pot and cook for a few seconds, then throw in drained beans and the rest of the ingredients here. Bring to boil and simmer until beans are tender (adding a little water, if necessary). This should take approx 1–1½ hours.
8–12 sausages of any variety, blanched (see opposite page) chopped parsley	Pan-fry or grill the sausages until browned all over, place on plates with a good dollop of the beans and a sprinkling of parsley.

The fart factor

'Beans, beans, good for the heart, but the more you eat the more you fart.'

Beans, as we all know, can cause what could be politely called a slight flatulence problem. This is due to the potassium oxide in beans, which is easily negated if the beans are soaked, as has been suggested, in cold water overnight.

The perfect roast chook

When it comes to my favourites, the perfect roast chicken with a crisp, buttery skin and tender, moist flesh has to be about at the top of the list. But to achieve that result is not always easy, so here are a few hints which will help you achieve that perfect chook every time.

- First of all, keep in mind that a highly commercial mass-produced bird will rarely produce the perfect roast chicken. So search out the best available product: if you can find one, a free-range number which has been fed on grain rather than on pellets is right there at the top of the tree.
- For a crisper skin, leave the bird uncovered on a sheet of foil in the fridge overnight.
- And, please forget the diet for this one day, because if there is one thing a roast chicken needs it is butter, and lots of it.
- There is nothing worse than an over-cooked bird. So, when its time in the oven appears to be up, check by piercing the bottom of the thigh: when the juices are almost clear, with just the slightest hint of pink, turn off the oven and rest it for 15 mins with the oven door ajar.
- Last, but not least—a warning. Chicken meat is highly susceptible to the bacteria associated with food poisoning. So immediately after preparing raw poultry, always wash all utensils and cutting surfaces thoroughly, only ever defrost frozen product in the fridge (never on the kitchen bench, where any bacteria will rapidly multiply), and keep for no more than 2 days in a domestic refrigerator, ensuring that none of the chicken's liquids fall on any other foodstuffs.

The perfect roast chook (for 4)

**2 whole lemons
several sprigs of fresh thyme
2 unpeeled garlic cloves, lightly crushed**

**1 x 1.8 kilo chicken
soft unsalted butter
freshly ground salt and pepper**

Preheat oven to 230°C.

Put lemons in microwave on high for 15 secs, remove, pierce all over with a fork and place in chicken cavity with the thyme and garlic.

Fold the chicken wings under the body and put a skewer through the legs and tip of the breast. Season chook well and smear generously with butter. Place breast-side down in a baking tray which is only slightly larger than the chicken. Place in preheated oven, instantly turn heat down to 200°C and cook for 30 mins. (Putting the chook breast-side down may seem rather strange and it does result in a slightly untidy bird, but it will be moister because all the juices will flow into the breast during that first roasting period and stop it from drying out.)

Then turn breast-side up and cook for another 25–30 mins, basting two or three times and turning heat back up to 230°C for the final 15 mins. When almost ready (see opposite page), turn off oven and leave for 15 mins with the oven door ajar. Serve with the buttery juices poured over the top.

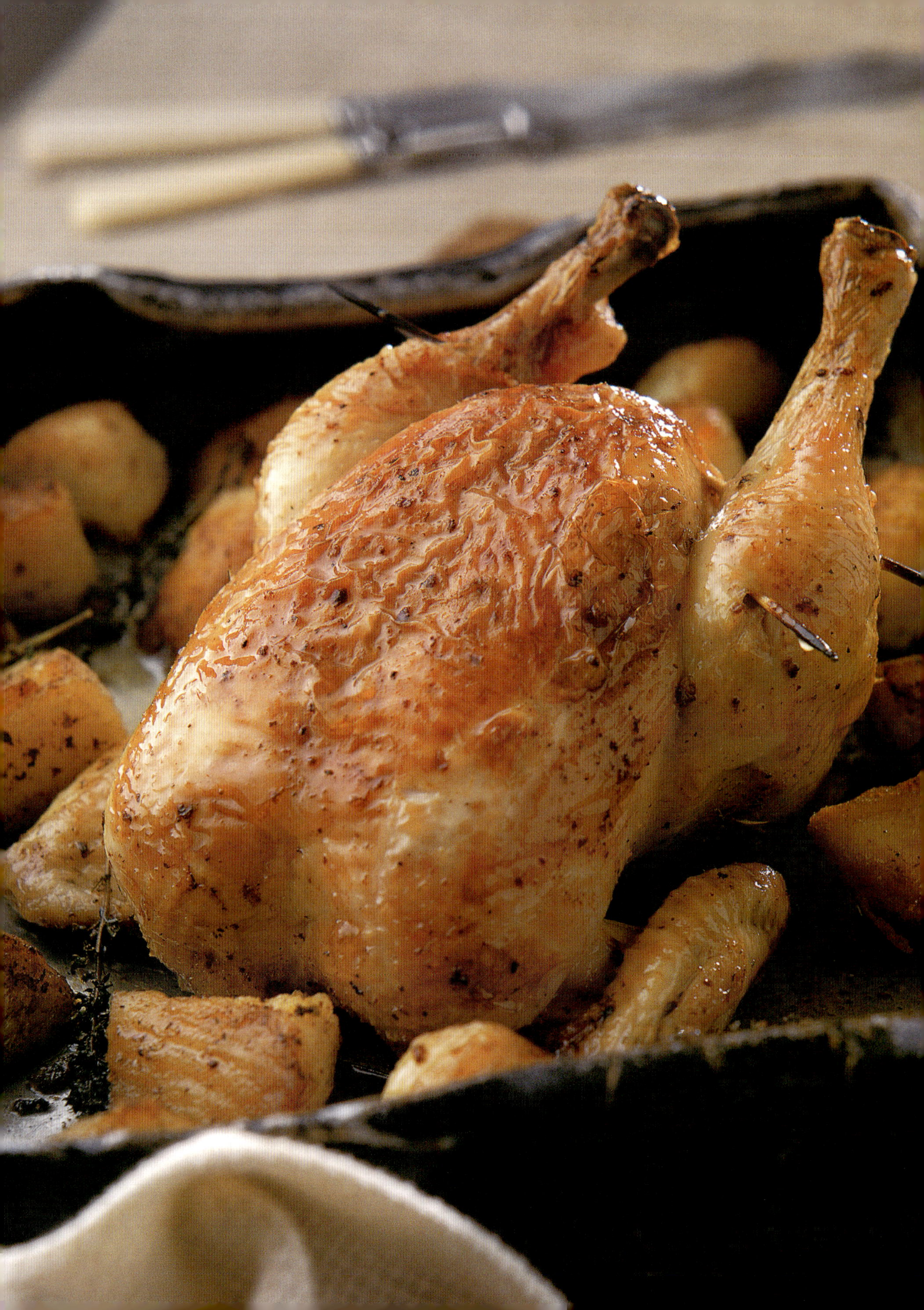

And let's not forget some crispy, crunchy roast spuds

6 medium-sized potatoes, peeled and quartered

Place spuds in a pot of boiling water and cook for 5 mins. Drain well and cool. Then scrape all the surfaces quite vigorously with the prongs of a fork.

freshly ground salt and pepper
olive oil or melted butter

Place spuds in their own baking tray, season well and toss with oil or butter. Then put in oven at the same time as chicken and cook, turning 2 or 3 times.

Roast chicken and crudités in lettuce cups (for 4)

I remember my first experience with crudités (which are little more than a selection of raw vegetables served with a tangy sauce). It was in Paris in 1975 and my good mate, Sig Jorgensen, and I were amazed that something so simple could taste so bloody good. Of course, it may have had a little to do with the sheer quality of the vegies itself, but the fact that the waiters prepared the dish to order right there in the dining room obviously made a difference as well. Still, simple it certainly was. But unfortunately, when crudités came into vogue in Australia, in most cases, we buggered them up. With one notable exception (Clichy, which Siggy and I owned), the vegetables were rarely chosen carefully, they were prepared way too far in advance and the sauce was usually bland and boring.

So here is a chance for crudités to achieve another fifteen minutes of fame. To make it even simpler, you could even use a bought barbecued chicken or duck.

1 iceberg lettuce	Remove damaged leaves and discard. Remove core, carefully separate leaves and set aside for another purpose any that are torn or damaged. Cut leaves into round cups, then wash and put into iced water.
a selection of vegies, such as celery, tomatoes, capsicum, beans, cucumber, radishes and spring onions (green onions)	Clean vegies, cut into neat shapes and place, in individual piles around your best platter.
1 roast chicken (see page 263)	Bone chook and cut into even pieces. Place in centre of platter.
any Asian-flavoured dipping sauce	Drain and dry lettuce cups and mound them on a plate. Allow guests to help themselves, wrapping the vegies and chicken in the lettuce cups with a dollop of the sauce.

Chicken schnitzel with pesto mash (for 4)

4 skinless chicken breasts	Gently flatten out the breasts to an even thickness.
slivers of zest from 1 lemon **1½ cups fresh breadcrumbs** **¾ cup grated parmesan** **1 tbsp chopped parsley** **1 tbsp chopped basil**	Mix all these together.
plain flour **freshly ground salt and pepper** **2 eggs** **a little milk**	In one bowl mix the flour and seasonings and in another the eggs and milk.
	Crumb the chicken by pressing each portion into the flour, then into the eggwash and finally into the crumbs. Set aside until needed.
olive oil	Heat a little oil in a large non-stick pan and fry the breasts, two at a time, until golden and firm to the touch. Drain well on paper towels and keep hot in a low oven.
pesto mash (see page 115) **lemon wedges**	Serve with pesto mash (which can be reheated in the microwave) and lemon wedges.

> **Make your own breadcrumbs in the food processor with day-old bread, crusts removed.**

Chicken Maryland with crispy bacon and sauce béarnaise (for 4)

When I first began in restaurants, no self-respecting establishment could hold its head high unless the menu contained staples such as Wiener Schnitzel, Oysters Kilpatrick, Steak Diane, Carpetbag Steak and Prawn Cocktails (with that bloody awful Sauce Marie Rose).

And almost all of them, due mainly to a lack of care in purchasing and/or cooking, were pretty terrible. Actually, one that I haven't mentioned but which was probably the worst of the lot was Chicken Maryland. Boiled within an inch of its life and then carelessly crumbed with a piece of banana and thrown into an overcrowded fryer, it was invariably dry and greasy and tasted of little apart from rancid fat. But simply dusted with flour and cooked either in the oven or in a pan (as they do in Maryland), this is a delicious recipe which proves that some golden oldies really do deserve another chance.

Preheat oven to 200°C.

300 g unsalted butter

Melt gently in a small pot, skim foam off top and pour butter off leaving impurities behind on bottom of pot.

100 ml white wine
100 ml tarragon vinegar
1 tbsp chopped onion
2 tbsp dried tarragon

Put these in a pot and boil until reduced by half. Cool slightly and transfer to a stainless-steel bowl.

4 egg yolks

Add yolks to liquid in bowl and put over a pot of simmering water. Whisk until lightly thickened and fluffy (this is the most important part of the process—don't overcook). Then cool slightly and add butter little by little, whisking continually. Season sauce to taste and keep in a warm (not hot) spot.

flour freshly ground salt and pepper 1 tsp mild paprika 8–12 chicken drumsticks or thighs—on the bone with skin on milk	Mix flour with seasonings and paprika. Dip chicken in milk and then in the seasoned flour.
¼ cup olive oil	Heat oil in a large heavy-bottomed pan and brown chicken pieces all over. Drain well and put in oven tray. Place in oven and cook, turning over once or twice until ready. (To check if chicken is cooked, make a small cut next to the bone: the juice should be clear.)
4 rashers rindless bacon	When chicken is almost ready, grill bacon until crispy. Then place chicken on plate with bacon, a good dollop of béarnaise on the top and a simple salad on the side.

> **Instead of the béarnaise, barbecued sweetcorn salsa (see page 94) would also work well.**

Chateaubriand of beef fillet with a mustard, soy and fresh herb crust and roasted kumara mash (for 4)

Preheat oven to 200°C.

1 kilo whole kumara (or sweet potato), unpeeled

Put kumara on rack in oven and cook for about 45 mins, until tender when pierced with a skewer. Remove from oven, and peel when cool enough to handle.

a good dollop, or two, of butter
freshly ground salt and pepper

Whiz up in the processor with the kumara. (This can be done in advance and reheated, with another dollop of butter, in the microwave.)

Turn oven to its highest setting and leave for 15 mins.

750 g centrecut beef fillet, trimmed of all fat and sinew
2 tbsp Dijon mustard
2 tbsp soy sauce
3 tbsp chopped fresh herbs (parsley, tarragon, mint)

Place beef on a small roasting tray. Whiz up remaining ingredients in a processor and smear over the beef. Put in preheated oven and cook to the desired degree (approx. 12–15 mins for medium rare). Then set aside, loosely covered, in a warm spot for 5 mins. Cut into thick slices and serve with the mash and any juices poured over the top.

Peppered steak casserole (for 4–6)

Preheat oven to 200°C.

1 kilo chuck steak, well trimmed and cut into 1.5 cm cubes
cracked black pepper
vegetable oil

Season the steak generously with the pepper. Heat some oil in a large, heavy-bottomed pot and seal steak, in two or three lots, on all sides. Remove.

2 medium-sized onions, sliced
2 garlic cloves, crushed
6 large mushrooms, sliced
2 rashers rindless bacon, diced

Add these to the pot, along with a little more oil if necessary, and cook over moderate heat until soft, scraping the brown bits from the bottom as it all cooks.

1 tbsp tomato paste
3 tbsp flour

Add tomato paste, mix in well and cook for 3 mins. Mix flour in well, turn heat right down and cook for a further 4–5 mins.

¾ bottle shiraz
beef stock (packet is fine)
2 tbsp chopped parsley
8 small baby spuds, scrubbed well and halved

Add wine to pot with an equal amount of stock, and bring to the boil. Add parsley and spuds to the casserole along with the beef. Cover tightly, put in oven and cook for approx 1¼ hours until beef is tender. Remove, add a splash of fresh wine to heighten the flavour, and check the seasoning.

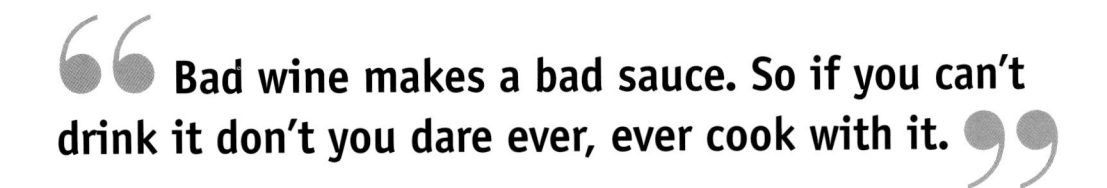

> **Bad wine makes a bad sauce. So if you can't drink it don't you dare ever, ever cook with it.**

Huey's true blue Aussie burger (for 6 or more)

I may appear a little slow, but after many years I have finally discovered why I am not overly fond of commercial burgers. At first, I thought it was the sweet bun, but after discarding this in favour of a good old-fashioned Aussie number I still felt there was something lacking. Next, I took a dislike to the pickles, salad and dressing. But even after replacing these with a pile of crisp lettuce, some barbecued onion, the odd slice of ripe tomato and some home-made mustardy mayo, it still wasn't quite right.

So out went the so-called burger pattie and in came a thick rissole chock-full of sautéed onion and my very best chutney. At last my burger was beginning to have real flavour (and, noticeably, none of the original ingredients), but still it appeared to be lacking a certain zing. Then it dawned on me—there was no beetroot. How could we have a true-blue Aussie burger without a couple of slices of the blessed purple stuff—and surprise, surprise, the minute I whacked that on (along with an egg and a rasher or two of bacon) all was right with the world.

---

vegetable oil
1 onion, chopped
2 garlic cloves, crushed
750 g minced beef
150 g tomato chutney
2 eggs, lightly beaten
2 tbsp Worcestershire Sauce
freshly ground salt and pepper

Heat a little oil and sauté onion and garlic until soft. Then place in a bowl with rest of the ingredients and mix well. Form into 6 or more patties.

vegetable oil
1 large onion, peeled and cut into 6 thick slices
6 rashers of rindless bacon
6 eggs
grated tasty cheese
6 burger buns, cut in half

Preheat BBQ.

Cook burger patties on oiled grill plate. At the same time, oil moderate part of the grill and cook onions. Then cook the bacon and eggs, and lightly oil the buns and grill them. When patties are almost cooked, put some grated cheese on top.

mayonnaise (see page 182)
crisp lettuce leaves (iceberg or cos)
12 thick slices ripe tomato
6–12 slices beetroot
tomato chutney (bought or homemade)

Smear bottom halves of buns with mayo, top with lettuce, tomato, beetroot, onion, bacon, patty, eggs and chutney. Top with upper half of bun and serve with salad or piles of fries.

> **Bar-room Slaw also goes well with burgers. Finely slice cabbage and onion, grate a little carrot and mix with, to taste, a generous amount of both mustard vinaigrette (see page 210) and alioli (see page 246).**

Pretentious claptrap

During the late seventies, I visited the three-star restaurants of France on every possible occasion. And I was not the only one. Because the dining rooms were full to overflowing with Aussies talking knowledgeably about the pros and cons of nouvelle cuisine, which side of the hill the mushrooms came from and whether the scallop on a large white plate with two tiny snowpeas looked a little lonely or not.

Meanwhile, at the same time, the streets of Asia were being overrun by a somewhat more casual (and obviously smarter) brand of Aussie, brandishing bottles of Fosters and not giving a stuff about their crispy noodles, satays and sambals, except whether they tasted good or not.

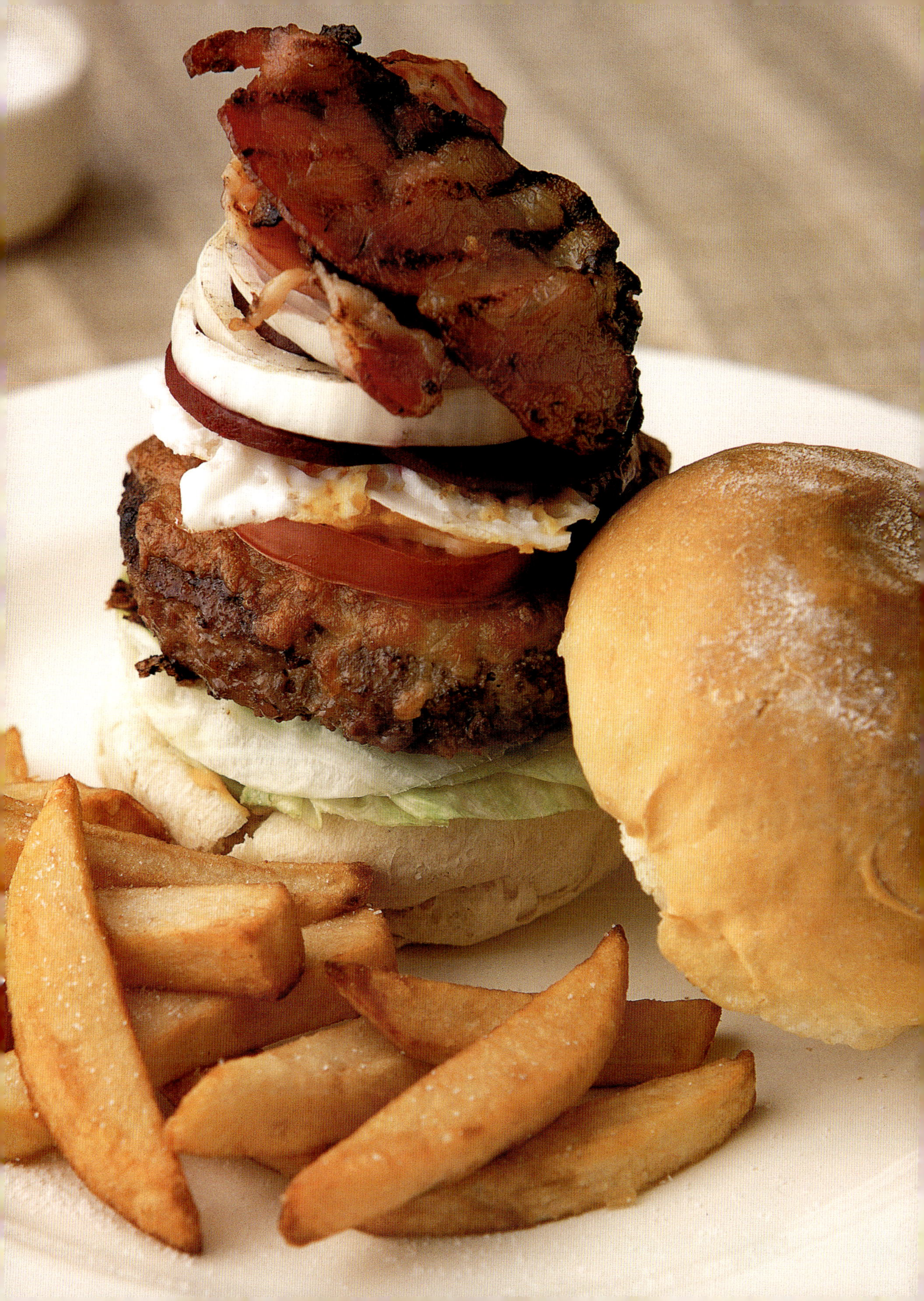

Steak diane (for 4)

olive oil
4 x 120 g pieces beef porterhouse, trimmed of all fat and sinew and battened out a little
olive oil
freshly ground salt and pepper

1 small red onion, finely chopped
1 garlic clove, crushed
2 tbsp brandy
½ tbsp Dijon mustard
a splash of Worcestershire sauce
½ cup cream
1 cup beef stock (packet is fine)
1 tbsp chopped parsley

Heat a little oil in a pan and quickly sear the steaks on both sides. Remove, season and set aside (keep separate from each other).

Add a little more oil, if necessary, and cook onion and garlic until lightly browned. Add brandy, allow to catch alight and, when flames go out, add the other ingredients. Mix well, scraping any brown bits from the bottom of the pan, and simmer until almost sauce-like. Then return steaks to the pan and cook to the desired degree. Serve with mash or chips.

> **The Steak Diane of the fifties and sixties was always the province of the head waiter. And his main purpose in life appeared to be to impress all and sundry by getting the flames from the brandy to reach the ceiling without setting the nearby curtains on fire.**

Spag bog with a beef and chicken liver ragu

(for 4–6)

4 tbsp olive oil
4 tbsp butter
2 onions, finely chopped
2 garlic cloves, crushed

Heat oil and butter in a heavy-bottomed pot and sauté onions and garlic until soft.

3 rindless bacon rashers, diced
1 large carrot, diced
2 celery stalks, diced

Add these and cook until lightly browned.

500 g coarsely ground lean beef
4 chicken livers, cleaned and finely chopped
1 cup dry white wine
2 cups beef stock (packet is fine)
1 cup tomato purée, canned
1 strip lemon zest
2 bay leaves
freshly ground salt and pepper

Add meats and stir well until they brown evenly. Add remaining ingredients, turn down heat, cover and simmer for approx 40 mins, stirring occasionally. When ragu has thickened, remove the zest and bay leaves, and set aside.

400 g spaghetti
olive oil
freshly grated parmesan

Cook spaghetti in plenty of lightly salted boiling water until al dente. Drain well, toss with a little olive oil and parmesan, and mound in 4–6 bowls. Top with reheated ragu and serve with more cheese on the side.

Crumbed cutlets with a blue-cheese stuffing

(for 4)

4 x 4-cutlet racks of lamb, trimmed of all fat and sinew slivers of any good blue cheese	Cut racks into cutlets, lay them on a board and give a good whack to flatten slightly. Then make a cut through each cutlet parallel to the board and almost to the bone. Insert slivers of cheese and re-form the cutlets.
2 tbsp chopped herbs (parsley, basil and mint) 2 cups fresh breadcrumbs plain flour salt and pepper 2 eggs ¼ cup milk	Combine herbs and breadcrumbs. Mix flour with seasonings and whisk eggs with the milk. Dip cutlets into flour, then into eggwash and finally press them into the crumbs.
olive oil	Heat ¼ cup oil in a large heavy-bottomed pan and sauté cutlets in two or three lots, until golden on both sides, adding more oil as necessary. Drain well and keep warm in oven until all the cutlets are cooked.
lemon wedges	Serve cutlets with lemon wedges and a simple salad dressed with olive oil and balsamic vinegar.

> **My mother always served another old-time favourite with crumbed cutlets—carrot and parsnip mash. You simply boil equal quantities of carrot and parsnip until tender, then drain well and mash coarsely (Mum always used a fork) with a generous dollop of butter and some freshly ground salt and pepper.**

> **The most remarkable thing about my mother was the fact that for 30 years she served the family nothing but leftovers—the original meals have never been found.**

American author Calvin Trillin

Braised lamb shanks with osso bucco sauce and gremolata (for 4)

This dish works well in the pressure cooker, if you happen to have one. The cooking time is almost halved.

Preheat oven to 200°C.

2 tbsp slivers of orange zest
2 tbsp slivers of lemon zest
4 tbsp chopped parsley
1 tbsp chopped garlic

Make gremolata by chopping all these together. Set aside.

vegetable oil
8 lamb shanks, French-cut
2 large onions, chopped
2 garlic cloves, crushed
2 celery stalks, diced
2 medium carrots, diced

Heat ¼ cup oil in a large heavy-bottomed pot and brown shanks on all sides. Remove. Add onion and garlic to pot, sauté gently for 2–3 mins, then add the celery and carrots. Cook gently for 5–10 mins, until soft.

2 tbsp chopped parsley
2 bay leaves
2 sprigs thyme
½ bottle white wine
3 tbsp balsamic vinegar

Add these to pot and reduce liquid by about one-third.

1 cup canned peeled tomatoes, drained and chopped
2 cups beef stock (packet is fine)
2 tbsp soy sauce
freshly ground pepper

Finally add these, mix in well and bring to the boil. Return shanks to pot, cover and cook in oven for 1½–2 hours, until meat is almost falling off the bones.

creamy mash (see page 260)

Serve shanks on mash, with the sauce poured over the top and a sprinkling of the gremolata.

A 'lite' breakfast

I remember meeting, admittedly a fair number of years ago, the proprietor of Amsterdam's leading restaurant, who had, as a youngster, worked as a shearer's cook throughout the Antipodes. And I will always remember his look of dismay when I informed him that shearers no longer ate eighteen or so lamb chops for breakfast. Obviously he had dined out on that story for a number of years, but at least he perked up a little when I admitted that we still did smear that strange black stuff on our morning toast.

Roast leg of lamb with olive oil roasted vegetables (for 6–8)

1 leg of lamb, approx. 2 kilos
2–3 garlic cloves, cut in slivers
4 anchovies, cut into 12 strips
12 small sprigs of rosemary
freshly ground salt and pepper
1 lemon
olive oil
1 cup beef stock (packet is fine)

8 brussels sprouts, cleaned and a cross cut on the stalk base
8 baby turnips, cleaned and peeled
8 baby beetroot, cleaned and peeled
8 baby carrots, cleaned and peeled
12 baby onions, peeled
8 baby spuds, scrubbed and cut in half
12 baby corn
extra olive oil
freshly ground salt and pepper

a dollop of butter

Preheat oven to 220°C.

Trim lamb of any excess fat and make 12 small cuts in the top, about 1 cm deep. Into each cut poke a sliver of garlic, a piece of anchovy and a sprig of rosemary. Put lamb on a rack over a roasting pan, season, and sprinkle with lemon juice and olive oil. Pour stock into pan, place in oven and cook to the desired degree (approx 50–60 mins for pink), using a bulb baster to baste lamb with the pan juices every 15 mins or so.

Toss vegies in another large roasting pan with a little oil and seasonings. After lamb has been cooking for 30 mins, place vegie pan at bottom of oven and cook, turning two or three times.

When lamb is ready, remove and place in a warm spot for 15 mins, loosely covered. Check vegies and, if need be, place at top of oven to finish cooking while lamb is resting (or leave them in turned-off oven). At same time, skim fat from the pan juices and reduce juices over high heat, adding butter at the end to give a little body. Then slice lamb and serve with the vegies and pan juices.

> Oh all right—if you don't like anchovies (or garlic), just leave them out. And to check the degree of cooking, just insert a metal skewer into the thickest part of the lamb. If the juices are pink, the lamb is around medium, if clear it will be well done—but do keep in mind that as the lamb rests it will continue to cook a little.

Lamb-shank hotch-potch (for 6–8)

A favourite of my Scottish grandmother's—this may have had something to do with the fact that she had brought up, in difficult times, a family of coal miners, and a generous bowl of this was one of the rare numbers that actually filled their bellies and was cheap. (She also, when times were really tough, replaced the shanks with bacon bones—a variation which I loved.)

¼ cup vegetable oil
1½ kilos lamb shanks, French cut

Heat oil in large heavy-bottomed pot and brown shanks in two or three lots. Set aside.

2 medium-sized onions, chopped
3 celery stalks, diced
1 large swede, diced
3 medium-sized carrots, diced

Add vegies to pot and cook gently for 10 mins.

chicken stock (packet is fine)

Return shanks to pot with enough stock to cover. Simmer until shanks are tender (approx 1½–2 hours). Remove shanks and set aside.

½ small cauliflower, cut into small florets
2 zucchini, diced

Add these vegies to liquid and cook in pot for another 20 mins. Remove meat from shanks, dice, and add to the pot.

freshly ground salt and pepper
¼ green cabbage, finely sliced
1 cup thawed frozen green peas
2 tbsp chopped parsley

Check and adjust seasoning, add cabbage, peas and parsley to pot and boil for 5 mins.

Canned salmon patties for Mavis (for 4)

Mavis, a delightful 82-year-old, approached me at a cooking show and told me that her salmon patties were, unlike her mum's, always stodgy. She asked me the secret to whipping up those light and fluffy little numbers. Well, I had to admit I didn't know the answer but, after some trial and error came up with this version which I then happily cooked, just for Mavis, on 'Healthy, Wealthy & Wise'.

Preheat oven to 200°C.

a good cup of canned salmon, well drained
just under 1 cup mashed potato (see page 260)
2 heaped tbsp mayonnaise
1 spring onion, finely chopped

Mash salmon roughly and mix with the other ingredients.

flour
freshly ground salt and pepper
2 eggs
milk
1 cup breadcrumbs

Put flour in one bowl with the seasonings. In another bowl, mix the eggs with a little milk, and in a third put the crumbs. Form salmon mix into patties about 6 cm in diameter and 1 cm thick. Then flour, dip in eggwash and carefully crumb.

vegetable oil

Heat oil in a large pan which can go into the oven and seal patties on both sides. Place pan in oven and cook patties for 4–5 mins, turning halfway through.

a handful of baby rocket leaves
virgin olive oil
balsamic vinegar
tartare sauce (see page 290)
lemon wedges
chopped parsley

Place leaves on plates, sprinkle with oil and balsamic, and top with patties. Add lemon wedges and tartare, and sprinkle with parsley.

Fish fingers with home-made tomato sauce (for 6–8)

I believe that commercially produced fish fingers are one of the abominations of the western world and should be avoided at all costs. And what I would like to know is: *where do all the square fish come from?* Because it is scientifically impossible to make such neat and even fingers from any fish known to man—and I should know, because I have tried time and time again.

2 kilos ripe tomatoes, cored and coarsely chopped
500 g Granny Smith apples, peeled, cored and coarsely chopped
500 g onions, peeled and coarsely chopped
1¼ cups white vinegar
400 g sugar
3 tsp allspice
2 tsp ground cloves
2 tbsp salt
1 pinch cayenne
freshly ground black pepper

Make the sauce at least a couple of days beforehand. Put all the ingredients in a heavy-bottomed pot, mix well and simmer for 1½ hours. Then blend, allow to cool, and put in sterilised jars or bottles (or, if you are using the sauce within a week, in a bucket).

500 g boneless, skinless firm fish fillets, such as blue eye cod, groper or snapper

Cut fish into even 'fingers' across the fillet.

1–2 cups flour
salt and pepper
2 eggs
¼ cup milk
2 cups fresh breadcrumbs

Put flour in one bowl, the eggs and milk in another, and crumbs in a third. Flour the fish fingers, then dip them in the eggwash and crumb carefully. Then set aside until ready to cook.

4 cups vegetable oil
salt
lemon wedges

Heat oil to 180°C in a wok or deep-sided pot, and cook the fish fingers in three or four lots (don't overcrowd). Drain well, salt and serve with lemon wedges and bowls of the tomato sauce.

> **A deepfrying thermometer is a worthwhile investment but, if you don't happen to own one, you can just throw in a cube of bread to check when the oil is ready. If the cube sinks to the bottom the oil is not hot enough, if the cube shrivels up and dies within seconds, it is obviously too hot but, if it sizzles gently and turns golden around the edges in a minute or so, you are ready for action.**

Dad's day

The Hewitson family were not the greatest of fishermen, although I do remember spending many a peaceful day on the piers and wharves of New Zealand, pole in hand, waiting for that elusive bite. But, to be honest, those bites were few and far between, in fact, I can't actually remember ever catching anything. (My brother Don did a little better: I certainly remember him, on one auspicious occasion, catching my finger with his hook during the middle of a highly complicated casting process.)

Still, even if we were not the greatest fishing family one thing we could do was cook the blessed stuff. On most occasions, this meant little more than a quick dusting of flour before pan-frying with butter, lemon juice and chopped parsley. But on very special days, Dad would don the apron and whip up the family favourite—good old-fashioned fish and chips. Of course, these were not just any old fish and chips, because he not only made large hand cut chips, which actually tasted of potato (unlike today's commercial versions which taste of nothing in particular), but also produced a wonderful crispy beer batter—a recipe which is still used to this day by family and friends alike and which also featured on the menu of my 'Last Aussie Fishcafs'.

Johnny Hewitson's fish and chips (for 4)

4 large floury potatoes, peeled

Cut spuds into thick chips lengthways, place under running water and leave until the water runs clear. Drain and dry carefully.

4 cups vegetable oil

Heat oil in a wok or deep-sided pot to 160°C and cook the chips for 4–5 mins, until lightly coloured but not brown. Drain well and set aside.

1 stubby of lager (330 ml), freshly opened
cold water
½ tsp salt
2 tsp baking powder
350–400 g self-raising flour

Put beer in a large bowl with half as much water. Mix salt, baking powder and flour together, then whisk into beer, little by little, mixing continually. (Do this slowly and don't ever stop mixing.) When batter coats a finger lightly, set aside.

salt

Reheat oil to 180°–190°C and fry chips until golden. Drain well, sprinkle with salt and keep warm in oven.

8 x 80 g pieces of boneless, skinless fish
lemon wedges
tartare sauce (see page 290)

Dip fish pieces into the batter and fry in 2 lots until golden. Drain well on paper towels, salt and serve with the chips, lemon and tartare.

> Just a couple of hints—a deep-frying thermometer is pretty essential for this dish. And to stop the fish sinking to the bottom and sticking, use tongs to hold each battered piece until it floats before letting it go completely into the hot oil. Also, most extra-fresh fish works well but my favourite varieties would have to be flathead, King George whiting and snapper.

Tartare sauce

Home-made tartare (even made with bought mayo) will always be far superior to the pre-made numbers. Just start off with 1 cup of mayonnaise and add a generous squeeze of lemon, ½ tbsp chopped capers, 2 chopped gherkins, 2 tsp chopped parsley and 1 tbsp very finely chopped red onion.

Fishermen's baskets circa 1969

Although I can be quite a fan of fried food (as long as it is not dripping with oil, and the oil itself is spotlessly clean), there was a period in my life when I could hardly face the thought of anything which had even gone near a deep-fryer. And this aversion had nothing whatsoever to do with allergies or even the thought that a diet of fried food, fried food and fried food was maybe not the perfect way to eat.

Instead, as they would say in the movies, it started with a particularly vicious storm that threatened to shut the doors of a New Zealand restaurant where I was working at the time. Thankfully, by late afternoon the storm had abated somewhat and the pretty resilient Saturday night crowd turned up as per their bookings. After negotiating the fallen trees and the overflowing gutters, they soon settled into the spirit of things and appeared quite content. Then disaster struck in the kitchen. A stream of water suddenly gushed out of the overhead exhaust system into the fryer. A combination of water and hot oil is, of course, highly dangerous, so there were many sighs of relief when, after about ten minutes of threatened eruptions, the fryer settled down and it was back to churning out 'Fishermen's Baskets', those awful yet oh-so-popular restaurant numbers from the late sixties.

Next day the storm had disappeared but, just in case there was still water in the exhaust system, the maintenance man was asked to check. And can you imagine his surprise when he found himself face to face with one very frightened possum. Obviously, the less said about the previous night's 'water' the better, but I do think it's pretty easy to understand why I immediately developed the aforementioned aversion to the deep-fryer and anything that had even passed within 10 feet of it.

Yabby and cheese crepes (for 4–6)

Do you remember when seafood crepes were all the go? Seemingly featured on every restaurant menu, they quickly became the darling of the home cook and, dare I say it, went downhill from there. Because, what both restaurant and home chefs quickly forgot was that no matter whether you used a spicy tomato or mornay sauce, or just some cheese and cream as in this recipe, the quality and freshness of the seafood was all-important. So forget those marinara and seafood mixes, and instead think the best prawns, crabs, yabbies, scampi or oysters and, if you have just won Lotto, the odd chunk of crayfish. Or instead, as I have done here, use just one of the above.

4–6 dozen yabbies, depending on their size
beer

Bring a large pot of lightly salted water to the boil and add the yabbies, along with a generous slurp of beer. Cook until yabbies change colour and are firm when squeezed. Remove and dunk in cold water. Leave until cool and then drain well. Peel and remove black track. Set aside.

105 g flour
2 eggs
300 ml milk
good pinch of salt
good pinch of sugar

At same time, make the crepes. Put the flour in a bowl, make a well in centre and add the eggs. Beat together gradually with a wooden spoon. Add milk, little by little, whisking continually, then add the salt and sugar. Leave batter to stand for 1 hour.

30 g butter

Melt butter in a crepe pan and whisk into the prepared batter. Then make 8–12 crepes by pouring a small amount of batter into pan and cooking on both sides, turning when brown spots appear. (Any leftover batter can be covered tightly and refrigerated for another day.)

Preheat overhead grill.

grated tasty cheese
thick cream

In a large, square ovenproof dish, lay a crepe at one end and top with some yabbies, some grated cheese and a sprinkling of cream. Roll up, position seam underneath, and repeat until dish is full. Sprinkle more cheese and cream over the top and cook under grill until golden and bubbling.

Kippers with a Lyonnaise potato salad

(for 4)

vegetable oil
4 kippers

Put a little oil in a large non-stick pan and fry the kippers, two at a time, for 3–4 mins on each side. Keep warm in a low oven.

10–12 small waxy potatoes, scrubbed and boiled until just tender
1 large onion, sliced

At same time, in another large pan, sauté the potatoes and onion until golden. Keep them warm in the oven too.

mustard vinaigrette (see page 210)
chopped parsley

Divide potato sauté between 4 plates, top with a kipper and sprinkle the lot with the vinaigrette and parsley.

> ❝ I know kippers are traditionally breakfast fare, but this is terrific for a light lunch or brunch. And, if you can find them, Spring's kippers (from South Australia) are brilliant. ❞

Pork stroganoff (for 4)

3 pork fillets, trimmed of all fat and sinew
vegetable oil
freshly ground salt and pepper

1 garlic clove, chopped
8 button mushrooms, sliced
1 large onion, sliced

1 cup beef stock (packet is fine)
1 heaped tbsp Dijon mustard
1 tsp mild paprika
freshly ground salt and pepper
2 tbsp chopped parsley

2 tbsp sour cream
fettuccine
chopped parsley

Rub the fillets with oil, season and grill them or pan-fry until just pink in the centre. Set aside, loosely covered, in a warm spot.

At the same time, in another large pan, heat a little oil in a large, heavy-bottomed pot and sauté vegies until soft.

Add these to pot and simmer until of a sauce-like consistency.

Slice the pork and add to the pot along with the sour cream. Bring to just below the boil and serve on fettuccine (or rice) with a sprinkling of parsley.

> **Another of those old restaurant favourites, where the meat was invariably overcooked and chewy. This version succeeds because the meat is cooked separately and then sliced. And, if you are feeling in a traditional sort of mood, in Russia stroganoff is served with *kartoplia solimkoi*—which may sound fancy but are, in essence, very thin crispy matchstick chips.**

A modern-day pea and ham soup (for 6–8)

4 large potatoes, peeled and chopped
4 large onions, peeled and chopped
2 leeks, well washed and chopped
1–2 smoked pork hocks
1 tbsp chicken stock powder

1 kilo super-fresh snowpeas or sugar peas, topped and tailed

a little cream
freshly ground salt and pepper

Put all this in a large heavy pot, cover with water and simmer for about 40 mins. Remove hocks and when cool enough to handle, peel and discard skin, remove and dice meat and set aside in a warm spot.

Bring contents of pot to rapid boil, add peas, bring back to boil and blend or process immediately.

Return soup to pot with the cream and the reserved ham and check seasoning. Serve soup the minute it boils with a swirl of extra cream on top.

> **When blending, keep some of the liquid back, only adding if the soup is too thick.**

Asparagus soup with a touch of orange (for 4)

For years I would not touch asparagus, because I thought it was limp and mushy like the canned stuff. And even after I discovered that asparagus was really crispy and crunchy, I still thought that asparagus soup was a disaster because most of my fellow chefs thought of it as a way to use up the woody stalks. But when cooked with the best bits, as in this recipe, I am pleased to say asparagus soup can be truly delectable.

vegetable oil **1 large potato, peeled and cubed** **2 medium-sized onions, peeled and cubed**	Heat a little oil in a large pot and sauté vegies over low heat until onion is soft.
¼ cup freshly squeezed orange juice **chicken stock (packet is fine)** **freshly ground salt and pepper**	Add to the pot the orange juice and enough stock to cover vegies well. Season, and boil for 10 mins.
2–3 bunches medium thick asparagus	Prepare asparagus by bending spears until they snap and then discarding the bottom parts. Peel upper section with a sharp knife or vegie peeler, and cut each into three pieces. Add to boiling liquid in pot and cook for 4–5 mins. Then blend until smooth, return to pan and bring back to the boil.
½ cup yoghurt **strips of zest from 1 orange** **1 tbsp chopped parsley** **orange juice to taste**	Mix yoghurt, zest and parsley, along with the juice to taste into soup. Serve in bowls, with a dollop of yoghurt on top.

A few asparagus tips

- Only buy asparagus when the tips are tightly closed and the spears are firm and crisp. To test, wait until the greengrocer's back is turned and then bend a spear: if it snaps crisply, it is worth buying, if not turn your mind to something else. (Prime season September–December.)
- Asparagus, more than almost any other vegie, needs to be ultra fresh to be good. So don't be tempted by out-of-season imports— normally from Asia or America, they are almost always lacking in flavour due to their long journey.
- To keep asparagus, simply place upright in a tall container with the bottom parts of the stalks in very cold water, but only for a day or two.
- Forget those silly asparagus steamers. Instead, cook your asparagus in plenty of lightly salted, rapidly boiling water, making sure you don't overcrowd the pot. And if serving it cold, remove from the pot the minute the water returns to the boil and then plunge into iced water.

Corned beef bubble and squeak (for 6–8)

Preheat oven to 220°C.

rock salt
2 large potatoes, scrubbed
2 medium-sized sweet potatoes, scrubbed
¼ butternut pumpkin

Lay a generous layer of rock salt on a tray. Place vegies on top and bake in oven until tender when pierced with a skewer. Set aside and, when cool enough to handle, peel and coarsely mash.

1 large onion, sliced
¼ green cabbage, sliced
vegetable oil

Sauté onion and cabbage in a little hot oil for 4–5 mins. Then add to above mash and mix in well.

500 g cooked corned beef, cubed (see below)
2 eggs
freshly ground pepper

Mix these ingredients into mash and form into 6–8 patties approx. 10 cm in diameter and 2–3 cm thick.

flour
vegetable oil

Flour patties of bubble and squeak lightly and seal on both sides in a lightly oiled frying pan. Place in oiled baking dish and cook in the oven until crusty on both sides, turning once or twice (approx. 10 mins).

6–8 eggs
½ green cabbage, finely sliced
tomato relish or chutney
vegetable oil
chopped parsley

Fry or poach the eggs, and sauté the cabbage briefly in a pan in a little oil. Place cabbage on plates, top with the patties, chutney and eggs, and sprinkle with parsley.

" **To cook corned beef, place in a pot, cover with cold water and bring to a gentle boil. Discard this water, rinse both meat and pot and cover again with fresh cold water. Add 1 large onion and 1 large carrot, both quartered, ½ cup white vinegar, 1 tsp mustard seeds, 6 cloves, 2 garlic cloves and 1 tbsp brown sugar. Then simmer gently for approx 1 hour per kilo of meat. When tender, turn off heat and let meat cool in the liquid.** "

YORKSHIRE
TEA ROOMS
Shepherds of Shambles
The Noted Jewellers of York
Truffles

The bashing of the neep

The swede is a vegetable which has been rarely treated with much respect. The French serve them to their cattle, Aussies just plain ignore them and even the great cooking author, Jane Grigson, advised us that they were a vegie to be avoided at all costs.

Yet the swede, the result of crossbreeding a cabbage and a turnip, can be truly delicious. My father, a passionate gardener, always said they weren't much good until after the first frosts—a fact which is reflected in their name, which suggests the swede's ability to thrive in the icy soil of countries like Sweden.

Swedes are also a hit in Scotland, where the natives have developed the rather strange habit of calling the poor thing a neep and then bashing (mashing) the hell out of it. This rough purée is then traditionally served with that other Scottish classic, haggis, along with a decent jolt of whisky, preferably a single malt. Sadly, even though of Scottish heritage I must admit that I am not a great fan of haggis and am far more likely to serve my neeps with a good sausage or three. But to compensate for such behaviour, I could always have a wee dram of the Macallan 12-year-old or my father's favourite, Laphroaig, but I must say a glass of my very best pinot would be even better.

Country sausages with bashed neeps

(for 4)

8 thick country sausages

Blanch bangers in a pot of simmering water until just firm when squeezed. Drain and set aside.

2–3 swedes, peeled
soft unsalted butter
freshly ground salt and pepper

Cut swedes into even cubes and cook in lightly salted water until tender. Drain well, mash coarsely and stir in plenty of butter and seasonings.

vegetable oil

At same time, pan-fry, grill or BBQ the sausages until brown all over.

chopped parsley

Mound the bashed neeps on 4 plates, place sausages alongside, sprinkle with parsley, and if you are feeling really naughty why not plop another piece of butter on top of the mash.

In search of a real Aussie dish

On radio one Australia Day, I was asked to come up with a true-blue Aussie recipe. And, I must admit, it was quite a task.

Obviously, I could have just given the Huey version of a Vegemite sandwich (Vegie on both sides and tasty cheese in between), but I had the vague idea that this was not quite what they were looking for. And while roast lamb and three veg was another obvious choice, with its strong Anglo-Saxon roots that could hardly be deemed to be true-blue. Even the pav, which we claim to be our very own, is also claimed by those upstarts across the Tasman as their very own. While Paul Hogan's famous prawns on the barbie are nothing special without a splash of sauce or marinade with a distinctive Asian or Mediterranean bent.

But eventually it dawned on me—this is actually what Australian food is about. Sure, it may not be completely original and may include influence and flavours from throughout the world, but it is in essence this mixture which makes modern Oz cooking so appealing. And then, just to confuse the issue, I actually did give a true-blue Aussie dish.

Beer damper

(for 1 loaf)

Preheat oven to 220°C.

3 cups self-raising flour
1 level tsp salt
¾ cup milk
¾ cup draught beer

Mix flour and salt together. Add enough of the liquids to form a thick, sticky dough.

extra flour

Dust hands with flour and form dough into a round loaf. Dust lightly with flour then cook in oven for approx. 45 mins or until it sounds hollow when base is tapped with knuckles.

I hate desserts

ACTUALLY, THIS IS not quite true. What I really hate is making desserts, because you have to follow the recipe and even weigh those bloody ingredients. And while in most things in life I can be as disciplined as the next guy, when it comes to cooking (as you may have, surprise, surprise, noticed) I am more of the handful-of-this, slurp-of-that school.

Still, there are some desserts I don't mind whipping up, most of which are, of course, pretty simple little numbers. But I would also have to say that when the end result is fail-safe, even I can be tempted on occasion to measure that odd bit of flour and sugar.

- Vanilla bean ice-cream
- Peach Melba shortbreads

- Italian raspberry trifle
- Christmas ice-cream pudding
- Me mum's pavlova
- Gateau of crepes with apple and almond filling
- Poor Suzette
- A hot chocolate mint pudding
- Chocolate cream caramel
- George's chocolate marshmallow ice-cream
- Tamarillo upside-down cobbler
- Cherry clafoutis
- Barbecued pineapple with spiced rum butter sauce
- Hot fruit salad with a brûlée glaze
- Poached figs with Armagnac syrup
- The simplest apple tart in the world
- Huey's hot banana and passionfruit split
- Paris brest stuffed with fresh fruit and cream
- Bread and butter pudding
- George Biron's rhubarb and jasmine fool

Vanilla bean ice-cream

6 egg yolks
250 g caster sugar

Whisk egg yolks and sugar in a stainless-steel bowl until pale and thick.

250 ml milk
seeds from 1 vanilla bean

Put these in a heavy-bottomed pot and heat to just below boiling point. Then whisk the milk into the egg mixture and cook over simmering water until the custard coats a wooden spoon.

250 ml double cream

Cool custard over ice. Mix in the cream and churn in an ice-cream machine, following the maker's instructions.

Peach Melba shortbreads (for 4)

The Peach Melba was created by the king of chefs, Auguste Escoffier, in honour of Australia's own Dame Nellie (he also created Melba Toast for her when she had partaken of too many portions and was consequently on a diet).

Like almost all great recipes, this is a simple combination of the very finest, freshest ingredients. But sadly, it is also a recipe which has been abused and misused, with many a cook throwing together canned peaches and frozen raspberries and then having the cheek to call the result Peach Melba.

Preheat oven to 160°C.

125 g plain flour
65 g cornflour
65 caster sugar
¼ tsp vanilla essence

To make biscuit dough, first combine flours and sugar and then mix in the vanilla.

130 g soft unsalted butter

Rub butter into above mixture to form a soft dough and then roll out to 1 cm thick. Cut into rounds with a pastry cutter approx. 8 cm in diameter. Put these on a greased oven tray and cook for 15–20 mins. Place on a rack to cool.

50 g caster sugar
1 litre water
½ cinnamon stick
¼ lemon, sliced

Put these in a large pot and stir until sugar dissolves.

4 fresh peaches, unpeeled

Add peaches to syrup, weight with a plate and simmer very gently for 5 mins. Turn off heat and leave to cool in the liquid, turning frequently. When cool, peel, stone and cut in half. Return to liquid until needed.

best vanilla ice-cream, bought or home-made (see page 307)

Allow ice-cream to soften slightly then form into 4 rounds with a pastry cutter approx. 6 m in diameter. Return to freezer on a tray in one layer.

2 punnets raspberries
a little sugar
Framboise (raspberry liqueur) or brandy

Pick out the best half of the raspberries and set aside. Purée the rest with sugar and Framboise to taste.

icing sugar
4 mint sprigs

To serve, place shortbreads on 4 plates and top each with ice-cream rounds, then 2 peach halves, a scattering of whole raspberries and a sprinkling of raspberry sauce. Garnish with a dusting of icing sugar and a sprig of mint.

Italian raspberry trifle (for 10–12)

Chocolate sponge

Preheat oven to 180°C.

5 eggs
150 g caster sugar

Put these in a stainless-steel bowl and whisk over boiling water until just warm. Take off heat and whisk until doubled in volume, pale and foaming.

35 g unsalted butter, melted and cooled
150 g plain flour, sifted
1 tbsp Dutch cocoa

Mix a little of the egg mixture into the butter and then pour this back into the remaining egg mix. Fold through carefully and then, also carefully, fold in the flour and cocoa. Pour into a greased cake tin and bake for 25–30 mins. Unmould and cool on rack.

Mascarpone cream

7 eggs
300 g caster sugar
30 ml brandy
30 ml Frangelico (Italian hazelnut liqueur)

Put these ingredients in a stainless-steel bowl and whisk over a saucepan of simmering water for 15–20 mins, until light and fluffy.

2 gelatine leaves
2–3 tsp water

Dissolve gelatine in water and add to above custard. Cool over ice.

500 g mascarpone
500 ml cream

Whisk these into the cooled custard and set aside.

Coffee syrup
1 cup hot black coffee
1 cup caster sugar
20 ml brandy

Combine these and allow to cool. Then split sponge in half and sprinkle with the coffee syrup.

To assemble
3 punnets raspberries
3 tbsp Framboise (raspberry liqueur) or Cointreau
powdered chocolate (or Dutch cocoa)

Assemble the trifle in a large bowl or individual glasses. Break the sponge into pieces and dip them into any leftover syrup. Sprinkle the raspberries with the liqueur. Then make layers of the mascarpone cream, the berries and the chocolate sponge continuing until bowl is full and ending with mascarpone. Sprinkle with the chocolate or cocoa.

> **You could use other berries (or a mixture), or even stewed rhubarb, plums or tamarillos.**

Christmas ice-cream pudding (for 10+)

This was one of 'Healthy, Wealthy & Wise's' greatest hits, with strangers even stopping me in the street to ask for the recipe. I was, of course, happy to oblige and began carrying a box of recipe sheets with me wherever I went (only joking, folks). But, jokes aside, it is a terrific simple Christmas dessert which can truly be whipped up at the drop of a hat.

2 cups mixed dried fruits 100 g chopped glacé pineapple 100 g chopped glacé cherries 50 g chopped glacé ginger zest of 2 oranges ¾ cup chocolate bits 2 tbsp brandy 2 tbsp Grand Marnier	Mix everything together.
4 litres softened bought vanilla ice-cream	Add fruit mixture to ice-cream and combine well. Line a large bowl with kitchen wrap, spoon in the mix and cover with more wrap. Place in freezer overnight and, when required, remove top wrap, invert and wrap a hot towel around the bowl until the ice-cream comes out.

❝ **You could serve this as is or with a purée of berries sweetened with a fruit liqueur, or even with a mixture of fresh berries sprinkled generously with Grand Marnier.** ❞

Me mum's pavlova (for 8–12)

My mother, like most Australian and New Zealand housewives of her generation, made a wonderful pav which was wheeled out at any half-way special meal. She took great pride in the fact that this was a Kiwi creation and certainly got a little upset by those 'bloody Aussies' (the only time I ever heard her swear) who, according to her, had attempted to claim the credit. But that's another story and certainly not one that a coward like me is prepared to tackle. Still, whatever its origins, the pavlova is a delicious dessert, especially if piled high with kiwi fruit, strawberries and passionfruit—which to me, are the essential garnishes.

Preheat oven to 150°C.

250 g egg whites
a pinch of salt

Whisk whites with the salt until soft peaks form.

500 g caster sugar
1 tsp cream of tartar
½ tsp vinegar
1 tsp vanilla essence

Add sugar to the egg whites, little by little, until peaks are firm, then fold in the rest gently. Grease an oven tray and gently shape the meringue mixture into a 7–8 cm high circle. Place in oven and cook for 1–1¼ hours, until set.

whipped cream (with a little vanilla and sugar)
kiwi fruit, peeled and sliced
passionfruit pulp
strawberries, quartered

Allow meringue to cool and then top with cream and fruit.

> **You may have to try this once or twice to get it perfect, as oven temperatures and hot spots do vary. But, just to help, if liquid is oozing the meringue is undercooked and if you can see caramelised drops or lines it has been cooked too quickly.**

Gateau of crepes with apple and almond filling

(for 8)

My first-ever kitchen experience was gained in the sixties in the Coachman Restaurant in Wellington (admittedly as a dishwasher). The restaurant was head and shoulders above anything else in New Zealand (and with the cleanest pots and pans). This was one of chef Des Britten's special desserts.

1 kilo cooking apples, peeled, cored and thickly sliced 120 g sugar	Cook apples with a little water, stirring occasionally, until tender. Then add sugar and boil for 10 mins. The purée should be thick and solid when lifted on a spoon.
2 tbsp cream 2 tbsp apple brandy (or standard brandy) ½ tsp cinnamon ½ tsp almond extract 1 tsp each grated lemon and orange zest	Mix these into the apple purée.
90 g ground almonds crepe batter (see page 292) soft butter	Make crepes, then place one on a lightly buttered ovenproof serving dish. Spread on a layer of the purée, about 5 mm thick, and sprinkle with 1 tbsp of the ground almonds. Repeat the process, finishing with a crepe.
1 tbsp slivered almonds 45 g melted butter 3 tbsp sugar	Sprinkle on the almonds, gently pour the melted butter over and sprinkle with the sugar. Set aside until needed. Preheat oven to 190°C.
60 ml apple brandy (optional)	Put gateau into oven for approx 30 mins, until heated through. Then, if you like, heat the brandy, set it alight and pour it over the top of the gateau.

> **Cut the gateau into portions, as you would an ordinary cake, and serve with plenty of whipped cream.**

Poor Suzette

Crepes Suzette is another delicious recipe which has almost disappeared from our culinary repertoire because of waiters' leanings towards pyromania. (I even remember Tiger Johnson, an old mate of mine, impressing the whole dining room when, on his first night in the restaurant industry, he not only set the crepes on fire but the tablecloth as well.) But when made correctly they really can be truly delicious and it's always a bit of fun to bring back an old favourite.

---

6 sugar cubes
2 large oranges

200 ml fresh orange juice (and I do mean fresh)
70 g unsalted butter
2 tbsp Grand Marnier
1 tbsp brandy

12 crepes (see page 292)
sugar
Grand Marnier

Rub sugar cubes hard over orange skin until they are well soaked with its oils.

Strain the juice and put in a large pan along with the sugar cubes and butter. Bring to the boil, add liqueur and brandy, and turn down to simmer.

Add the first crepe to the pan and when it is hot fold it in four and push to the side. Tip pan so that sauce runs back into centre and repeat process with another crepe. When all the pancakes are piping hot, place on 4 plates, sprinkle with a little more sugar if you like and pour some flaming Grand Marnier over them.

> **By the way, this is another creation from the king of chefs, Escoffier.**

The perfect head waiter

My first-ever visit to a three-star Michelin establishment was in the early seventies when I went to La Tour d'Argent in Paris with my sister-in-law Jean. Having spent weeks practising my French and not getting far, I was pretty relieved to discover that all the staff spoke English. In fact, our section's head waiter even had a distinct Australian lilt and explained that he had spent a number of years working in Sydney. Imagine my surprise when I revisited the restaurant a few years later, in the company of a group of English people, and discovered that the same head waiter this time had a rather plummy English accent because he had worked at the Savoy for a number of years. As yet, I have not visited with a party of Americans, but I do wonder whether that waiter would have a southern or northern accent—or maybe he'd have both!

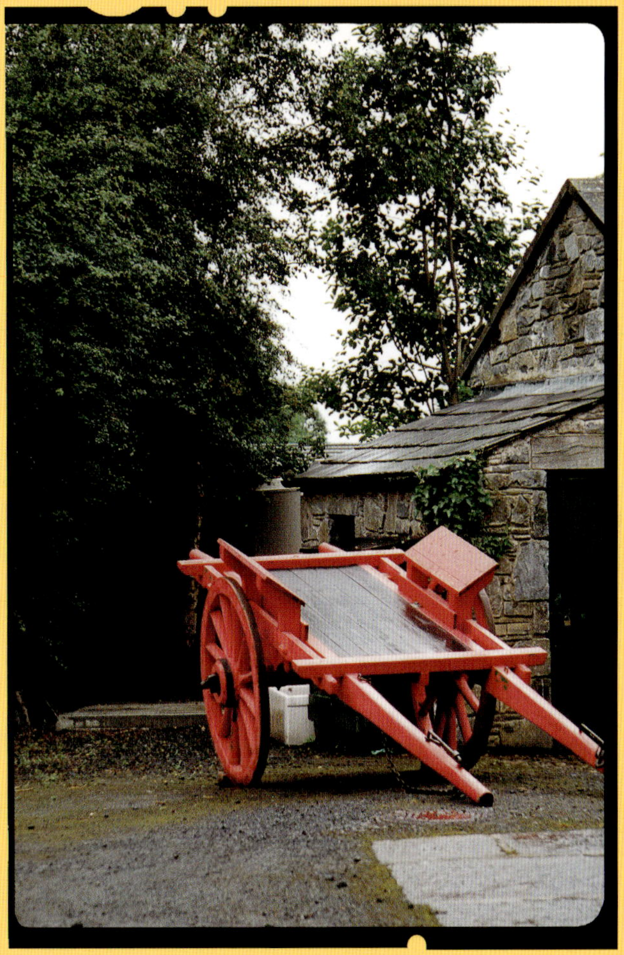

A hot chocolate mint pudding (for 6)

Halfway between a soufflé and a pudding. As with a soufflé, all utensils must be clean and dry, without even a skerrick of water.

	Preheat oven to 200°C.
180 g dark cooking chocolate **3 tbsp Crème de Menthe**	In a pan, melt these together over a very gentle heat.
4 egg yolks **90 g sugar**	Beat eggs with the sugar in an electric mixer until thick and pale. Then stir in the chocolate mix. Remove from bowl and set aside.
12 egg whites	Wash and thoroughly dry the electric mixer. Then beat whites to medium-firm peaks and gently fold in chocolate mix. Divide between 6 soufflé dishes and cook for 12 mins.
icing sugar	Dust puddings with icing sugar and serve immediately with vanilla ice-cream or whipped cream.

> **And while we're on the subject of chocolate puddings, English chef Antony Worrall Thompson makes about the simplest one. He just whips cream and thick yoghurt and then stirs in grated chocolate. Poured into individual soufflé dishes, it is chilled overnight with a sprinkling of brown sugar on top—delicious!**

Chocolate cream caramel (for 6)

	Preheat oven to 175°C.
1 cup sugar **1 cup water**	Put in a small heavy-bottomed pot and cook, swirling at regular intervals (don't whisk or stir), until caramelised but not burnt. Then pour into a large gratin dish and distribute to cover bottom.
220 g dark cooking chocolate **750 ml milk**	Melt, very gently, over low heat.
5 egg yolks **2 whites** **1½ cups sugar**	Whisk these until thick and then add to chocolate mixture.
5 amaretti biscuits (Italian almond macaroons), crushed	Sprinkle these over the caramel in the gratin dish and then top with the chocolate mix. Put in a deep baking tray on folded newspaper, and add hot water ¾ of the way up the sides of the gratin dish. Cook for approx 60 mins, until a skewer comes out clean.
whipped cream	Cool, unmould and serve with whipped cream.

George's chocolate marshmallow ice-cream

My girlfriend's father George, unlike me, loves whipping up desserts. And he is very good at it too. To the extent that his labrador Madison, who obviously shares George's love of sweet things, has to go to a health farm every time he travels overseas (which is, fortunately for Madison, on a fairly regular basis).

600 ml milk 600 ml double cream ¾ cup sugar 1 tsp vanilla sugar	Put milk and cream in a heavy-bottomed pot, place over a moderate heat and bring to just below the boil. Add both sugars and stir until dissolved.
6 egg yolks	Beat yolks until thick and pale and then gradually add to the milk mix, stirring continually. Cook either over a low heat or in a stainless-steel bowl over a pot of simmering water until custard lightly coats a wooden spoon (80°C). Remove from heat.
1 packet white marshmallows 300 g dark cooking chocolate	Add marshmallows to custard and stir until they dissolve. Add chocolate and also stir until dissolved.
2–3 tbsp Creme de Cacao	Add to custard and set aside mixture to cool. Then churn in an ice-cream machine; if you don't have one, cover and refrigerate overnight, then stir until smooth and refrigerate overnight again.

> **Vanilla sugar is made by simply storing a vanilla bean in a covered canister of caster sugar.**

> **Using this recipe, you can make truly wonderful Baci by shaping the ice-cream, once frozen, into balls and topping each one with a hazelnut. Then melt some dark chocolate, pour over the top and return to the freezer.**

Tamarillo upside-down cobbler (for 6–8)

	Preheat oven to 180°C.
500 ml water 300 g sugar 1 cinnamon stick 12 tamarillos, peeled	Bring water and sugar slowly to the boil. Add cinnamon stick, boil for 10 mins and then throw in the tamarillos, poaching them until tender (approx. 10–12 mins). Drain and place in a gratin dish.
¼ cup sugar 1 egg	Beat these until thick.
1 cup flour 1 tbsp baking powder 1 tbsp vanilla extract ½ cup milk	Add to the egg mixture and beat well with a whisk until smooth. Pour over the tamarillos and bake until golden (approx. 35–40 mins).
vanilla ice-cream	Serve as is, or leave for 10 mins and turn out. Serve with ice-cream.

" Cobblers are American puddings which are fairly similar to our sponge-topped fruit puddings, but a little lighter in texture. "

Cherry clafoutis (for 2)

	Preheat oven to 200°C.
4 eggs 100 g sugar 1 vanilla bean a pinch of salt a splash of dark rum	Beat eggs and sugar until frothy. Scrape seeds from vanilla bean and add seeds to egg mix along with the salt and rum.
100 g flour 350 ml milk	Stir above egg mixture into the flour with a whisk. Then add the milk, whisking well.
400 g pitted cherries soft butter	Grease an ovenproof dish, throw in the cherries and pour the batter over the top. Cook until golden and risen (approx. 40 mins).
icing sugar	Dust clafoutis with icing sugar before serving.

> **A delicious, yet simple, French dessert which also works well with other fruits, such as apples or pears.**

Barbecued pineapple with spiced rum butter sauce

(for 6–8)

1 small, fairly ripe pineapple	Cut into rings (see below).
1 cup brown sugar ½ cup dark rum 200 g unsalted butter a pinch each of ground nutmeg, cinnamon and allspice	Put in a small pot and simmer for 10 mins. Then keep warm on the side of the barbie or on a low heat on the stove.
lightly whipped cream	Barbecue or grill the pineapple on a ridged grill until attractively marked and hot. Then serve with the rum butter and whipped cream on top.

> **An easy way to prepare pineapple rings. Cut the pineapple into thick slices and use an appropriately sized pastry cutter to cut each slice almost at the skin. Then, with a small cutter, take out the core.**

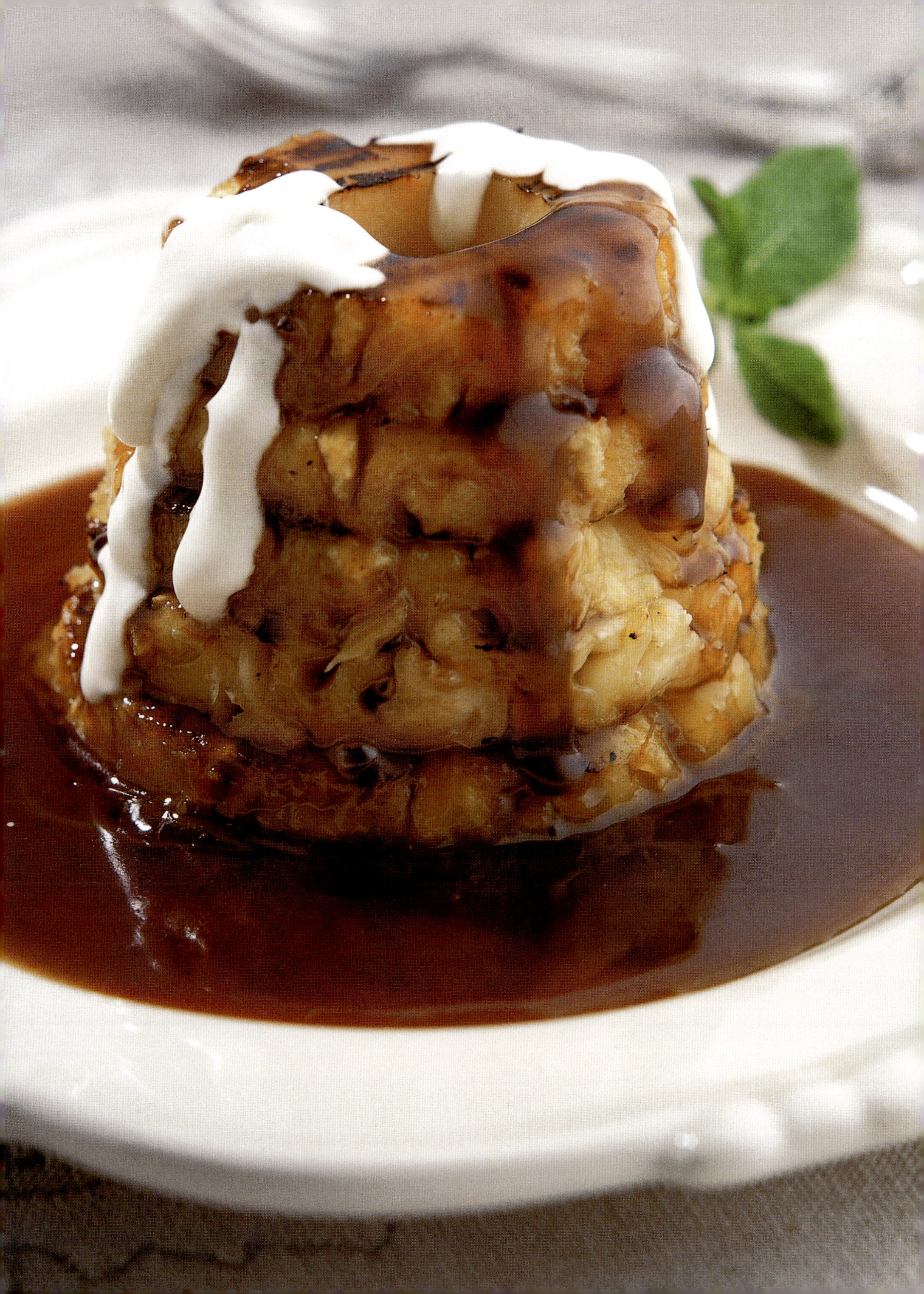

Hot fruit salad with a brûlée glaze (for 6)

½ **vanilla bean**
1 **cup cream**
5 **egg yolks**
60 g **caster sugar**

First make the brûlée. Scrape seeds from vanilla bean and add to cream. Bring to the boil. At same time, whisk yolks and sugar until thick and pale. Add hot cream to egg mixture, little by little, whisking continually. Pour back into pot and whisk until lightly thickened *(do not boil)*. Strain into bowl and refrigerate overnight.

4–5 **cups of a mixture of exotic fruit, such as mango, kiwi, paw paw, lychees, berries, etc., etc.**
3 **tbsp honey**
juice of ½ **lemon**

Peel and cut all the fruit into smallish neat slices or chunks. Then, in a pan, heat the honey and lemon juice until melted. Add fruit and heat a little.

brown sugar

Place in a gratin dish and top with the brulée mix. Sprinkle sugar over the top and caramelise with a blowtorch or under the grill.

> **You can also, instead of the brûlée mix, just whip some cream, spread it on top of the fruit and sprinkle with the brown sugar before glazing.**

Poached figs with Armagnac syrup (for 4)

4 cups water
2 cups sugar
½ lemon, finely sliced
1 cinnamon stick

12 figs, peeled but left whole
a generous splash of Armagnac
    (or cognac)

vanilla ice-cream or whipped cream
icing sugar

In a large pot, heat water and sugar until sugar dissolves. Then add lemon and cinnamon, and bring to the boil.

Add the figs to above syrup, turn off heat and add the Armagnac. Leave to cool in the liquid, turning frequently.

Cut a cross in each fig, down through the top almost to the bottom. Spread open then place 3 figs one on top of each other, like the petals of a flower. Sprinkle with a little of the poaching liquid, place a scoop of ice-cream or whipped cream on top, and dust with icing sugar.

The simplest apple tart in the world

Place a sheet of bought puff pastry on a baking tray. Peel, core and slice some cooking apples and place the slices in rows, overlapping slightly, on the pastry leaving a 1.5-cm border all round. Sprinkle the apples with sugar, dot with unsalted butter and then brush the border with a simple eggwash (egg yolk mixed with milk). Bake in a fairly hot oven until pastry border is golden-brown. Serve with whipped cream.

Huey's hot banana and passionfruit split

(for 4)

good knob of butter
4–6 bananas, peeled and sliced
pulp of 2–3 passionfruit

juice of 2 oranges
1 tbsp brown sugar
a generous splash of dark rum

8–12 scoops vanilla ice-cream
whipped cream
slivers of zest from 1 orange
4 sprigs of mint

Melt butter in a pan, add fruit and stir for 1–2 mins.

Add these to the pan, cook gently to reduce the liquid and then divide between 4 sundae dishes.

Place ice-cream on top of fruit, pipe whipped cream around, scatter with orange zest and garnish with mint.

> **If you are more of a traditionalist than me, just cut the bananas in half and be very careful, during the cooking process, that they don't collapse.**

Paris brest stuffed with fresh fruit and cream

(for 6–8)

Preheat oven to 200°C.

½ litre water
2 tsp salt
240 g unsalted butter

Bring these to the boil in a heavy-bottomed pot until all butter has melted.

2 cups plain flour

Remove from heat, add all the flour at once and stir vigorously until paste is smooth. *Don't over-beat:* this step should only take a few seconds. Allow to cool for 5 mins.

8 eggs

Transfer paste to an electric mixer and add the eggs one at a time, beating between each addition. When they have all been added, beat for a further 3 mins until smooth and glossy. Put mixture into a piping bag and make a circular cake by piping mixture on a baking sheet in a continuous circle starting with a small circle in the centre. Bake for 20–30 mins, until risen and a light golden-brown. Remove from oven, place on rack and make a small hole in each side to release any steam.

whipped cream
fruit, such as berries, kiwi fruit, mangoes, etc.

When pastry is cool, cut in half crossways and smear base with whipped cream. Then layer with chosen fruit, spread with another layer of cream and place top half on.

icing sugar

Dust with icing sugar and cut into wedges to serve.

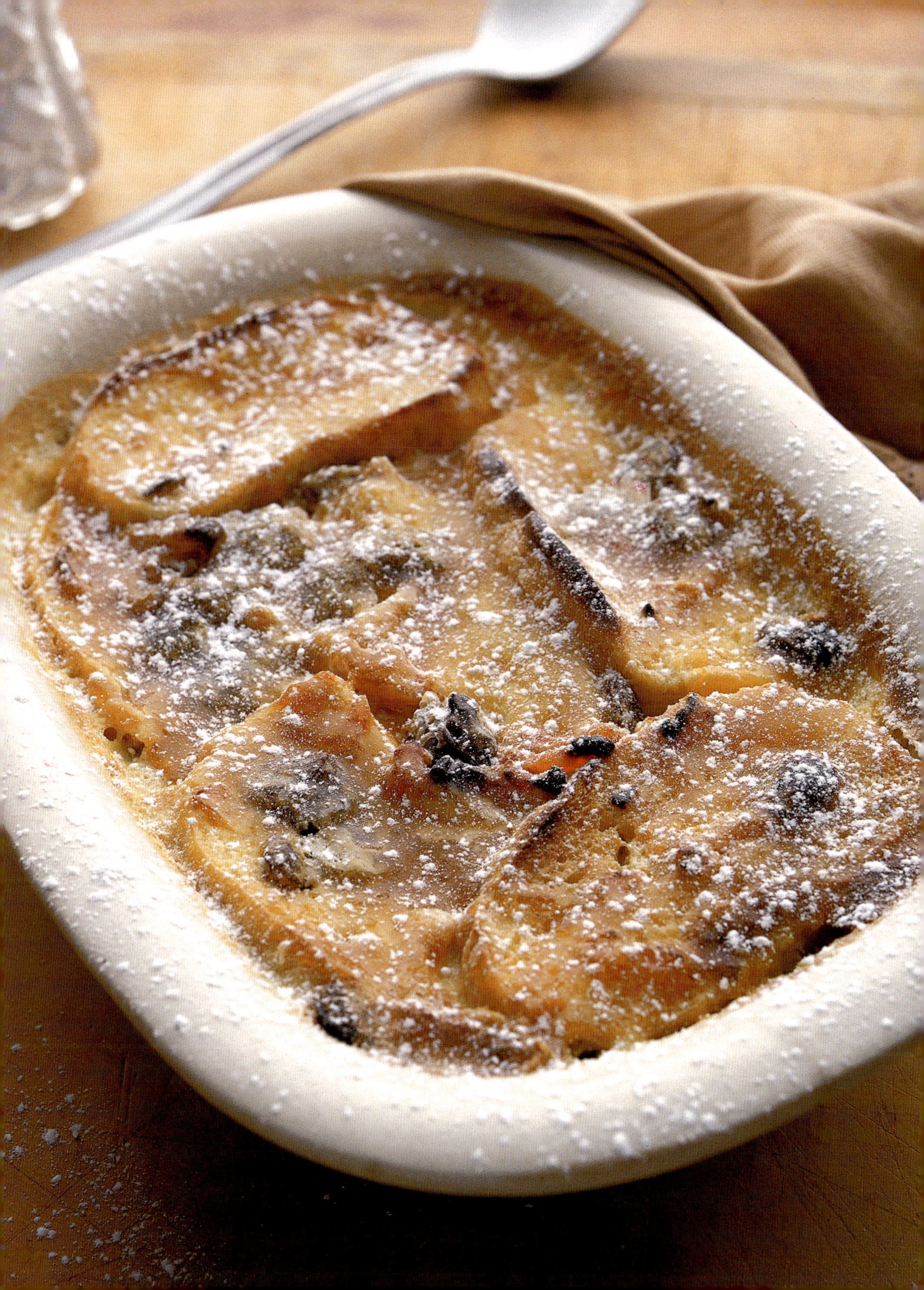

Bread and butter pudding (for 6–8)

My favourite TV program is *Pie in the Sky* (which, hopefully, will return to our screens soon). Of course, it is understandable why this is my absolute favourite—as a fan of detective novels and a passionate foodie, how could I resist a show where the detective is sensibly proportioned, just happens to be a chef, and most mysteries appear to somehow involve his restaurant?

Which brings me to bread and butter pudding. In one of my favourite episodes, detective-cum-chef Henry Crabbe was on the track of a pair of elderly female embezzlers who invariably cooked the most sublime of bread and butter puddings for their victims before proceeding to rip them off. Needless to say, our intrepid dick caught up with the pair and discovered not only that the embezzlement wasn't really their fault (what a surprise!) but that the secret ingredient of the pudding was a generous dollop of Scotland's famous Dundee marmalade. And it really does work rather well, especially in this version which is a bit of a mixture of the recipes of two of London's finest chefs, Richard Shepherd and Anton Mosimann. (Pictured on page 331.)

Preheat oven to 160°C.

8 tbsp chopped dried apricots
4 tbsp golden raisins
whisky

Put fruit in a bowl, cover with whisky and set aside to soak for 15 mins or so.

soft unsalted butter
4–6 bread rolls

Butter an oval or square gratin dish and place the fruit on the base and sprinkle with all the juices. Slice rolls thickly, butter on both sides and layer into the dish until about four-fifths full.

250 ml milk
250 ml double cream
1 vanilla bean, split
3 large eggs
125 g caster sugar

Bring milk, cream and vanilla bean to boil. At same time, whisk eggs and sugar in a mixer until thick and pale. Then, with mixer on low, add milk and cream mix to the eggs. Strain into a new bowl and then pour carefully over the bread.

Place a sheet of folded newspaper in a deep oven dish (this stops the pudding from catching on the bottom). Then carefully place the gratin dish on top and add enough boiling water to come halfway up the sides. Cook for 45–50 mins: when ready, it should have risen and be golden but still wobbly in the centre. Remove, and allow to settle for 5 mins.

3 tbsp Dundee orange marmalade (or apricot jam)
icing sugar

Melt the marmalade over a low heat, adding a little water if necessary. Then brush over the pud and dust with the icing sugar.

> **Never eat more than you can lift.**

Miss Piggy

George Biron's rhubarb and jasmine fool

(for 4)

I have always been intrigued by fools (the culinary, not human, versions). In her book *Good Things*, author Jane Grigson showed a similar interest and she presumed that the name comes from the French word 'fouler', which means to crush. But she was then forced to admit in her *Fruit Book* that this is dead-wrong, because she had since discovered that a fool is simply a whimsical bit of nonsense in the same vein as a trifle or a whim-wham (which, I am told, is a trifle without the custard).

Well, whatever the name's origins, fruit fools are a bit of fun and none more so than this version from culinary genius George Biron, whose restaurant Sunnybrae in Birregurra in south-west Victoria was, as they say in the Michelin Guide, well worth a journey. But no longer, I sadly have to report, because George has decided to shut the doors and move on to new things (where hopefully this delicious fool will also feature).

100 ml cream **1 tbsp jasmine tea leaves (not a bag)**	Warm together and then set aside to infuse.
350 g rhubarb, chopped **75 g sugar** **30 ml water**	Cook rhubarb with sugar and water in a pot until soft.
1 vanilla bean, seeds scraped out **2 tsp orange blossom water or** **1 piece orange zest**	Add these to the rhubarb and allow to cool. Remove vanilla bean.
75 g sugar **6 egg yolks**	Whisk together until thick and pale.
extra 500 ml cream **1 vanilla bean, seeds also scraped out**	Strain the jasmine infused cream into a cooking pot, add the extra cream and vanilla bean, and bring to a simmer. Stir this into egg mix, return to pot and heat gently until it coats a wooden spoon lightly—*do not boil*. Remove from heat, cool and then discard vanilla bean. Then layer, alternately with the rhubarb, into parfait glasses or a bowl.

Index

A brick-pressed Mediterranean sandwich 132
A calamari salad with eastern flavours 193
A cheat's cassoulet from the south of France 141
A crispy noodle cake with wok-fried beef and vegetables 156
A flavoursome roasted tomato and basil soup 123
A flavoursome vegetable stock 237
A hot chocolate mint pudding 318
A lamb, sweet potato and coconut curry 219
A lo-cal lamb salad with minted yoghurt 68
A minute steak in an Italian fashion 117
A minute steak of kangaroo with a tangy apple salad 170
A modern day pea and ham soup 296
A Moroccan orange, fennel and olive salad 29
A mousse of home-salted cod 245
A mozzarella salad with gazpacho overtones 207
A pasta 'omelette' with the leftovers 129
A piquant BBQ mayo 86
A pot of Italian lamb chops 118
A Provençal seafood stew with a splash of Pernod 138
A ripper warm salmon salad with anchovy mayo 192
A salad of barbecued vegies, orange couscous and harissa yoghurt 28
A salad of pink livers and spinach in a Dubonnet, orange and cranberry dressing 186
A salad of raw vegies with a garlic and herb mayo 182
A stack of northern Indian vegetable cutlets 215
A tangy apple salad 170
A vegetarian lasagne from Provence 140
A warm rabbit, orange and chorizo salad 242
Aherne's pot of seafood 14
alioli
    preparation of 246
    Sardines with sea salt and alioli 246
almond
    Gateau of crepes with apple and almond filling 314
An Asian oyster and vegetable 'omelette' 168
An Indian cucumber, tomato and onion salad with mint yoghurt 228
anchovy
    Anchovy and onion pizza from Provence (pissaladière) 136
    A ripper warm salmon salad with anchovy mayo 192
    Potato and anchovy tortilla 244
    Roasted capsicum, anchovy and soft-dried tomato salad 201
Anchovy and onion pizza from Provence (pissaladière) 136
apple
    A minute steak of kangaroo with a tangy apple salad 170
    Gateau of crepes with apple and almond filling 314
    Lamb's fry and crispy bacon with apple stew and a mustard and thyme butter 256
    Tagine of pork chops with spicy apple 30
    The simplest apple tart 328
Armagnac
    Poached figs with Armagnac syrup 327
artichoke
    Olive oil braised artichoke salad 208
asparagus
    Asparagus soup with a touch of orange 297

asparagus
    buying and cooking tips 298
    Microwave risotto with asparagus and peas 126
Asparagus soup with a touch of orange 297
avocado
    Avocado salsa 88
    BLT salad with avocado and a poached egg 179
    Kick-arse chicken tortilla with avocado salsa 88

Baby potatoes, mashed 119
Baby pumpkin stuffed with a Thai pumpkin and bean curry 145
Baci 321
bacon
    Barbecued potatoes with crispy bacon and sour cream 103
    Chicken Maryland with crispy bacon and sauce Béarnaise 268
    Lamb's fry and crispy bacon with apple stew and a mustard and thyme butter 256
Bahamian baby fish 91
Baked beans and sausages 261
balsamic
    Peppered beef salad with rocket, balsamic and parmesan 188
banana
    Honey-drenched bananas 84
    Huey's hot banana and passionfruit split 329
Bangers and mash with golden onions 260
Bar-room slaw 273
Barbecue roasted rib-eye of beef with mustard crust and horseradish sour cream 73
Barbecued beetroot salad with spicy yoghurt 108
Barbecued corn on the cob with gremolata butter 101
Barbecued octopus with olive oil roasted vegetables 189
Barbecued oysters with sausages 98
Barbecued pineapple with spiced rum butter sauce 324
Barbecued potatoes with crispy bacon and sour cream 103
Barbecued sweet corn salsa 94
Barbecued sweet potato 62
basil
    A flavoursome roasted tomato and basil soup 123
    Basil-infused olive oil 125
    Big juicy mushrooms with basil oil 106
    Lemon and basil crusted chicken salad 183
BBQ, tips for success 87
bean
    Baby pumpkin stuffed with a Thai pumpkin and bean curry 145
    Baked beans and sausages 261
    Chicken and beans in a spicy gumbo sauce 45
    Green beans with soft-dried tomatoes and crispy prosciutto 203
    Vanilla bean ice-cream 307
Béarnaise sauce 268
beef
    A crispy noodle cake with wok-fried beef and vegetables 156
    A minute steak in an Italian fashion 117
    Bangers and mash with golden onions 260
    Barbecue roasted rib-eye of beef with mustard crust and horseradish sour cream 73
    Beef in Guinness 5
    Beef on a stick 76
    Blackened fillet steak on a bed of corn and peas with garlic and chilli butter 54
    Chateaubriand of beef fillet with a mustard, soy and fresh herb crust and roasted kumara mash 270
    Corned beef 299
    Corned beef bubble and squeak 299
    Fidel Castro's favourite Cuban beef salad 184
    Huey's terrific steak sanga
    Huey's true blue Aussie burger 272
    Mixed grill—Italian style 74
    Peppered beef salad with rocket, balsamic and parmesan 188
    Peppered steak casserole 271
    Spag bog with a beef and chicken liver ragu 277
    Steak diane 276
    T-bone steak with Maggie Beer's slow roasted onions 72
    Texas style BBQ baby back ribs 80
    Thai beef and cranberry salad 185
    Tripe and onions 259
    Tuscan fillet of beef with mushrooms and olive butter 67
Beef in Guinness 5
Beef on a stick 76
Beer damper 304
beetroot
    Barbecued beetroot salad with spicy yoghurt 108
Big juicy mushrooms with basil oil 106
Black pudding with Irish creamy mash (champ) 7
Blackened fillet steak on a bed of corn and peas with garlic and chilli butter 54
BLT salad with avocado and a poached egg 179
Blue cheese stuffing 278
Blue swimmer crabs with aromatics 171
bok choy
    Stir-fry of baby bok choy, snowpeas and shiitake mushrooms 154
Boxty with smoked salmon and horseradish and chive sour cream 11
Braised lamb shanks with osso bucco sauce and gremolata 280
bread
    Beer damper 304
    Bread and butter pudding 332
    Homemade pita bread 37
    Indian pork and veal koftas in flat bread 78
    K-Paul's cheese and chilli bread 56
    Myrtle Allen's Irish brown bread 9
    Pa amb tomaquet (bread and tomato) 248
Bread and butter pudding 332
breadcrumbs
    how to make 267
brest
    Paris brest stuffed with fresh fruit and cream 330
broad beans
    how to prepare 235
Brown lemon and caper butter 258
brûlée glaze 326
    Hot fruit salad with a brûlée glaze 326
Brussel sprout colcannon 10
bugs
    Roasted bugs with a red capsicum butter 114
butter
    Barbecued corn on the cob with gremolata butter 101
    Barbecued pineapple with spiced rum butter sauce 324
    Blackened fillet steak on a bed of corn and peas with garlic and chilli butter 54
    Bread and butter pudding 332
    Huey's favourite BBQ butter 71
    Lamb's brain with a brown lemon and caper butter 258
    Lamb's fry and crispy bacon with apple stew and a mustard and thyme butter 256
    Roasted bugs with a red capsicum butter 114

Salmon on a bed of charred radicchio with a tapenade butter 89
Spatchcocked chicken with garlic butter and fresh basil 83
Tuscan fillet of beef with mushrooms and olive butter 67
Butterflied leg of lamb in a mustardy marinade 62

Cajun groper fillets with fried watermelon and raita 46
cajun roux
    preparation of 44
calamari
    A calamari salad with eastern flavours 193
    preparation of 93
    Stuffed squid (calamari) with Sicilian parsley, garlic and olive oil dressing 92
Calamari salad with eastern flavours 193
Calypso chook 84
Candied sweet potatoes 62
Canned salmon patties for Mavis 285
Cantonese-style whole baby fish 150
capsicum
    Curried root vegetable soup with purée of roasted capsicum 217
    Parmesan crumbed veal with roasted capsicum salad 119
    Roasted bugs with a red capsicum butter 114
    Roasted capsicum, anchovy and soft-dried tomato salad 201
caramel
    Chocolate cream caramel 319
Carpaccio of mushrooms with rocket, parmesan and virgin olive oil 195
carrot
    Middle eastern chickpea, date and carrot salad 209
Cashel blue cheese and vegetable soup 6
casseroles and stews
    A cheat's cassoulet from the south of France 141
    Aherne's pot of seafood 14
    A pot of Italian lamb chops 118
    A Provençal seafood stew with a splash of Pernod 138
    Beef in Guinness 5
    Dublin coddle 12
    Harira with kefta and ham hock 34
    Irish stew with a touch of Paris 3
    Lamb tagine with sweet potatoes 38
    Peppered steak casserole 271
    Pork stroganoff 295
    Tagine of pork chops with spiced apples 30
champ (Irish mashed potatoes)
    Black pudding with Irish creamy mash (champ) 7
Char Siu rack of lamb 146
Chateaubriand of beef fillet with a mustard, soy and fresh herb crust and roasted kumara mash 270
cheese
    A fillet of roasted salmon on pesto mash with shavings of parmesan 115
    A mozzarella salad with gazpacho overtones 207
    Carpaccio of mushrooms with rocket, parmesan and virgin olive oil 195
    Cashel blue cheese and vegetable soup 6
    Crumbed cutlets with a blue cheese stuffing 278
    Eggplant almost parmigiano 130
    K-Paul's cheese and chilli bread 56
    parmesan, buying and storage 195
    Parmesan crumbed veal with roasted capsicum salad 119
    Peppered beef salad with rocket, balsamic and parmesan 188
    Prawn and cheese hush puppies 52
    shaving tip 115
    Twice-baked cheese soufflés with plumped oysters and blue mascarpone cream 120
    Yabby and cheese crepes 292
Cheese soufflés with plumped oysters and blue mascarpone cream 120
Chermoula-marinated chicken in the style of Huey 19
Cherry clafoutis 323
chicken
    A salad of pink livers and spinach in a Dubonnet, orange and cranberry dressing 186
    Calypso chook 84
    Chermoula-marinated chicken in the style of Huey 19
    Chicken and beans in a spicy gumbo sauce 45
    Chicken breast fillets in a fresh orange and soy marinade 158
    Chicken crackling 149
    Chicken in cava 238
    Chicken Maryland with crispy bacon and sauce Béarnaise 268
    Chicken satays with macadamia nut sauce 155
    Chicken schnitzel with pesto mash 267
    Chicken with dates and a lemon yoghurt 224
    Chicken with sherry vinegar and cloves of garlic 240
    Japanese chicken 'sausage' with stirfried snowpeas 174
    Kick-arse chicken tortilla with avocado salsa 88
    Lemon and basil crusted chicken salad 183
    Malay chicken wings 162
    Meena Pathak's chicken korma 221
    My ever-changing warm salad 181
    Real simple chicken breast with a lemon-spiked herb marinade 85
    Roast chicken 262
    Roast chicken and crudités in lettuce cups 266
    Spag bog with a beef and chicken liver ragu 277
    Spatchcocked chicken with garlic butter and fresh basil 83
    Thai garlic and chilli drumsticks 163
    Vietnamese chicken salad 148
Chicken and beans in a spicy gumbo sauce 45
Chicken breast fillets in a fresh orange and soy marinade 158
Chicken crackling 149
Chicken in cava 238
Chicken Maryland with crispy bacon and sauce Béarnaise 268
Chicken satays with macadamia nut sauce 155
Chicken schnitzel with pesto mash 267
Chicken with dates and a lemon yoghurt 224
Chicken with sherry vinegar and cloves of garlic 240
chickpea
    Middle eastern chickpea, date and carrot salad 209
    preparation of 39
chilli
    Blackened fillet steak on a bed of corn and peas with garlic and chilli butter 54
    K-Paul's cheese and chilli bread 56
    Thai garlic and chilli drumsticks 163
chocolate
    A hot chocolate mint pudding 318
    Chocolate cream caramel 319
    Chocolate whip 318
    George's chocolate marshmallow ice-cream 320
Chocolate cream caramel 319
Chocolate whip 318
chorizo (Spanish sausage)
    A warm rabbit, orange and chorizo salad 242
Christmas ice-cream pudding 312
cobbler

Tamarillo upside-down cobbler 322
Cochin prawns in a spiced coconut sauce 213
coconut
    A lamb, sweet potato and coconut curry 219
    Cochin prawns in a spiced coconut sauce 213
cod
    A mousse of home-salted cod 245
coddle
    Dublin coddle 12
Coleslaw
    Me mum's coleslaw recipe 108
corn
    Barbecued corn on the cob with gremolata butter 101
    Barbecued sweet corn salsa 94
    Blackened fillet steak on a bed of corn and peas with garlic and chilli butter 54
    Oyster and corn macque choux 42
Corned beef 299
Corned beef bubble and squeak 299
Country sausages with bashed neeps 302
couscous
    Couscous salad 22
    A salad of barbecued vegies, orange couscous and harissa yoghurt 28
Couscous salad 22
cranberry
    A salad of pink livers and spinach in a Dubonnet, orange and cranberry dressing 186
    Thai beef and cranberry salad 185
crepes
    Gateau of crepes with apple and almond filling 314
    preparation of 292
    Yabby and cheese crepes 292
Crispy bacon with barbecued potatoes and sour cream 103
Crumbed cutlets with a blue cheese stuffing 278
Crumbed veal with parmesan and roasted capsicum salad 119
cucumber
    An Indian cucumber, tomato and onion salad with mint yoghurt 228
    Mint and cucumber raita 220
Curried root vegetable soup with purée of roasted capsicum 217
curry
    A lamb, sweet potato and coconut curry 219
    Baby pumpkin stuffed with a Thai pumpkin and bean curry 145
    Curried root vegetable soup with purée of roasted capsicum 217
    Mussels in a light green curry broth 161

dhal
    Sudhakaran Meetinay's dhal makhani 229
date
    Chicken with dates and lemon yoghurt 224
    Middle eastern chickpea, date and carrot salad 209
Dead-easy duck 165
desserts
    A hot chocolate mint pudding 318
    Baci 321
    Barbecued pineapple with spiced rum butter sauce 324
    Bread and butter pudding 332
    Cherry clafoutis 323
    Chocolate cream caramel 319
    Chocolate whip 318
    Christmas ice-cream pudding 312
    Gateau of crepes with apple and almond filling 314
    George Biron's rhubarb and jasmine fool 334
    George's chocolate marshmallow ice-cream 320
    Hot fruit salad with a brûlée glaze 326
    Huey's hot banana and passionfruit split 329
    Irish whiskey syllabub 15
    Italian raspberry trifle 310
    Me mum's pavlova 313
    Paris brest stuffed with fresh fruit and cream 330
    Peach Melba shortbreads 308
    Poached figs with Armagnac syrup 327
    Poor Suzette 315
    Tamarillo upside-down cobbler 322
    The simplest apple tart 328
    Vanilla bean ice-cream 307
Devilled lamb's kidneys on toast 255
dressings
    Orange and cranberry dressing 186
    salad dressings 210
drinks
    Irish coffee 15
    Tolarno's bloody mary oyster shooters 99
Dublin coddle 12
Dubonnet
    A salad of pink livers and spinach in a Dubonnet, orange and cranberry dressing 186
duck
    Dead-easy duck 165

Easy favourite pasta 126
Eggplant almost parmigiano 130
eggs
    An Asian oyster and vegetable 'omelette' 168
    A pasta 'omelette' with the leftovers 129
    BLT salad with avocado and a poached egg 179
    how to hard boil 192
    poached eggs, how to cook 179
    eggwash 56

fennel
    A Moroccan fennel, orange and olive salad 29
Fidel Castro's favourite Cuban beef salad 184
figs
    Poached figs with Armagnac syrup 327
fish
    A calamari salad with eastern flavours 193
    A fillet of roasted salmon on pesto mash with shavings of parmesan 115
    A mousse of home-salted cod 245
    A Provençal seafood stew with a splash of Pernod 140
    A ripper warm salmon salad with anchovy mayo 192
    An onion and anchovy pizza from Provence (pissaladière) 136
    Bahamian baby fish 91
    Boxty with smoked salmon and horseradish and chive sour cream 11
    Cajun groper fillets with fried watermelon and raita 46
    Canned salmon patties for Mavis 285
    deep frying, how to 289
    Fish fingers with home-made tomato sauce 286
    Grilled marlin with roasted salsa 95
    Johnny Hewitson's fish and chips 289
    Kippers with a Lyonnaise potato salad 294
    Mediterranean tuna steaks 111
    Moroccan swordfish steaks with preserved lemon salsa 23
    Mustapha's hot and spicy steamed fish 21
    purchasing 150
    Salmon on a bed of charred radicchio with a tapenade butter 89

Salmon, preparation tip 192
Sardines on toast with a twist 96
Sardines with sea salt and alioli 246
Slow-roasted tuna tonnata 113
Snapper steamed in banana leaves 214
Spicy fresh salmon tartare in witloof boats 190
Steamed salmon with a crackling dressing 145
Tandoori swordfish 225
Thai salmon patties 166
Tolarno's bloody mary oyster shooters 99
Tuna steaks with a Spanish green-olive relish 235
Whiting with an Italian herb relish 90
Whole baby fish Cantonese-style 152
Yabby and cheese crepes 292
Fish fingers with home-made tomato sauce 286
fruit
    Hot fruit salad with a brûlée glaze 326
    Paris brest stuffed with fresh fruit and cream 330

garlic
    A salad of raw vegies with a garlic and herb mayo 182
    Blackened fillet steak on a bed of corn and peas with garlic and chilli butter 54
    Chicken with sherry vinegar and cloves of garlic 240
    Preserved lemon and garlic mayonnaise 32
    Sardines with sea salt and alioli
        (garlic mayonnaise) 246
    Stuffed squid (calamari) with Sicilian parsley, garlic and olive oil dressing 92
    Thai garlic and chilli drumsticks 165
Gateau of crepes with apple and almond filling 314
George's chocolate marshmallow ice-cream 320
George Biron's rhubarb and jasmine fool 334
Greek salad 107
Green beans with soft-dried tomatoes and crispy prosciutto 203
gremolata
    Braised lamb shanks with osso bucco sauce and gremolata 280
Gremolata butter 101
Grilled marlin with roasted salsa 95
Guinness
    Beef in Guinness 6
    history 4
gumbo
    Chicken and beans in a spicy gumbo sauce 45
    Prawn and sausage gumbo ya ya 43

ham
    A modern day pea and ham soup 296
    Harira with kefta and ham hock 34
Harira with kefta and ham hock 34
harissa
    A salad of barbecued vegies, orange couscous and harissa yoghurt 28
    homemade 26
Herb relish 90
Herby Moroccan marinated lamb cutlets 64
Home-made mayonnaise 182
Home-made pita bread 37
Home-made tomato sauce 286
Honey-drenched bananas 84
horseradish
    Barbecue roasted rib-eye of beef with mustard crust and horseradish sour cream 73
    Boxty with smoked salmon and horseradish and chive sour cream 11
Hot fruit salad with a brûlée glaze 326

Huey's favourite BBQ butter 71
Huey's hot banana and passionfruit split 329
Huey's terrific steak sanga 70
Huey's true blue Aussie burger 272

Iain's salad in the style of Caesar 197
ice-cream
    Baci 321
    Christmas ice-cream pudding 312
    George's chocolate marshmallow ice-cream 320
    Vanilla bean ice-cream 307
Indian pork and veal koftas in flat bread 78
Irish coffee 15
Irish stew with a touch of Paris 3
Irish whiskey syllabub 15
Italian raspberry trifle 310

Japanese chicken 'sausage' with stir fried snowpeas 174
jasmine
    George Biron's rhubarb and jasmine fool 334
John Wilson's hot-smoked lamb topside 63
Johnny Hewitson's fish and chips 289

K-Paul's cheese and chilli bread 56
kangaroo
    A minute steak of kangaroo with a tangy apple salad 170
    Wolfgang Puck's marinated kangaroo with mint vinaigrette 82
kebabs
    Beef on a stick 76
    Spanish pork kebabs (pinchos morunos) 241
keftas (meatballs)
    Moroccan keftas in tomato sauce 33
    Harira with kefta and ham hock 34
Kick-arse chicken tortilla with avocado salsa 88
Kippers with a Lyonnaise potato salad 294
kitchen tools vii
    meat thermometer, use of 73
    woks 172
koftas
    Lamb koftas in rogan josh sauce 222
kumara
    Chateaubriand of beef fillet with a mustard, soy and fresh herb crust and roasted kumara mash 270

lamb
    A cheat's cassoulet from the south of France 141
    A lamb, sweet potato and coconut curry 219
    A lo-cal lamb salad with minted yoghurt 68
    A pot of Italian lamb chops 118
    Braised lamb shanks with osso bucco sauce and gremolata 280
    Butterflied leg of lamb in a mustardy marinade 62
    Char Siu rack of lamb 146
    Crumbed cutlets with a blue cheese stuffing 278
    Devilled lamb kidneys on toast 255
    Garlic and rosemary studded leg of lamb 66
    Herby Moroccan marinated lamb cutlets 64
    Irish stew with a touch of Paris 3
    John Wilson's hot-smoked lamb topside 63
    Lamb's brains with a brown lemon and caper butter 258
    Lamb chops in the style of Catalonia 233
    Lamb cutlets 'scottadito' 60
    Lamb koftas in rogan josh sauce 222
    Lamb-shank hotch-potch 284
    Lamb tagine with sweet potatoes 38

Lamb's fry and crispy bacon with apple stew and a
    mustard and thyme butter 256
Mixed grill—Italian style 74
Moroccan keftas (meatballs) in tomato sauce 33
Roast leg of lamb with olive oil roasted vegetables 282
Shepherd's pie 252
Spiced lamb with pita bread and mint yoghurt 36
Lamb's fry and crispy bacon with apple stew and a mustard
    thyme butter 256
Lamb's brains with a brown lemon and caper butter 258
Lamb chops in the style of Catalonia 233
Lamb cutlets 'scottadito' 60
Lamb koftas in rogan josh sauce 222
Lamb tagine with sweet potatoes 38
Lamb-shank hotch-potch 284
lasagne
    A vegetarian lasagne from Provence 140
Lemon and basil crusted chicken salad 183
Lemon and basil marinade 180
Lemon yoghurt 224
Lemon-spiked herb marinade 85
lemongrass, how to prepare 159
lettuce cups 266
Lettuce salad 108
liver
    A salad of pink livers and spinach in a Dubonnet, orange
        and cranberry dressing 186
Lyonnaise potato salad 294

macadamia
    Chicken satays with macadamia nut sauce 155
Madhur Jaffrey's perfect rice pilaf 226
Malay chicken wings 162
Malaysian noodle soup 151
marinades
    Butterflied leg of lamb in a mustardy marinade 62
    Chermoula marinated chicken in the style of Huey 28
    Chicken breast fillets in a fresh orange and
        soy marinade 158
    Herby Moroccan marinated lamb cutlets 64
    Lemon and basil marinade 180
    Real simple chicken breasts with a lemon-spiked herb
        marinade 85
marlin
    Grilled marlin with roasted salsa 95
marshmallow
    George's chocolate marshmallow ice-cream 320
mayonnaise
    A piquant BBQ mayo 86
    A ripper warm salmon salad with anchovy mayo 192
    A salad of raw vegies with a garlic and herb mayo 182
    Homemade mayonnaise 182
    Preserved lemon and garlic mayonnaise 32
    Sardines with sea salt and alioli
        (garlic mayonnaise) 246
Me mum's pavlova 313
meat thermometer
    how to use 73
meatballs
    Moroccan keftas (meatballs) in tomato sauce 33
Mediterranean tuna steaks 111
Meena Pathak's chicken korma 221
Microwave risotto with asparagus and peas 126
Middle eastern chickpea, date and carrot salad 209
mint
    A hot chocolate mint pudding 318
    Mint and cucumber raita 220
    Mint yoghurt 228

Wolfgang Puck's marinated kangaroo with mint
    vinaigrette 82
Mint and cucumber raita 220
Mint yoghurt (Indian style) 228
Minted yoghurt (lamb accompaniment) 68
Minted zucchini salad 209
Mixed grill—Italian style 74
Moroccan keftas (meatballs) in tomato sauce 33
Moroccan swordfish steaks with preserved lemon salsa 23
mozzarella
    A mozzarella salad with gazpacho overtones 207
mushrooms
    Big juicy mushrooms with basil oil 106
    Carpaccio of mushrooms with rocket, parmesan and
        virgin olive oil 195
    preparation of 106
    Stir-fry of baby bok choy, snowpeas and shiitake
        mushrooms 154
mussels
    cleaning of 155
    Mussels in a light green curry broth 161
    Pasta with mussels and citrus crumble 128
Mustapha's hot and spicy steamed fish 21
mustard
    Chateaubriand of beef fillet with a mustard, soy and
        fresh herb crust and roasted kumara mash 270
    Lamb's fry and crispy bacon with apple stew and a
        mustard and thyme butter 256
My ever-changing warm salad 181
My very own Caesar pasta 198
Myrtle Allen's brown bread 9

neeps (swedes)
    Country sausages with bashed neeps 302
noodles
    A crispy noodle cake with wok-fried beef and
        vegetables 156
    Malaysian noodle soup 151
    Vegetarian Hokkien noodles 176
Not even close to a minestrone 124

oil temperature, how to check 287
olive
    A Moroccan fennel, orange and olive salad 29
    how to marinate 125
    Tuna steaks with a Spanish green-olive relish 235
    Tuscan fillet of beef with mushrooms and olive butter 67
olive oil
    Basil-infused olive oil 25
    Barbecued octopus with olive oil roasted
        vegetables 189
    health benefits of 94
    Roast leg of lamb with olive oil roasted vegetables 282
    Tapenade olive oil 125
Olive oil braised artichoke salad 208
onions
    An Indian cucumber, tomato and onion salad with mint
        yoghurt 228
    An onion and anchovy pizza from Provence
        (pissaladière) 136
    Bangers and mash with golden onions 260
    T-bone steak with Maggie Beer's slow roasted onions 72
    Tripe and onions 259
orange
    A Moroccan fennel, orange and olive salad 29
    A salad of pink livers and spinach in a Dubonnet, orange
        and cranberry dressing 186
    A warm rabbit, orange and chorizo salad 242

Asparagus soup with a touch of orange 297
Chicken breast fillets in a fresh orange and
    soy marinade 158
osso bucco
    Braised Lamb shanks with osso bucco sauce and
        gremolata 280
Oyster and corn macque choux 42
oysters
    An Asian oyster and vegetable 'omelette' 168
    Barbecued oysters with sausages 98
    Tolarno's bloody mary oyster shooters 99
    Twice-baked cheese soufflés with plumped oysters and
        blue mascarpone cream 120

Pa amb tomaquet (bread and tomato) 248
Paris brest stuffed with fresh fruit and cream 330
parmesan
    A fillet of roasted salmon on pesto mash with shavings
        of parmesan 115
    buying and storage 195
    Carpaccio of mushrooms with rocket, parmesan and
        virgin olive oil 195
    Peppered beef salad with rocket, balsamic and parmesan
        188
passionfruit
    Huey's hot banana and passionfruit split 329
pasta
    A pasta 'omelette' with the leftovers 129
    My very own Caesar pasta 198
    Real simple pasta 196
Pasta insalata (pasta with salad) 196
Pasta with mussels and citrus crumble 128
pavlova
    Me mum's pavlova 313
pea
    A modern day pea and ham soup 296
    Blackened fillet steak on a bed of corn and peas with
        garlic and chilli butter 54
    Microwave risotto with asparagus and peas 126
    Potato and green-pea pastries in the style
        of samosas 216
Peach Melba shortbreads 308
Peppered beef salad with rocket, balsamic and parmesan 188
Peppered steak casserole 271
Pernod
    A Provençal seafood stew with a splash
        of Pernod 140
pesto 115
    A fillet of roasted salmon on pesto mash with shavings
        of parmesan 115
    Chicken schnitzel with pesto mash 267
pilaf
    Indian rice pilaf 227
    Madhur Jaffrey's perfect rice pilaf 226
    Spanish vegetable pilaf 236
pineapple
    Barbecued pineapple with spiced rum butter sauce 324
pita bread
    Homemade pita bread 37
    Indian pork and veal koftas in flat bread 78
    Spiced lamb with pita bread and mint yoghurt 36
pizza
    An onion and anchovy pizza from Provence
        (pissaladière) 136
    toppings 134
Poached eggs, how to cook 179
Poached figs with Armagnac syrup 327
Poor Suzette 315

pork
    Dublin coddle 12
    Indian pork and veal koftas in flat bread 78
    Pork stroganoff 295
    Spanish pork kebabs (pinchos morunos) 241
    Tagine of pork chops with spiced apples 30
    Tuscan barbecued rolled pork 81
Pot roasted quail with lemons and raisins 25
potato
    A fillet of roasted salmon on pesto mash with shavings
        of parmesan 115
    Bangers and mash with golden onions 260
    Barbecued potatoes with crispy bacon and
        sour cream 103
    Black pudding with Irish creamy mash (champ) 7
    Chicken schnitzel with pesto mash 267
    John Hewitson's fish and chips 289
    Kippers with a Lyonnaise potato salad 294
    Potato and anchovy tortilla 244
    Potato and green-pea pastries in the style
        of samosas 216
    Potato salad with a tangy lemon dressing 107
    selecting the best potato 107
    Roast spuds 265
Potato and anchovy tortilla 244
Potato and green-pea pastries in the style of samosas 216
Potato salad with a tangy lemon dressing 107
prawn
    Cochin prawns in a spiced coconut sauce 213
    Prawn and cheese hush puppies 52
    Prawn and sausage gumbo ya ya 43
Preserved lemon
    how to make 24
    Moroccan swordfish steaks with preserved
        lemon salsa 23
    Preserved lemon and garlic mayonnaise 32
    Preserved lemon salsa 23
prosciutto
    Green beans with soft-dried tomatoes and crispy
        prosciutto 203
pudding
    A hot chocolate mint pudding 318
    Bread and butter pudding 332
    Christmas ice-cream pudding 315
    Tamarillo upside-down cobbler 322
pumpkin
    Baby pumpkin stuffed with a Thai pumpkin and bean
        curry 145
    Pumpkin with soy-honey caramel 105
    Roasted pumpkin seeds 105
Pumpkin seeds, roasted 105

quail
    Pot roasted quail with lemons and raisins 25
    Red Emperor's twice-cooked spicy quail 159
rabbit
    A warm rabbit, orange and chorizo salad 242
radicchio
    Salmon on a bed of charred radicchio with a tapenade
        butter 89
raita
    Cajun groper fillets with fried watermelon and raita 46
    mint and cucumber raita 220
raspberry
    Italian raspberry trifle 310
Real simple chicken breast with a lemon-spiked herb
    marinade 85
Real simple pasta 196

Red capsicum butter 114
Red Emperor's twice-cooked spicy quail 159
relish
    Tuna steaks with a Spanish green-olive relish 235
    Whiting with an Italian herb relish 90
rhubarb
    George Biron's rhubarb and jasmine fool 334
Ribs, baby back, Texas style 80
rice
    Madhur Jaffrey's perfect rice pilaf 226
risotto
    Microwave risotto with asparagus and peas 126
Roast chicken 262
Roast chicken and crudités in lettuce cups 266
Roast leg of lamb with olive oil roasted vegetables 282
Roast spuds 265
Roasted bugs with a red capsicum butter 114
Roasted capsicum, anchovy and soft-dried tomato salad 201
Roasted capsicum salad 245
Roasted kumara mash (sweet potato) 270
Rogan josh sauce 221

salad
    A calamari salad with eastern flavours 193
    A lo-cal lamb salad with minted yoghurt 6
    A minute steak of kangaroo with a tangy apple salad 170
    A Moroccan fennel, orange and olive salad 29
    A mozzarella salad with gazpacho overtones 207
    A ripper warm salmon salad with anchovy mayo 192
    A salad of barbecued vegies, orange couscous and harissa yoghurt 28
    A salad of pink livers and spinach in a Dubonnet, orange and cranberry dressing 186
    A salad of raw vegies with a garlic and herb mayo 182
    A warm rabbit, orange and chorizo salad 242
    Almost a true blue Greek salad 107
    An Indian cucumber, tomato and onion salad with mint yoghurt 228
    Barbecued beetroot salad with spicy yoghurt 108
    Barbecued octopus salad with olive oil roasted vegetables 189
    Bar-room slaw 273
    BLT salad with avocado and a poached egg 179
    Carpaccio of mushrooms with rocket, parmesan and virgin olive oil 195
    Chermoula-marinated chicken salad in the style of Huey 19
    Couscous salad 22
    dressings 210
    Fidel Castro's favourite Cuban beef salad 184
    Green beans with soft-dried tomatoes and crispy prosciutto 203
    Iain's salad in the style of Caesar 197
    Lemon and basil crusted chicken salad 183
    Lettuce salad 108
    Kippers with a Lyonnaise potato salad 294
    Me mum's coleslaw 108
    Middle eastern chickpea, date and carrot salad 209
    Minted zucchini salad 209
    My ever-changing warm salad 181
    Olive oil braised artichoke salad 208
    Parmesan crumbed veal with roasted capsicum salad 119
    Pasta insalata (pasta with salad) 196
    Peppered beef salad with rocket, balsamic and parmesan 188
    Potato salad with a tangy lemon dressing 107
    Roasted capsicum salad 245
    Roasted capsicum, anchovy and soft-dried tomato salad 201
    Spicy fresh salmon tartare in witloof boats 190
    Thai beef and cranberry salad 185
    The simplest of tomato salads 200
    tomato salads 205
    Vietnamese chicken salad 148
salad dressings 210
salmon
    A fillet of roasted salmon on pesto mash with shavings of parmesan 115
    A ripper warm salmon salad with anchovy mayo 192
    Canned salmon patties for Mavis 285
    preparation tip 192
    Spicy fresh salmon tartare in witloof boats 190
    Steamed salmon with a crackling dressing 145
    Thai salmon patties 166
Salmon on a bed of charred radicchio with a tapenade butter 89
salsas
    Barbecued sweetcorn salsa 94
    Grilled marlin with roasted salsa 95
    Kick-arse chicken tortilla with avocado salsa 88
    Preserved lemon salsa 23
    Roasted salsa 95
sandwiches
    A brick-pressed Mediterranean sandwich 132
    Huey's terrific steak sanga 70
    The peacemaker 51
    The po-boy 50
Sardines on toast with a twist 96
Sardines with sea salt and alioli 246
sauces
    Braised lamb shanks with osso bucco sauce and gremolata 280
    Chicken Maryland with crispy bacon and sauce Béarnaise 268
    Chicken satays with macadamia nut sauce 155
    Cochin prawns in a spiced coconut sauce 213
    Home-made tomato sauce 286
    Lamb koftas in rogan josh sauce 222
    Spiced coconut sauce 213
    Spiced rum butter sauce 324
    Tangy lemon dressing 107
    Tartare sauce 290
    Tomato sauce 33
sausage
    A warm rabbit, orange and chorizo salad 242
    Baked beans and sausages 261
    Bangers and mash with golden onions 260
    Barbecued oysters with sausages 98
    Country sausages with bashed neeps 302
    Japanese chicken 'sausage' with stirfried snowpeas 174
    Mixed grill—Italian style 74
    Prawn and sausage gumbo ya ya 43
seafood
    A Provençal seafood stew with a splash of Pernod 138
    Aherne's pot of seafood 14
    An Asian oyster and vegetable 'omelette' 168
    Barbecued octopus with olive oil roasted vegetables 189
    Barbecued oysters with sausages 98
    Blue swimmer crabs with aromatics 171
    Cochin prawns in a spiced coconut sauce 213
    mussels, how to clean 155
    Mussels in a light green curry broth 161
    Oyster and corn macque choux 42
    Pasta with mussels and citrus crumble 128

Prawn and cheese hush puppies 52
Prawn and sausage gumbo ya ya 43
Roasted bugs with a red capsicum butter 114
Stuffed squid (calamari) with Sicilian parsley, garlic and olive oil dressing 92
Twice-baked cheese soufflés with plumped oysters and blue mascarpone cream 120
Yabby and cheese crepes 292
Shepherd's pie 252
shortbreads
  Peach Melba shortbreads 308
Simplest apple tart 328
Slow roasted onions 72
Slow-roasted tuna tonnata 113
Snapper steamed in banana leaves 214
snowpeas
  Japanese chicken 'sausage' with stirfried snowpeas 174
  Stir-fry of baby bok choy, snowpeas and shiitake mushrooms 154
Soft-drying tomatoes at home 201
soup
  A flavoursome roasted tomato and basil soup 123
  A modern day pea and ham soup 296
  Asparagus soup with a touch of orange 297
  Cashel blue cheese and vegetable soup 6
  Chicken and beans in a spicy gumbo sauce 45
  Curried root vegetable soup with purée of roasted capsicum 217
  Malaysian noodle soup 151
  Mussels in a light green curry broth 161
  Not even close to a minestrone 124
  Prawn and sausage gumbo ya ya 43
sour cream
  Barbecue roasted rib-eye of beef with mustard crust and horseradish sour cream 73
  Barbecued potatoes with crispy bacon and sour cream 103
  Boxty with smoked salmon and horseradish and chive sour cream 11
Spag bog with a beef and chicken liver ragu 277
Spanish pork kebabs (pinchos morunos) 241
Spanish vegetable pilaf 236
Spatchcocked chicken with garlic butter and fresh basil 83
Spiced lamb with pita bread and mint yoghurt 36
Spiced rum butter sauce 324
Spicy fresh salmon tartare in witloof boats 190
spinach
  A salad of pink livers and spinach in a Dubonnet, orange and cranberry dressing 186
squid (calamari)
  preparation of 93
  Stuffed squid (calamari) with Sicilian parsley, garlic and olive oil dressing 92
Steak diane 276
Steak in an Italian fashion 117
Steamed salmon with a crackling dressing 145
stews
  A pot of Italian lamb chops 118
  A Provençal seafood stew with a splash of Pernod 138
  Lamb-shank hotch-potch 284
Stir-fry of baby bok choy, snowpeas and shiitake mushrooms 154
stock
  A flavoursome vegetable stock 237
Stuffed squid (calamari) with Sicilian parsley, garlic and olive oil dressing 92
Sudhakaran Meetinay's dhal makhani 229

sugar
  vanilla sugar 320
swedes (neeps)
  Country sausages with bashed neeps 302
sweet potato
  A lamb, sweet potato and coconut curry 219
  Candied sweet potatoes 62
  Chateaubriand of beef fillet with a mustard, soy and fresh herb crust and roasted kumara mash 270
  Lamb tagine with sweet potatoes 38

T-bone steak with Maggie Beer's slow roasted onions 72
tagine
  description of 35
  Lamb tagine with sweet potatoes 38
  Tagine of pork chops with spiced apples 30
Tamarillo upside-down cobbler 322
Tandoori swordfish 225
Tapenade olive oil 125
Tartare sauce 290
Tea-smoked tomatoes 204
Texas style BBQ baby back ribs 80
Thai beef and cranberry salad 185
Thai garlic and chilli drumsticks 163
Thai salmon patties 166
The peacemaker 51
The po-boy 50
The simplest of tomato salads 200
Tips for a successful barbie 87
Tolarno's bloody mary oyster shooters 99
tomatoes
  A flavoursome roasted tomato and basil soup 123
  An Indian cucumber, tomato and onion salad with mint yoghurt 228
  Fish fingers with home-made tomato sauce 286
  Green beans with soft-dried tomatoes and crispy prosciutto 203
  how to peel and seed 95
  how to purée 236
  how to roast 123
  Moroccan keftas (meatballs) in tomato sauce 33
  Roasted capsicum, anchovy and soft-dried tomato salad 201
  soft drying tomatoes at home 201
  Tea-smoked tomatoes 204
  The simplest of tomato salads 200
  tomato salads 205
tortilla
  Kick-arse chicken tortilla with avocado salsa 88
  Potato and anchovy tortilla 244
trifle
  Italian raspberry trifle 310
Tripe and onions 259
tuna
  Slow-roasted tuna tonnata 113
  Mediterranean tuna steaks 111
  Tuna steaks with a Spanish green-olive relish 235
Tuscan barbecued rolled pork 81
Tuscan fillet of beef with mushrooms and olive butter 67
Twice-baked cheese soufflés with plumped oysters and blue mascarpone cream 120

Vanilla bean ice-cream 307
vanilla sugar 320
veal
  Indian pork and veal koftas in flat bread 78
  Parmesan crumbed veal with roasted capsicum salad 119
Vegetable soup, not even close to a minestrone 124

Vegetable stock 237
vegetables
- A flavoursome vegetable stock 237
- A brick-pressed Mediterranean sandwich 132
- A crispy noodle cake with wok-fried beef and vegetables 156
- A salad of barbecued vegies, with orange couscous and harissa yoghurt 28
- A stack of northern Indian vegetable cutlets 215
- An Asian oyster and vegetable 'omelette' 168
- Barbecued sweet potato 62
- Barbecued corn on the cob with gremolata butter 101
- Barbecued octopus with olive oil roasted vegetables 189
- Barbecued potatoes with crispy bacon and sour cream 103
- barbecued vegie ideas 104
- bashed neeps (swedes) 302
- Big juicy mushrooms with basil oil 106
- Black pudding with Irish creamy mash (champ) 7
- broad beans, preparation of 235
- Brussel sprout colcannon 10
- Cashel blue cheese and vegetable soup 6
- Corned beef bubble and squeak 299
- Curried root vegetable soup with purée of roasted capsicum 217
- Eggplant almost parmigiano 130
- Marinated olives 125
- Mashed baby potatoes 119
- mushrooms, how to clean 106
- pumpkin seeds, roasted 105
- Pumpkin with soy-honey caramel 105
- Roast leg of lamb with olive oil roasted vegetables 282
- Roast spuds 265
- Slow roasted onions 72
- Stir-fry of baby bok choy, snowpeas and shiitake mushrooms 154
- Tea-smoked tomatoes 204
- Vegetable stock 237
- Witloof in an Italian manner 102

vegetarian
- A Moroccan fennel, orange and olive salad 29
- A salad of barbecued vegies, orange couscous and harissa yoghurt 28
- A salad of raw vegies with a garlic and herb mayo 182
- A stack of northern Indian vegetable cutlets 215
- A vegetarian lasagne from Provence 140
- Baby pumpkin stuffed with a Thai pumpkin and bean curry 145
- barbecue tips 100
- Carpaccio of mushrooms with rocket, parmesan and virgin olive oil 195
- Cashel blue cheese and vegetable soup 6
- Couscous salad 22
- Curried root vegetable soup with purée of roasted capsicum 217
- Eggplant almost parmigiano 130
- Microwave risotto with asparagus and peas 126
- Middle eastern chickpea, date and carrot salad 209
- Potato and green-pea pastries in the style of samosas 216
- Spanish vegetable pilaf 236
- Stir-fry of baby bok choy, snowpeas and shiitake mushrooms 154
- Sudhakaran Meetinay's dhal makhani 229

Vegetarian Hokkien noodles 176
Vietnamese chicken salad 148
vinaigrette
- Wolfgang Puck's marinated kangaroo with mint vinaigrette 82

watermelon
- Cajun groper fillets with fried watermelon and raita 46

whiskey
- Irish coffee 15
- Irish whiskey syllabub 15

Whiting with an Italian herb relish 90
Whole baby fish Cantonese-style 152
witloof
- Spicy fresh salmon tartare in witloof boats 190
- Witloof in an Italian manner 102

Wolfgang Puck's marinated kangaroo with mint vinaigrette 82

Yabby and cheese crepes 292
yoghurt
- A lo-cal lamb salad with minted yoghurt 68
- An Indian cucumber, tomato and onion salad with mint yoghurt 228
- Chicken with dates and a lemon yoghurt 224
- Barbecued beetroot salad with spicy yoghurt 108
- Spiced lamb with pita bread and mint yoghurt 36
- mint yoghurt 228

zucchini
- Minted zucchini salad 209